PEOPLE'S CHINA

People's China

A BRIEF HISTORY

Craig Dietrich

New York   Oxford
Oxford University Press
1986

Oxford University Press

Oxford   New York   Toronto
Delhi   Bombay   Calcutta   Madras   Karachi
Petaling Jaya   Singapore   Hong Kong   Tokyo
Nairobi   Dar es Salaam   Cape Town
Melbourne   Auckland

and associated companies in
Beirut   Berlin   Ibadan   Nicosia

Published by Oxford University Press, Inc.,
200 Madison Avenue, New York, New York 10016
Oxford is a registered trademark of Oxford University Press

Library of Congress Cataloging in Publication Data
Dietrich, Craig.
People's China.
Bibliography: p.
Includes index.
1. China—History—1949–   .   I. Title.
DS777.55.D52   1986   951.05   85-15217
ISBN 0-19-503688-3
ISBN 0-19-503689-1 (pbk.)

Printing (last digit): 9 8 7 6 5 4 3

Printed in the United States of America

To Helen and
to the memory of Harold

Acknowledgments

I wish to acknowledge a debt of gratitude to the many people who helped me complete this book. There are too many to mention individually, but I especially want to thank the following persons. Ramon H. Myers of the Hoover Institution on War Revolution and Peace provided me with helpful comments and encouragement at an early stage of the project. Two anonymous readers who evaluated my manuscript for Oxford University Press provided extensive constructive criticism, thereby helping to improve the book's accuracy and utility. Whoever they are, I thank them and take full responsibility for those errors that remain. My editor, the indefatigable Nancy Lane, receives my deep appreciation for championing the half-completed manuscript and shepherding it through the many phases of publication. I also wish to thank Benjamin Harrison for his portraits, Kristen Sommer for her cartography, Winston Barton and Lesley Jones-Holloway for the graphs, Judith Manton for providing the cover illustration, and John Major of the Asia Society for introducing Ms. Manton to Oxford. Finally, I thank Sherilyn Dietrich, my long-suffering "book widow," who cultivated the garden while I wrote.

Portland, Maine   C. D.
June 1985

Contents

**A NOTE ON THE ROMANIZATION OF
CHINESE WORDS, xiii**

INTRODUCTION, 3

1   OLD CHINA AND YOUNG REVOLUTIONARIES, 10

Village China and Young Mao, 10
China: Vast Agrarian Empire.   Poor China.
Haves and Have-nots.   The Family.

To the City, 17
Urban China.

Unification, Invasion, and Civil War, 22
Postwar China: 1920–36.   The Yanan Years: 1937–45.
Civil War: 1945–49.

Personalities and Causes, 32
Liu Shaoqi (1889–1969): Organization Man.   Zhou Enlai (1898–
   1976): Premier.   Zhu De (1886–1967): Commander in
Chief.   Chen Yun (1905–): Economic Expert.   Chen Boda
(1904–): Theoretician.   Lin Biao (1908–71): Battlefield Genius
   and Radical.   Chen Yi (1901–72): Field Commander.   Deng
Xiaoping (1904–): Apparatchik Supreme.   Peng Dehuai (1898–
   1974): General.   Jiang Qing (1914–): Rebel Actress.

Was China Ripe for Revolution?   43
Marxism.   Other Views.

2   REVOLUTIONARIES SEIZE POWER: 1949–52,   50

Establishing Sovereignty,   51
Military Victory.   Leaning to One Side.

Installing the New Order,   55
Restoring Normalcy.   The Party.   Party Center and Party Cadres.
The State Bureaucracy.   The Military.

The Korean War,   65

Campaigns,   68
Land Reform.   Resist America, Aid Korea.   Marriage Law.
Oppose Counterrevolutionaries.   Thought Reform.
Oppose Bureaucracy.   Oppose Corruption.

Disappointments, Ironies, and Contradictions,   79
The Sweet and the Bitter.   Institutional Development Versus
Revolutionary Transformation.

3   SOCIALIST TRANSFORMATION: 1953–57,   83

The First Five-Year Plan,   85
Industrialization.   Agriculture.   Education.   Health.

The High Tide of 1955,   91
Mao Counterattacks.   High Tide in Industry and
Commerce.   Implications of Socialist Transformation.   A New
Political Climate.   Retreat From the Reckless Advance.

The Eighth Party Congress, September 1956,   102

The Hundred Flowers Campaign,   105

4 THE GREAT LEAP FORWARD: 1958–60,   110

Initial States of the Great Leap,   111
The Summer of 1957.   Revival of the Radical Agricultural
Program.   Mao's Trip to Moscow.

The Great Leap in the Ascendant, 120
The First Phase: December 1957–May 1958.
Exerting Our Utmost Efforts: June 1958–November 1958.

The Great Leap in Decline, 132
Readjustment: November 1958–June 1959.   Showdown at Lushan:
July 1958–August 1958.   End of the Great Leap: 1960.

**5 DEPRESSION, RECOVERY, AND STRUGGLE AT THE
TOP: 1960–65, 142**

The Immediate Repercussions of the Great Leap, 143
Depression.   Adjustment.   Recovery.

Political Crisis, 150
The Tenth Plenum.   The Socialist Education
Movement.   Education.   Culture.   The PLA and Foreign
Policy.   The Crisis of 1965.

6 THE CULTURAL REVOLUTION: 1966–69, 178

Participants, 178

Tidal Wave, 181
Ominous Breakers: May 1966–August 1966.   Inundation: From
August 1966 to the February 1967 Adverse Current.   Resurgent
Tidal Wave: Summer 1967.

The Flood Recedes, 194
Turbulent Reflux: September 1967–April 1969.   Final Assessments.

The Cultural Revolution in Retreat: 1969–76, 205

Failure to Consolidate Radical Rule: 1969–71, 206
Economic and Social Policy.   A New Global Strategy.
Party Rebuilding.   The Fall of Lin Biao.

The Uneasy Regime of the Moderates: 1972–75, 216
The Radicals Lose Ground.   Zhou Enlai Takes Charge.   Persisting
Radical Influence.

Mao's Final Months and the Arrest of the Gang of Four: 1976, 229

An End and a Beginning, 235

8 RETURN TO PRAGMATISM: 1976–84, 236

After Mao: Politics and Problems, 236

Power Struggle: October 1976–December 1978, 237
The Uneasy Prominence of Hua Guofeng.   Deng Xiaoping
Redivivus: 1977–78.   Party Meetings and the Third Plenum of
December 1978.

Deng Takes Charge: 1979–81, 247
Liberalization and Democracy Wall.   The Clampdown Against
Democracy Wall.   Vietnam.   Economic Reforms.   Deng's
Triumph and Political Reforms.   The Trial of the Gang of Four
and the Sixth Plenum.

**9 SOCIALIST MODERNIZATION AND ITS
DISCONTENTS, 273**

**Achievements and Dilemmas of Socialist Modernization:
1981–85, 273**
The Economy.   Political Reforms.
Foreign Relations.   Education.   Population Control.
Environmental Damage.

Looking Backward, 293

NOTES, 299

SUGGESTED READINGS, 309

INDEX, 319

A Note on the Romanization of Chinese Words

No doubt every reader of this book will be at least dimly aware that Chinese writing is based on radically different principles from our own phonetically based alphabet. Already two millennia ago, the Chinese had developed a script comprised of several thousand "characters," which either singly or in pairs constitute the words of the language. Essentially the same system is still in use today.

The difficulties of learning Chinese are evident enough, but readers may not have had occasion to realize the problems that such a system creates for Western scholars whose audience has no familiarity with these characters and yet must be introduced to various Chinese names. It is a problem that goes back to sixteenth-century Christian missionaries and even to Marco Polo in the fourteenth century.

Because these characters all have spoken pronunciations, the obvious answer to the difficulty is simply to adopt phonetic conventions, using Roman letters to represent the sounds. Such is the answer that has been pursued from the start. Inherently this is not a bad solution, even though the several "tones" that constitute part of the pronunciation are usually lost, and despite the fact that the many homonyms of Chinese make the phonetic spelling more ambiguous than the written characters.

The most annoying difficulty has been the fact that Western scholars, never satisfied with their predecessors' efforts, have seemed unable to stop contriving new systems. There have been literally hundreds. The result is, for example, that the family name of one of the paramount leaders of modern China, which sounds much like the English name *Joe,* can be rendered *Jou, Tchou, Chow,* and *Cheo*—to name but a few. Responding to the need for standardization, in English-speaking countries a system known as Wade-Giles has been widely used for many decades. By its dictates the name in question is spelled *Chou*. More recently—and it is hoped for the last time—one more new Romanization scheme has been introduced. Since 1979 the Chinese government has officially promoted a system known as "pinyin," under whose rules the name is *Zhou*. Pinyin is coming into worldwide use and is employed throughout this book.

Unfortunately, pinyin conventions are not ideally suited to give English speakers an immediate idea of certain pronunciations. For example, how does one read *zhi* or *qi* or *ze*? In this book names, when first introduced, are accompanied by a pronunciation based on the closest sounds in common American words and spellings and without reference to any Romanization system. More rigorously inclined readers may wish to know the equivalencies of the various letters and combinations of pinyin. Most vowels are pronounced fairly close to how they would sound in English. A few consonants have special values:

> *c* sounds like *ts*
> *q* sounds like *ch*
> *x* sounds like something between *s* and *sh*
> *z* sounds like *ds*
> *zh* sounds like *j*

These rules may be enough to permit tolerably close approximations of the originals. To learn the finer points, the reader should consult texts on the language or general texts on Chinese civilization, which always include a page or two on pronunciation.

Because pinyin has only recently replaced the Wade-Giles system, it will be useful here to provide a list of names used in this book together with their Wade-Giles equivalents.

Personal Names

pinyin	*Wade-Giles*
Zhang Zhixin	Chang Chih-hsin
Chen Boda	Ch'en Po-ta
Chen Yun	Ch'en Yun
Chen Yi	Ch'en I
Chen Yongguei	Ch'en Yung-kuei
Deng Xiaoping	Deng Hsiao-p'ing
Deng Zihui	Deng Tzu-hui
Fu Yuehua	Fu Yueh-hua
Gao Gang	Kao Kang

Hu Yaobang	Hu Yao-pang
Hua Guofeng	Hua Kuo-feng
Jiang Qing	Chiang Ch'ing
Kang Sheng	K'ang Sheng
Lei Feng	Lei Feng
Lin Biao	Lin Piao
Liu Shaoqi	Liu Shao-ch'i
Luo Ruiqing	Lo Jui-ch'ing
Mao Zedong	Mao Tse-tung
Mao Yuanxin	Mao Yuan-hsin
Nie Yuanzi	Nieh Yuan-tsu
Peng Dehuai	P'eng Te-huai
Peng Zhen	P'eng Chen
Ren Wending	Jen Wen-ting
Wang Guangmei	Wang Kuang-mei
Wang Hongwen	Wang Hung-wen
Wei Jingsheng	Wei Ching-sheng
Wu Han	Wu Han
Yao Wenyuan	Yao Wen-yuan
Zhang Chunqiao	Chang Ch'un-ch'iao
Zhau Ziyang	Chao Tzu-yang
Zhou Enlai	Chou En-lai
Zhu De	Chu Teh

Place Names

pinyin	*Wade-Giles*
Beijing	Peking
Changsha	Changsha
Guangzhou	Canton
Nanjing	Nanking
Shanghai	Shanghai
Tianjin	Tientsin
Wuhan	Wuhan
Yanan	Yenan

Finally, the following names have become so familiar in their own idiosyncratic or Wade-Giles spellings that they have been retained in this book: Chiang Kai-shek, Sun Yat-sen, and Hu Shih.

| 0 | 500 | 1000 Miles |

S.

Irysh R.

Yenisey R.

Irk

U.

Lake Balkhash

MONGOLIAN

Alma Ata

A L T A I   M T S.

TIEN   SHAN

Urumchi

PAMIR MTS.

Tarim R.

S I N K I A N G

Hami

Yarkand

Lop Nor

K

A

N

KASHMIR

Koko Nor

KUNLUN   MTS.

TSINGHAI

Sining

H

I

M

A

T I B E T

Lanch

L

A

Y

Shigatse • Lhasa

CHAMDO

S Z E

A

Cheng

N E P A L

M

T

S.

Ganges R.

BHUTAN

SIKKIM

Brahmaputra R.

Mekong

I N D I A

E. PAKISTAN

Kunming

YUNNAN

R.

BURMA

L

A

PEOPLE'S REPUBLIC OF CHINA

☐ *Autonomous Regions*

+++ *Main railways (in China and Russia)*

THAILAND

S.
Lake Baikal
Nerchinsk
Komsomolsk
R.
Khabarovsk
Manchouli
Amur R.
HEILUNGKIANG
Ulan Bator
Tsitsihar
Sungari R.
Harbin
EPUBLIC
KIRIN
Ch'ang-ch'un
Vladivostok
Mukden
LIAONING
Yalu R.
NORTH KOREA
N
E
R
Huhehot
Peking
Port
Arthur
Pyongyang
Paotow
Dairen
Seoul
GREAT WALL
Tientsin
Chefoo
SOUTH KOREA
Taiyuan
Tsinan
SHANSI
SHANTUNG
Tsingtao
SHENSI
Yellow
Kaifeng
Sian
HONAN
KIANGSU
Nanking
Shanghai
N
HUPEH
Wuhan
Ningpo
hungking
Yangtze R.
Hangchow
CHEKIANG
Changsha
Nanchang
Wenchow
HUNAN
KIANGSI
Kweiyang
FUKIEN
Foochow
EICHOW
Kweilin
West R.
Taipei
KWANGSI
Amoy
TAIWAN (FORMOSA)
Nanning
Canton
Swatow
Nationalist China
KWANGTUNG
Hong Kong (Br.)
Macao (Port.)
RTH
NAM
HAINAN
PHILIPPINE
IS.
South China Sea
GREATER KHINGAN MTS.
MONGOLIA
HOPEH
ANHWEI
PESCADO
RYUKYU IS.
OKINAWA
Pacific
Ocean
JAPAN
Vaughn Gray

PEOPLE'S CHINA

Introduction

A long night stayed the dawn of China's crimson day.
Hundred-year hobgoblins galloped up and down.
But the people . . . oh the fragmented five hundred million . . .

Suddenly a crowing cock illuminates the world.
From far-off Yutian, from everywhere, musicians come.
What gathering of poets could equal this?

Mao Zedong addressed these verses to a fellow poet in 1949 during the celebrations marking the Communist victory in China.[1] The poem seemed to point both forward and backward. In form and diction, it recalled a traditional scholar-gentleman's literary amusement. But the content was new. Mao Zedong scarcely resembled a robed scholar sipping tea with friends and sharing poems in his exquisite garden. He was the redoubtable commander of an insurgency, the Chinese Communist Party and the Red Army, that had seized control of the world's most populous country. He had just proclaimed the birth of the People's Republic of China. It was a moment that marked the victory over numerous hobgoblins—the rulers, warlords, and foreign aggressors who had presided over a century of national humiliation. The curtain was now rising on some extraordinary historical scenes as China, under communism, sought to achieve social change, economic development, and power. To sketch these scenes briefly is the objective of this book.

Chapter 1 describes the genesis of revolution. One important ingredient was poverty: Pre-1949 China was scarred by want and

3

suffering. It was not a temporary or incidental poverty but a fundamental condition in the sense that land, labor, and capital were not yet "developed" to a degree capable of producing modern abundance for the entire society. It was a condition that could be ameliorated only through a sustained process of nation building, requiring commitment of resources to massive invest-ment, social orderliness and organization, foreign assistance, and wise policies. Just as material abundance was always crucial to Marxism, so economic development was a central objective of the Chinese revolution. Not surprisingly, economic issues figure prominently in the chapters that follow.

In the mid-1950s China adopted a Soviet central-planning ap-proach, which was embodied in its First Five-Year Plan. This plan called for the largest possible program of investment, es-pecially in "heavy" industry (iron, steel, machinery, and the like) at the expense of agriculture and consumer goods. But Mao soon soured on the plan for economic as well as other reasons, and he launched a radically different solution to the poverty prob-lem, called the Great Leap Forward (1958–60). When that ef-fort nearly wrecked the economy, Mao agreed to a tactical re-treat back to Soviet-style arrangements. For the next fifteen years (from the early 1960s to the mid-1970s), these two ap-proaches—the Soviet and the Maoist—jostled one another at policy-making tables. Not until after 1978, under Deng Xiao-ping, did the country experience sustained programs capable of reaching the elusive economic goal that had always seemed to recede like the horizon. Even into the mid-1980s, China was still a poor country with formidable difficulties along the road to abundance.

Speaking again of the pre-1949 era, one must say that want and suffering by themselves cannot breed successful revolu-tions. If poverty were sufficient, the world would surely witness the daily success of social upheavals. In addition to grievances, revolutions require leaders and a cause. In China the cause was communism, and the leaders were the men who fought to the top of the Chinese Communist party. Chapter 1 discusses the

principal tenets of Marxism-Leninism. It also provides information about Mao Zedong's early life and includes biographical
sketches of a handful of other prominent personalities. Both at
that time and later, the revolution was profoundly affected by
the relationship between the supreme chief and the rest of the
Party elite.

Few modern political figures can equal Mao Zedong. He was
active in the Chinese Communist party for fifty-five years, of
which forty were spent as the Party's undisputed leader. His influence compares in scope to the combined careers of Lenin, who
like him led a victorious insurgency, and Stalin, who like him
oversaw its subsequent development for a quarter century. Today the current official wisdom of the Chinese government, a
view widely shared by outside observers, is that Mao's contribution up to 1949, the Leninlike phase of his career, was of a
high and unique order. It is not too much to say that his audacious, decisive, and inspiring leadership was an absolutely crucial ingredient in the movement's success. However, after liberation he was responsible for some extremely costly and brutal
mistakes (for which he has been compared to Stalin).

As subsequent chapters show, the relationship between Mao
and his revolutionary colleagues began to change after 1949. His
position became ambiguous. He enjoyed unrivaled prestige, but
the others did not lack power to influence events. The People's
Republic became a great congeries of bureaucratic machines in
which some of the other leaders were rather more adept, and the
interaction between Mao and his old comrades grew strained.
Economic disagreements fed this estrangement as Mao's approach conflicted with the more systematic majority. Power
struggles also contributed as Mao resisted being pastured out to
honorific retirement and as a latent succession struggle developed. This split at the top first appeared during the Great Leap
Forward in 1959 and in the recovery years after that campaign.
It became acute in the Great Proletarian Cultural Revolution
(1966–69), at which time Mao nearly destroyed the Party. It was
known as a "two-line struggle": romantic revolution against or-

ganized development, mass campaigns versus bureaucracy, slogans as opposed to plans, zeal vying with structure, purity struggling with pragmatism. Only following Chairman Mao's death in 1976 were these polarities adequately resolved.

The struggles among the leaders corresponded to a vaster but less visible tension between the new regime's principles and the Chinese people. There can be little mistake about what the Chinese Communist party wished the people to accept as fundamental values: nationalism; rapid economic development; personal sacrifice for the nation; socialist ownership; central planning; class struggle against identified counterrevolutionaries; policies to promote equality between cities and villages, rich and poor, men and women, rulers and ruled. There can also be little doubt that these principles found some degree of acceptance throughout the society.

But exactly what was the official line, and how should it manifest itself in concrete policies? Was there not a contradiction between the push for economic development and the desire to promote equality through redistribution? Could the party that monopolized power also be responsive to the people in the absence of legally guaranteed rights and free public expression? Once, briefly under Mao's urging, the government encouraged public feedback only to retaliate harshly when the criticisms were deemed excessive. This was known as the Hundred Flowers movement (1957). The Anti-Rightist movement, which brought it to a close, resulted in the imprisonment of many thousands of intellectuals. There were other periods of excess, especially that of the Cultural Revolution (1966–69), in which mob violence was encouraged in the name of lofty Marxist principles. Later the Cultural Revolution would be officially condemned. These changes, contradictions, and excesses inhibited popular acceptance of the regime and its doctrines—although it would be equally unjustified to conclude that the people utterly repudiated the People's Republic.

The Chinese revolution was also the product of outside pressure that was usually referred to as *imperialism* and had eco-

nomic, religious, cultural, and of course military aspects. Japan
was the last great aggressor (1932–45). Britain was the first—
in a conflict known as the Opium War (1839–42). At that time,
Chinese generals and admirals at Canton in south China noticed
a strange new warship. Her name was *Nemesis*. Double the ton-
nage of the typical Chinese war junk, her squat, flat-bottomed
hull enabled her to ply the shallowest waters. Protruding half-
way between her two masts was a smoke-belching funnel, and
amidships on either side turned a huge paddle wheel. Chinese
shot barely dented her iron-plated hull while fore and aft her own
pair of thirty-two-pound swivel guns dealt mayhem to any un-
lucky junk within range. Western science, technology, and ideas:
They were indeed a kind of nemesis that dogged the isolated
Chinese nation. Even the Chinese Communist movement, with
its ideological and organizational debt to Western Europe, was
a product of European influence.

It is not surprising then to discover that after 1949 China continued to be affected by the outside world. The Korean War
(1950–53), in which China fought against American-led United
Nations forces, and a military and economic alliance with the
Soviet Union produced the so-called "lean to one side" policy
of close friendship with Moscow and bitter hostility toward
Washington. In the early 1950s, China seemed well on the way
to becoming a carbon copy of the USSR. Then with the Great
Leap Forward Beijing (formerly Peking) began to chart its own
course. The two Communist powers drifted rapidly apart, and
by the early 1960s they were already deeply split.

China and the United States had nursed their mutual antagonism since the Korean conflict. Even though some sort of Sino-
American strategic relationship might have seemed logical by the
mid-1960s, when China and the USSR appeared to be on the
verge of open warfare, cooperation between the champion of
capitalism and the self-styled model for people's liberation
movements seemed out of the question. It became all the more
unlikely in the mid- to late 1960s, when China experienced the
radicalism of the Cultural Revolution and the United States drifted

into a large-scale war against Beijing's socialist ally Vietnam. Yet in the early 1970s, rather unexpectedly, China began to build relationships with America and the other developed nations. Since that time and especially since Mao's death in 1976, the People's Republic has abandoned its doctrinaire aloofness. Despite impediments and setbacks, relations with the United States, Japan, and all the other industrialized democracies have blossomed. Concurrently with this "open door," Marxism and especially Mao's version of it have been given fresh interpretations to permit pragmatic modernization policies, making the People's Republic a rather different society from what it was under the sterner hand of Mao Zedong.

These are the outlines of the narrative found in the following pages. It is a vast story for which there exists a correspondingly massive literature. An increasingly sophisticated phalanx of historians, sociologists, anthropologists, economists, political scientists, geographers, and humanists has, in the last quarter century, written articles, monographs, and books by the hundreds on every facet of contemporary Chinese life. This is not to suggest that there is not a great deal yet to be learned. But it is clear that for the interested learner, even one confined to materials in English, there exists a wealth of scholarship on China.

Why, then, a book such as this which attempts to compress in a few pages such a vast subject? From personal experience as a teacher of college undergraduates, experience confirmed by my colleagues, I am convinced of the need for an abbreviated account of the history of the People's Republic, a book that can be integrated into various courses (political, historical, comparative) and do a tolerably good job of representing the subject. In addressing this need, I have been under no illusion that a condensed version can fully replace fuller analyses of events. Because human affairs are complex and their causes and relationships elusive, the treatment possible in a few hundred pages necessarily oversimplifies, glosses over, and even ignores important points. Competing interpretations of events and different perspectives necessarily cannot all be represented. Thus, the reader is cautioned to treat this book as no more than an introduction to a subject so vast that its study could consume many lifetimes.

And yet, all that being said, it may still be possible for a brief account to give the reader a reasonably good idea of the general contours of historical events in China over the last several decades. That, at any rate, is my hope. The student who wishes to pursue certain questions further may begin by consulting the Suggested Readings at the end of this book.

1

Old China and
Young Revolutionaries

Village China and Young Mao

China: Vast Agrarian Empire

On December 26, 1893, a first son, Mao Zedong, was born into a peasant family in Hunan Province. Neither background nor upbringing marked him as other than a typical son of the soil. The odds were that he would live out his life, as did so many others, in a single landscape of terraced hills that glistened brilliantly in the spring, grew richly green in summer, and, barring floods, droughts, and infestations, turned brown with ripe grain in the fall.

China then was a vast, feeble agrarian empire whose population was concentrated in the eastern half of the country in nine greater regions[1] (see Fig. 1). These regions were the economic building blocks of the empire. They differed from each other in size and wealth, but each contained a central, populous, fertile core located on an important river system. Each was largely self-sufficient in food and fiber although there was also a great deal of trade between the regions. Collectively, they were home to about 397 million people in the year of Mao's birth. This was perhaps one-quarter of the earth's population.

Mao was born in central China in the heart of the second most

FIG. 1 Greater agricultural regions of China.

populous of these nine regions. Through it flowed China's long-est river, the Yangzi. The rich soils and abundant rains of the three provinces that comprised this region produced a grain sur-plus for export to other parts of China. Mao's father was a rice farmer and broker. Besides rice, which was the staple crop in six of the nine regions, the products of China consisted almost entirely of other agricultural commodities and handicraft manufactures. They included wheat, millet, maize, potatoes, sweet potatoes, peanuts, rapeseed, tobacco, tea, opium, silk, cotton, processed foods, paper, furniture, rugs, salt, and coal. The economic system was a vast, complex, essentially self-contained one, almost entirely lacking in science and industrial technology.

The peasants who grew these crops and made most of these handicrafts constituted an overwhelming majority of the population. About 94 percent of all Chinese lived in the country's 800,000 villages.[2] These villages were typically clusters of mud or brick houses with thatched or tiled roofs and dirt floors. Each dwelling was enclosed by a wall. From fifteen to thirty of these small villages were arranged within walking distance around a larger village, where markets were held every few days. These markets were connected by road or water to still larger market towns, where more frequent, larger, and more specialized exchanges took place. Further up the scale, there was an ascending system of towns, small cities, and great cities. Mao's birthplace appears to have been a large market village. Thus he grew up in a community that was on the boundary between peasant China and the China of towns and cities.

Poor China

Outside observers were always struck by the miserable standard of living of most Chinese. Although Mao was certainly not among the poorest, he remembered later in life that as a child he virtually never got animal protein with his rice. His father, who may have been excessively stingy, gave his hired laborers eggs just once a month and meat never. Most people spent almost all their income just to eat. This poverty reflects principally one central fact about China: population density. With one-quarter of the world's people, China possesses only six percent of the earth's arable land. For example, in a typical southern community in the year 1929 just over half of all farm families owned plots of land totaling between one and two acres. Another third owned between two and eight acres. Eight percent of farms contained less than two acres while only five percent contained more than eight acres.[3] With land scarce and valuable, the peasant lavished attention upon his scattered strips of soil and managed to achieve, especially in rice cultivation, a high yield per unit of land.

Unfortunately the peasant's capital (some hand tools and perhaps an animal) and other inputs were the kind that had been used for centuries. Night soil, animal manures, and green manures were used but no chemical fertilizers. Chemical pesticides and scientifically bred seeds were unknown. Human or animal labor pumped the water and pulled the plow without the assistance of motors and engines. As a result, high per-acre yields were lower than they could have been by using modern inputs. Achieved at the cost of unremitting, backbreaking toil, these yields were very low in terms of labor inputs.

For generations China's harvests had just kept pace with her huge and slowly expanding population. There was little surplus. In most places over the long run, things didn't get much better, and they didn't get much worse. In the short run in a given region, a good year could be followed by a year of flood, drought, or pests; and hunger or even famine could result. For example, not long after sixteen-year-old Mao had first moved away from his native village, Hunan Province suffered a famine. In one incident, revolting peasants seized a grain shipment being sent to the city market. It belonged to Mao's father.

Haves and Have-nots

The career of Mao's father is an instructive example of the distribution of wealth and income among the peasantry. Before Mao's birth, his father had gone into debt and lost his land. The reason for his borrowing is not known, but it is known that peasants commonly pawned or mortgaged property to get working capital for farming or to pay for important occasions, particularly parents' funerals and children's weddings. Mao senior left his village, spent some years as a soldier, and later returned. Then he took up petty trading.

He prospered and saved enough to reclaim his land. At this point he owned about two and one-fourth acres, which raised his status from landless "poor peasant" to "middle peasant." Through hard work and watching every coin, his assets grew. When Mao Zedong was still a young boy, Mao senior bought an additional acre, thereby becoming a "rich peasant." He also began to use his savings to deal in grain. He bought up rice and shipped it to the city market. He also made loans to other peasants. He hired farm labor in order to free his own time for brokering and moneylending. He had every reason to consider himself a success. As a farmer he produced a profitable surplus of rice. His other enterprises also made money. As he came up in the world, he replaced his thatched roof with tile; but, according to his son's later testimony, he never relaxed his stinginess.

This case history exemplifies the distribution of wealth. Every village had its landless or nearly landless peasants who scratched out a living through day labor, tenant farming, handicrafts, or service occupations. Above them on the economic ladder were families who owned enough land to sustain themselves through agriculture, and those considered "rich" because they owned more land than they could personally cultivate and were able to rent some of it out. At the top of the scale were wealthy landlord families who avoided all manual labor and lived on their rents and other business income. The larger their holdings, the more likely they were to live in the towns or cities.

Figure 2 represents one analysis of the distribution of farm land. The poorest 60 percent of households, corresponding roughly to what the Communists came to refer to as "poor peasants" and "lower-middle peasants," owned only about 18 percent of the land. Those whom the Communists would call "middle peasants," constituted about one-third of the households and owned one-third of the land—a proportion that would seem fair.

FIG. 2 Proportion of farmland held by poor, middle, and wealthy households (1936).

At the top of rural society, the "rich peasants" and landlords, who constituted 10 percent of all households, held title to nearly half of all the fields.[4] It is clear that a great economic gulf separated the mass of have-nots from the small minority of haves.

The case of Mao's father is also interesting because of its portrayal of economic mobility. From middle peasant to landless soldier to penny entrepreneur, then back up to middle peasant and ultimately to rich peasant, rice broker, and moneylender Mao senior had a career that covered a considerable range. Over time this sort of changing fortune was fairly typical. Hard work, investment, and good luck could pull a family up. But bad luck could drag a family down. The custom of equal inheritance by male heirs also tended to fragment accumulated wealth. Though it is true that some big families managed to stay prosperous for generations, a certain egalitarianism pervaded village China. Many poor peasants had once seen better times. Many rich peasants had risen, like Mao's father, from humbler circumstances. They all knew that these circumstances might easily be reversed.

The Family

Economically, socially, psychologically, and in every other way, the family system shaped and organized life in China. Since time immemorial the central focus of every person's life was the nuclear family into which he was born (or into which she was married) and the larger lineage or "clan" to which that family belonged. Most villages consisted of just a few lineages, and there were many villages that had but one. Succor in childhood, inheritance of land and skills, the acquisition of a suitable spouse, security in old age, and proper burial with the fullest possible rituals—these were among the important functions carried on exclusively in the family setting.

Each person was enjoined to cultivate the virtue of "filial piety" or deference toward parents and elders. Everyone was expected to marry, families often betrothing their offspring while they were still children; and the principal objective of conjugal life was to produce sons to carry on the family name. It was acceptable for a husband with means to take secondary wives for this purpose or merely for his greater pleasure. It was expected that wives would be fertile, strictly segregated from contact with other men, and confined to the home. They were expected to subordinate themselves to their parents-in-law, their husbands, and, when parents and husbands died, to their sons. Thus, the family system was both protective and demanding. It was hierarchical and conservative. For centuries it had been the bedrock on which Chinese civilization was built.

To the City

It was the intention of Mao's father that the boy remain at home. Having received a rudimentary education, he was supposed to help with the family accounts while also working the land. To this end, Mao was taken out of school at thirteen.

But the father had not counted on his son's rebelliousness. There had been some early signs of this. When Mao was only ten, he ran away for three days in protest against his teacher's harsh methods. Then, soon after being withdrawn from school, he got into a furious verbal exchange with his father in the presence of guests. Enraged by such filial disrespect, the father came after Mao. Mao ran off. The mother pursued them both, trying to calm the situation. When they got to the pond at the front of the house, the boy stopped and threatened to drown himself if his father came one step closer. With the mother mediating, negotiations resulted in a compromise: a limited apology from the son and no beating by the father.

Mao's father must have begun to realize that his hold on the boy was extremely weak. Mao continued his education through private reading. Before long he ran off to the nearby home of an unemployed law student and managed to find a teacher for further instruction in the classics. By fourteen or fifteen he was becoming aware of the wider world and was about to depart from Shaoshan. The succeeding stages of his career took him to the other arena of Chinese life, the towns and cities.

The first stage of that odyssey was a year (1910) at a "modern higher primary school" in the large town that served as the seat of the neighboring county. Mao was sixteen years old and still quite provincial. He was not even aware of the death, two years earlier, of the emperor of China. From then on his broadening and education accelerated. In 1911, Mao managed to enter another school in the city of Changsha. The county seat he had just come from was an important town, but it paled to insignificance beside Changsha, provincial capital and regional metropolis. He spent the next seven years, a very important period in his development, in that city.

A brief stint in a secondary school was interrupted by the dramatic events of the fall and winter of 1911. Revolutionary groups had been active for years, and one of their attempts to overthrow the Qing dynasty began on October 10 at Wuhan, the great tri-city metropolis to the north of Changsha. This uprising and the events that followed led to the abdication of the last Qing emperor in 1912. And while all this was still in progress, Mao decided to go up to Wuhan to serve in the revolutionary army. But the insurgency came to him in Changsha, where he served as a soldier for six months. Finally, the disturbances ceased, and he turned his attention to a future career. After considering police work, soapmaking, law, and commerce, he matriculated at the provincial normal school to train as a teacher.

In his five years at the First Provincial Normal School, Mao got not only an academic but also a political education. By the time he graduated in 1918, he had become a political writer and organizer with a growing reputation. Back in his army days, he had been introduced to newspapers and the steady diet of current affairs that they provided. He encountered socialist ideas. He also observed a great deal of social injustice. For example, in 1912 he came across the murdered bodies of the two populist leaders who had established the first revolutionary government at Changsha. They had been assassinated by conservative enemies.

The three years following graduation were still more eventful. In the summer of 1919, every city and town in China was convulsed with prolonged demonstrations and boycotts against the great powers. Workers and the middle classes joined students in protesting the Versailles treaties, which gave to Japan, as part of the settlement of World War I, Germany's former sphere of influence in Shandong Province. But as widespread and passionate as these demonstrations were, the ferment of these years went much deeper. In Russia the Bolshevik Revolution had occurred, and the optimism of this new regime infected some Chinese intellectual circles with a great interest in Marxism. Other currents of thought had a great vogue as well. For example, John Dewey and Bertrand Russell made extended speaking tours in China. Not even the Chinese language was immune to change; the difficult classical style was widely abandoned in favor of simpler colloquial writing. Chinese women took the first steps toward sexual equality.

The epicenter of this political and cultural disturbance was the national university at Beijing. Soon after graduating from normal school, Mao went to Beijing and briefly worked at the university as assistant librarian. Between that summer of 1919 and the summer of 1921, he spent two brief periods on the fringes of the university. He twice went to Shanghai, the greatest of China's commercial cities. Twice he returned to Changsha, first as a political organizer and later with the additional responsibility of directing a primary school.

By late 1919, Mao considered himself a Marxist and devoted his energies to writing and organizing for the new cause. The first great historic moment of his life occurred in the summer of 1921 although at the time it could not have seemed as significant as it later became. Having organized a small Communist group in Changsha, Mao journeyed once again to Shanghai. This time it was to participate in the First National Party Congress of the Chinese Communist party. This, in effect, brought the Party formally into existence.

Urban China

The towns and cities of China contained only a small proportion of the country's total population, but their influence on national life was great. It had always been the case that governmental functions—the imperial court, provincial offices, and county magistracies—had their headquarters in the empire's 1200 walled towns and cities. Also, interregional trade and specialized handicrafts tended to locate in urban settings. Then in the nineteenth century, Chinese cities acquired a new aspect. Increasing numbers of the largest ones became "treaty ports."

The first treaty ports were established in 1842. In accordance with the provisions of the Opium War settlement between Britain and the defeated Qing dynasty, five cities were designated as locations where foreign trade could be carried on and where Westerners could establish "concessions," virtually self-governing communities. More treaties followed, and by the time Mao was born there were dozens of treaty ports, large and small, on the coast and on navigable rivers. Changsha was one. Wuhan was another, which also had a British "concession." At the capital, Beijing, the foreign diplomatic community acquired an enclave protected by their own troops.

Shanghai led all other cities in foreign influence. At the turn of the century, Shanghai was already China's great international port and was rapidly becoming the largest center for light industry as well. Companies run by the English, the Japanese, and other foreigners, as well as by Chinese businesspeople, were rapidly expanding in the period from 1895 to about 1920. Down in the villages, peasants were still mired in the timeless cycles of sowing and harvesting. But the cities were experiencing a vigorous industrial growth. Between 1912 and 1920 industrial production increased nationally at an average rate of over 14 percent per year. During this period the major trunk lines of north China's still limited but very important railroad system were built. Telegraph lines connected major cities.

Urban change was not limited to economics. The Western cultural impact was also very great. Until about the time of Mao's birth, China's educated elites had generally resisted foreign culture, which they considered barbarian. The few open to new ideas were vastly outnumbered by an uninterested majority. But in 1895, China suffered a humiliating defeat at the hands of modernizing Japan. The Sino-Japanese War settlement imposed a huge indemnity and required China to relinquish Taiwan. Three years later Germany, Russia, England, and France forced the Qing government to grant them special "spheres of influence" in selected regions of the empire. Then in 1900 the United States and Japan joined these same powers in retaliating against government-encouraged, anti-Christian mobs. This was the Boxer incident, and it cost the dynasty a huge indemnity and further humiliation. As a succession of catastrophes, these incidents were unprecedented since the collapse of the Ming dynasty three hundred years earlier. Only after this succession of blows to their self esteem did the intelligentsia begin to take an interest in Western ideas.

Thus, when Mao was growing up, a great upsurge in foreign influence was underway. It was then widely recognized that Japan had made herself powerful by emulating the West. Unless China did the same, she would grow progressively weaker until the great powers decided to dismember her at will. Although the sense of crisis was particularly strong in the cities, it even reached Mao's Shaoshan village. "Alas!" said one of the pamphlets that young Mao read, probably without appreciating its full significance, "China will be subjugated."[5] A new, Western-influenced intelligentsia emerged from about 1900 to 1920. In school Mao's generation studied a curriculum that included increasing amounts of modern subject matter. Western technology, science, social philosophy, economics, political thought, literature, art, architecture, music, military organization, strategy and tactics, dress, social mores, business methods, administrative techniques—and much more—flooded into China. The impact of all this was principally felt in the cities.

But the Chinese not only admired and copied foreigners. They also resented and even hated them. They fumed inwardly against the national loss of face that had accumulated for decades and against Western arrogance and opportunism. In 1917, Mao attended a soccer match between his school and one that had links to Yale University. He jumped up and shouted, "Beat those slaves of foreigners!" Later in Shanghai, to persuade an old friend to stop wearing Western clothes, Mao led him to the British park and showed him the sign barring entry to dogs and Chinese.

Thus, in this period a few rays of hopeful economic, social, and intellectual change faintly illuminated a generally gloomy landscape. The cities experienced rapid economic, social, and intellectual changes, but the countryside was different. Agriculture was still dominated by vast populations toiling in tiny plots with simple tools. Politically, China suffered from two massive problems. First, the government was weak. Until 1911 the declining Qing dynasty was struggling to survive and could not play a vigorous leadership role. When it collapsed, there ceased to be any effective administration at all. Second, foreign meddling continued. In 1914 it actually intensified as Japan exploited the war to pursue imperialistic expansion in China.

Unification, Invasion, and Civil War

Postwar China: 1920–36

After World War I the economy entered troubled times. Industrial growth slowed down, and agriculture began to experience a prolonged crisis. The world economy was partly responsible for all this. The disappearance of wartime demand for Chinese products was followed by harmful international currency manipulations in the 1920s and world depression in the 1930s. The absence of strong, stable central government made it doubly difficult for the country to cope with this economic adversity.

Politically, the early 1920s saw the emergence of two significant movements: the Nationalist party and the Communist party. The Nationalist Party has for decades been referred to in the literature as the KMT. This acronym stands for the party's Chinese name, transcribed according to an older system of spelling. Although this spelling departs from the system used throughout the present text, it will be retained because of long usage. The same applies to the names of the party's two major leaders, Sun Yat-sen and Chiang Kai-shek, which have long been thus spelled in Western writings.

The KMT, as it existed in the 1920s and beyond, was reorganized by Sun Yat-sen in 1923 and 1924 out of earlier parties. Sun had been a well-known revolutionary since the turn of the century. Although his new organization had Soviet advisers and funding, its members ranged from moderate to conservative. The party quickly became the largest and strongest in the country. When Sun Yat-sen died in 1925, the KMT came under the control of General Chiang Kai-shek. He soon began to tower over the political landscape and remained China's acknowledged leader from 1927 through the late 1940s. From 1927 until war with Japan broke out in 1937, Chiang presided over a new government called the Republic of China with his capital in Nanjing on the Yangtze River. He achieved a loose reunification of the country.

Chiang had to cope with three extremely serious political enemies. One of them was the warlords. Ever since the collapse of the Qing in 1912, the problem of local militarists had been growing until, in the late 1910s and early 1920s, hundreds of warlords, large and small, dominated the entire country. Although Chiang was able to bring some of them into his government and to subdue others, local warlords continued to plague most provinces and to frustrate administrative unification. A second problem was Japan. Of all the factors that shaped China's destiny in those years, Japanese aggression was perhaps the most damaging. In 1928, Japanese generals and diplomats tried to block Chiang's efforts at reunification. Then, in 1931, Japanese troops occupied Manchuria, China's rich northeastern region. In 1932 they established the puppet state of Manchukuo there, and during the next few years they pushed southward into the provinces around Beijing. Finally, in 1937, they mobilized a full-scale invasion, which resulted in Japanese occupation of all the major cities, from Beijing in the north to Wuhan and Shanghai in the center to Canton in the south. As a result of this, in 1938, Chiang's government was driven deep into the western province of Sichuan where he remained for the duration of World War II (1938–45).

Chiang's third major headache in the 1920s and 1930s was the Communist movement. As noted earlier, in 1921 a handful of young radicals, including Mao Zedong, held the first congress of the Chinese Communist party (CCP). Back then, the fledgling Party seemed unlikely ever to rule China. Its members were few and young. It depended heavily on Moscow for doctrinal and financial support as well as for strategic and tactical direction. In classic Marxist fashion, it was preoccupied with the industrial proletariat and gave top priority to organizing unions and fomenting strikes. But despite some temporary successes, these efforts did not constitute a formula for long term victory because the number of factory workers in an underdeveloped country like China was too small.

In 1924, when Sun Yat-sen was building the KMT with Russian assistance, Moscow prevailed on the Chinese Communists to enter into a cooperative relationship with Sun's much larger party. All Chinese Communists joined the KMT as individual members and worked within the KMT. This collaboration continued during the first two years of Chiang Kai-shek's leadership and while Chiang's national reunification efforts got underway (1925–27). But Chiang and most of the KMT were essentially conservative whereas the CCP, which had begun to grow rapidly, pushed for socially radical policies such as land reform and labor unions. Conflict was inevitable. In the spring of 1927 these two forces had a violent falling out. Chiang took the initiative and attacked the radicals in a bloody purge that the Communists called the "White Terror." Hundreds of CCP and union members were executed. Communist counterattacks failed. So the remnants of a shattered party either went underground in the cities or took to the hills.

But Chiang was mistaken if he thought he had cured his CCP headache. In their adversity and cut off from Russian assistance and interference, the surviving Communists began to fashion a homegrown strategy for success. Having earlier ignored military action for purely political action, a disadvantage that allowed Chiang nearly to wipe them out, they now began to nurture a Red Army under close Party control. Second, they began to abandon their urban preoccupations, realizing that the cities were precisely where Chiang's strength was greatest and that their opportunity lay in the vast, suffering countryside.

At the center of this rethinking was Mao Zedong. He was one

of those who had retreated to the hills in 1927. By 1930 his peasant-based guerrilla strategy began to take shape. Together with other Communist rebels, he established a rural base area in the southeastern province of Jiangxi, named the Jiangxi Soviet. They began to work out land policies, military tactics, and other doctrines for success among the peasantry. Before long they were ruling perhaps nine million people. To Chiang Kai-shek's horror, the CCP had risen from the ashes.

Chiang renewed his attack in a series of five encircling campaigns. The first four went badly for Chiang, requiring him to pull back his columns, which had been badly mauled by Communist guerrillas. But by 1934 under German advisers, Chiang adopted a methodical, massive encirclement approach that threatened to crush the Communist movement once again. In desperation the Reds decided to break out. In October 1934 about 100,000 began a famous trek known to history as the Long March. It was to last a year and cover 6,000 miles as the beleaguered Communists fought their way to the northwest. Perhaps 90 percent of those who started out never made it to the end. It happened that, prior to this serious setback, Mao had been demoted by Moscow-backed Chinese Communists who had migrated to the Jiangxi Soviet from Shanghai and other cities. He thus escaped responsibility for the debacle.

Although the Long March was a tactical defeat, it had very beneficial psychological and organizational effects and gave the Communists an important strategic advantage. Psychologically, the Long March was not unlike Valley Forge in the American Revolution. The suffering and heroism actually strengthened the movement and proved that it was indomitable. Organizationally, the Long March clarified the leadership of the Party. Mao began to emerge as the undisputed leader. (One biographer describes him as a latter-day Moses.) With the support of several talented military and political men, some of whom had opposed him in earlier times, he reclaimed his position at the top.

To understand the strategic benefits of the Long March, one must remember that Japan's aggressiveness had been increasing throughout the 1930s. On the Long March, the CCP trumpeted a new purpose and thereby transformed a retreat into a holy cause. The Communists proclaimed that they were marching to fight Japan. People all over China had grown increasingly disturbed by Japanese incursions in the north. In the public mind, Chiang Kai-shek's standing diminished each time he bowed to Tokyo's insatiable demands. Why should Chinese fight Chinese, it was asked, while Japan was overrunning the country? The Communists seized this issue of anti-Japanese nationalism and thereby preempted an extremely powerful emotional force.

The Yanan Years, 1937–45

The Japanese invasion of 1937 ruined everything for Chiang. It drove him out of the big cities, which were his economic lifeline. His plan for consolidating Nationalist rule required large modern armies to crush the warlords and the Communists. Funding for these forces came from taxes and other impositions on commerce and manufacturing, especially in Shanghai. Without these urban revenues, where was he to get adequate support for this military consolidation? The invasion also crippled his rural strategy. Although agriculture was by far the largest sector of the economy, the government amazingly did not tax landowners. This was the price that a weak regime paid for their political support. Now, in addition to denying Chiang the cities, the invasion destroyed village stability in many places. Under Japanese occupation, many conservative local leaders fled, thereby removing their direct influence. Others collaborated with the invaders, thereby branding themselves with the traitor's mark. In either case, the old local hierarchy received a severe blow. A kind of political vacuum resulted, into which stepped the CCP.

In contrast to causing the Nationalists difficulties, World War II was a boon to the Communists, who were now able, in their northwest sanctuary under Mao's firm leadership, to practice guerrilla warfare. It was something they had become increasingly good at since they had taken to the hills in 1927. Japanese atrocities played into their hands by driving millions of peasants into active resistance. With the local notables frequently absent or weakened, as just described, the Communists were able to place themselves at the head of this movement. Thus, it was they—and not the government—who increasingly enjoyed the reputation of leading the nation's struggle against Japan.

But a full analysis of the CCP success must also take into account the political skills that they had sharpened in the preceding decade. The Party had schooled itself in promoting the interests of the ordinary people. It had learned how to give voice and muscle to popular demands for things like land, elemental fairness, and women's liberation. Its leaders did without offices, fine uniforms, and motorcars. Consequently, as Mao put it, the Party was like "fish" in the people's "water."

Mao had a theory covering this relationship. He called it "mass line," and it might be thought of as his answer to Western democracy (or "bourgeois democracy," as he called it). The goal was solidarity in the effort to achieve the goals of the people. Both disciplined leadership and responsiveness to the needs of the masses were indispensable. To do this, the Party must remain intimately involved with the masses, consult them about their problems, and work out appropriate courses of action. As the resulting policies were implemented, the Party would monitor their effects, consult with the people, and adjust them accordingly. Thus, instead of mere majority rule, Mao aimed at total solidarity between the CCP and the masses.[6]

Party organizational structures also adapted to the fragmented character of guerrilla warfare. The center at Yanan had to promote flexibility and decentralization while still maintaining control over general policy. Intense indoctrination was one tool for achieving this. Every member was required to participate in reading and discussions on such subjects as Marxist theory and guerrilla war. Strict party discipline was also vital. The leading group of every military and administrative unit contained its Party "fraction," and these people were expected to implement Party directives. As a result, broad strategy could be decided at the top and adapted tactically in the field.

The Party's popular image added to its organizational strength.

The superhuman feats of the Long March had already given the Communists a romantic glamour. Their cause was just. They could be battered but never beaten. The Yanan years only added luster to their reputation. Yanan was located in the poorest of China's eight agricultural regions. Even the Communist leaders lived in caves like ordinary peasants. Supplies were scarce; and luxuries, unknown. Everything seemed simple, wholesome, and honest. The troops were strictly taught to respect the people and pay for what they took. If one word could encompass their myth, the word would be "purity."[7] Consequently, the Communists built up a solid reputation as the one positive and effective political movement in China.

The cult of Mao was also forming. Certain other leaders won wide fame as well, but Mao was becoming preeminent. Already the messiah of the Long March, he was increasingly the personification of the Communist party. From his pen came a body of doctrines on guerrilla warfare and theoretical writings in which Marxism was applied to Chinese conditions. A rewritten Party history portrayed him as always central and always correct. In 1942 a move to consolidate Mao's position resulted in a "rectification" campaign. The entire Party was set to studying and discussing doctrine (mostly Mao's writings), criticizing comrades, accepting criticism of themselves, and rectifying their mistakes. At this same time, the propaganda apparatus came under Mao's control.

As a result of these favorable conditions, the CCP grew rapidly. Tables 1 and 2 show this dramatic expansion. The Party's original 1921 membership of fifty-seven had grown to about 58,000 by the spring of 1927. After the disastrous falling out with Chiang Kai-shek in that same year, the numbers went as low as 10,000 and only gradually recovered to 122,000 by 1930. In the early 1930s, the heyday of Mao's guerrilla base in the southeast, membership grew to about 300,000, but the Long March again reduced the ranks to 40,000 on the eve of the Japanese invasion. Then within three years of the onset of hostilities, the CCP boasted 800,000 members. Under severe military

Table 1. Growth of the CCP

1921	57
1922	123
1923	432
1925	950
1927 (April)	57,967
1927 (end)	10,000
1928	40,000
1930	122,000
1933	300,000
1937	40,000
1940	800,000
1945	1,200,000
1947	2,759,456
1948	3,065,533
1949	4,500,000
1956	10,730,000
1969	22,000,000
1973	28,000,000
1977	35,000,000
1982	39,000,000

Table 2. Growth of
the Red Army

1937	92,000
1939	320,000
1940	500,000
1941	440,000
1943	464,000
1945	860,000
1947	1,950,000
1949	4,000,000

pressure from both the Japanese and the Nationalists, they saw their numbers contract slightly in 1941 and 1942, but by 1944 they were once again on the upswing: over 1 million by 1945, more than 2 million by 1947, and almost 5 million by 1949.[8]

The Red Army experienced a similar expansion. From slightly

over 90,000 troops in 1937, the Communist forces reached half a million in 1940. The numbers then leveled off for four years and began to grow rapidly again toward the end of the war. There were almost 900,000 troops in 1945, and that number swelled to 4 million by 1949.[9]

Civil War, 1945–49

Still, Generalissimo Chiang Kai-shek and his KMT seemed to be in an enviable position at war's end. Recognized throughout the world as China's legitimate government, they had a large army and faced excellent prospects for returning to Nanjing in triumph. Two of the impediments to consolidation had now been eliminated: Japan lay in rubble under Allied occupation, and the remaining warlords were no match for Nationalist armies. United States aid could be counted on because a cornerstone of American foreign policy was a strong non-Communist government in China. When the United Nations was established, the United States insisted that China be considered a great power with a permanent seat on the Security Council.

Unfortunately for Chiang, the third of his three major stumbling blocks, the Communists, were stronger than ever. With their large party and army, they controlled the rural hinterland in most of north China and in many other regions as well. The populations under their control numbered perhaps 90 million. For Chiang to meet this serious challenge would require every material, organizational, and moral resource available to the government. His regime was simply not equal to the challenge. Although there were many decent and dedicated civil servants, the government as a whole was incompetent and corrupt. The generals, under the generalissimo's direction, pursued a losing strategy and proved tactically inept. "The world's worst leadership," one U.S. general called them.[10] They committed a massive error in attempting in 1946 to take and hold vast regions from the Communists. The result was well-equipped but overextended armies in Manchuria and elsewhere in the north. With such a strategic deficit and short on tactical brilliance, the Nationalist armies were a force that was doomed to defeat.

While the generals were thus engaged, the Nationalists' civil administration received inadequate resources. Above all, it could not solve the critical problem of hyperinflation. By late 1946 it took a million Chinese dollars to buy the equivalent of one 1937 Chinese dollar. And that was only the beginning. The wholesale price index topped 16 million in December, 1947, 21 billion a year later, and well over 2 trillion by the last report in March 1949. With this cancer eating at the morale of government and citizens alike, it was scarcely likely that the numerous other administrative problems would be solved. In fairness it should be noted that this same regime ruled Taiwan from 1950 on, providing stable administration and fostering economic development. What this might or might not prove about the causes for the Nationalist defeat is subject to debate. But it does perhaps suggest that the outcome of the civil war may be best accounted for by the momentum that the Communists had gained during the war. In smoother times, Chiang's regime might conceivably have proved adequate.

By 1945 the Communists were a completely rejuvenated movement. All the elements of a successful insurgency were present: leadership, organization, doctrine, and popular support. But their true strength was not then widely appreciated. When civil war erupted in 1946, few expected the Reds to achieve a rapid, sweeping victory. The CCP leaders themselves, although confident of the final outcome, overestimated the time they would need. Stalin, even after their decisive victory in November 1948, urged them to consolidate the north and leave south China to the Nationalists. But by that time the Communists could sense victory. They would not be denied.

Red armies were isolating and surrounding government forces. In the far northeast, entire government divisions surrendered in the fall of 1948, giving the Communists possession of Manchuria, China's greatest industrial prize. Then the Communists moved down into the north China plain. The government defenders of cities and strategic crossroads were defeated during the winter. In February 1949 the Communists occupied Beijing (Peking), China's capital until 1927 and soon to be restored to its former importance.

Would the government be able to hold south China? Militarily, it was possible. The Yangzi River, which cuts China into northern and southern halves, is a great natural bulwark. "The Nationalists could have defended the Yangzi River with broomsticks if they had the will to do so," said a senior American general.[11] But the crack armies of the KMT had already disintegrated, and the fighting spirit of what remained was spent. Demoralization was epidemic. Generals bungled. Troops surrendered or fled. By spring Communist armies had battled across the Yangzi. Waves of refugees washed across the landscape while officials shamelessly looked to their personal advantage and carried off what they could. In October 1949, China's southern metropolis, Guangzhou (Canton), was taken by the Reds. Appeals for more American aid fell on deaf ears. Finally, Chiang Kai-shek removed the remnants of his government and army to the island of Taiwan for a last stand.

Communist initiatives were moving forward in every sphere. In northern villages, land reform was under way. In national politics twenty-three non-Communist parties agreed to participate in a constitutional convention to be called, "The Chinese People's Political Consultative Conference." Conventions of labor confederations and women's and youth organizations convened. Then in Beijing on October 1, 1949, Mao Zedong, wearing a military tunic with a single decoration, proclaimed the establishment of the People's Republic of China (PRC).

Personalities and Causes

Mao did not stand alone on that podium on October 1, 1949. Nor were the Communist movement and the People's Republic his personal creations. Beside him, literally and figuratively, stood many personalities whose heroic contributions gave them a claim to important roles in the new regime. It would not be possible to understand the history of the People's Republic without meeting at least some of these figures. In the brief biographies that follow, the first five people came to Beijing in the spring of 1949 to set up the new central government. They are Liu Shaoqi, Zhou Enlai, Zhu De, Chen Yun, and Chen Boda. Next come five who served temporarily as Party and army commanders in the military regions overseeing the transition to permanent provincial administrations. They are Lin Biao, Chen Yi, Deng Xiaoping, Gao Gang, and Peng Dehuai. Finally, Mao's fourth wife must be introduced.

Liu Shaoqi (1898–1969): Organization Man

Liu Shaoqi (pronounced something like "Liew Shao Chee") was born into a rich peasant family in Hunan Province not far from Mao's home village. As a young Marxist he organized labor unions. By the late 1920s his duties had expanded to include establishing underground Party cells, supervising political work in the army, overseeing Party administration, and writing theoretical articles. During the anti-Japanese resistance he was out in the field perhaps more than any other senior leader, getting to know many of the second-level cadres and laying the groundwork for his later position as top organization man. As Mao consolidated his leadership of the Party at this time, Liu became one of his principal supporters. Liu was one of the first to hail Mao's contributions to Marxism.

By 1949, Liu had become the second-ranking leader in China. He was the number two man in the Party. He was also a vice-chairperson of the People's Revolutionary Military Council, which oversaw the armed forces. He played a leading role in the Chinese People's Political Consultative Conference, a united front assembly that legally established the People's Republic of China and that continued to meet in later years. That conference named an interim legislature, the Central People's Government Council. Liu was one of its six vice-chairpersons. He was the head of China's labor federation and chaired the important Sino-Soviet Friendship Association. He took over temporarily as head of state when Mao went to Moscow in late 1949.

Tall, seldom smiling, and prematurely gray, Liu had little public personality compared to some of his colleagues. One foreigner described him as "dour, unemotional, and colorless in manner but an intelligent man who is practical, thorough, and assiduous in his work." [12] Until 1966 the betting was that Liu would be Mao's successor.

Zhou Enlai (1898–1976): Premier

Zhou Enlai (pronounced something like "Joe Un-lie") was probably the most engaging public figure produced by China in this century. Although he came from a prosperous Tianjin family in north China, he became a leftist around 1920 like so many of his contemporaries. Zhou joined the wave of young Chinese who went to Europe in the 1920s and became a Communist there. Returning home in 1924, he immersed himself in radical politics both as a Communist and as a member Sun Yat-sen's Nationalist Party. His most notable exploit in these years was the 1927 workers' insurrection, which seized control of Shanghai. They delivered the city to Chiang Kai-shek's Nationalist troops, who were completing the first phase of reunification. Unfortunately, the bloody Nationalist-Communist split was in the offing. Within weeks Chiang turned on the workers. Zhou barely escaped with his life, and thousands of his comrades faced the KMT execution squads.

In the difficult years that followed, Zhou became increasingly prominent in the CCP. By the time of the Long March he joined Mao's faction. He became the Party's leading diplomat and negotiator. Because the Communist-Nationalist united front was reestablished to fight Japan, he spent much of the war as CCP liaison officer in Chiang's wartime capital. Beginning in 1949, Zhou began a long and distinguished career as premier, the head of China's government apparatus. He was particularly active in foreign affairs, concurrently holding the title of foreign minister for several years.

The handsome, charming Zhou was immensely liked by Chinese and foreigners alike. He was an inexhaustible worker, well suited to take on the administrative duties of premier. In addition he had a unique instinct for political survival. He remained influential and active through every swing to the left or right until the day he died.

Zhu De (1886–1976): Commander in Chief

When the revolutionaries entered Beijing in 1949, one of its two best-known figures was Zhu De (pronounced "Joo Duh"). Sixty-three years old at the time, he had been the CCP's senior soldier since the late 1920s and, more than any other person, was responsible for the growth and success of the Red Army. He had come to the calling of revolutionary as a result of a sort of mid-life career change. Originally he was an officer in warlord armies, enjoying wealth and concubines and able to indulge an opium addiction. But around 1920 he was affected by the cultural changes that transformed so many young people, and in 1922 he renounced his comfortable position to work for China's salvation. He had to break his narcotic habit, pension off his wives, and subordinate himself to much younger men. For example, when he joined the CCP in 1922 at the age of thirty-six, his sponsor was twenty-four-year-old Zhou Enlai. But pride could not stand in the way of his determination. He was a most appealing character, plain—even slightly ugly—in appearance, modest and unassuming, affable, undogmatic, and devoted to his troops.

After 1928 it was he and Mao who built up the Red Army and the guerrilla bases that enabled the CCP to survive against Chiang's attacks. Zhu excelled as commander in chief, as a field general, and as an inspiration to his soldiers. His name became legendary; peasants claimed he had superhuman powers. Yet his relationship to Mao exemplified Mao's famous dictum that political power grows out of the barrel of a gun and that the Party controls the gun.[13] Without the Red Army, the Communists could not have won China, and Zhu was the architect of that army. Yet, despite some serious disagreements, Zhu worked closely with Mao and never challenged the supremacy of Party leadership. He supplied the perfect combination of great talent and restrained ambition.

Zhu's principal contributions to the revolution were made in the 1930s and 1940s. After 1949 he continued as commander in chief of the army, which was renamed the People's Liberation Army (PLA). He played various other roles as one of the great luminaries of the Party, always counted among the highest circle of leaders.

Chen Yun (1905–   ): Economic Expert

Of all the leaders discussed here, Chen Yun (pronounced "Chun Ywin") was the only one who had actually been an industrial worker. As a labor union organizer, he entered the Party in the mid-1920s and soon found himself embroiled in Zhou Enlai's 1927 Shanghai uprising. He joined Mao in his soviet, participated in the Long March, and worked in Yanan during the anti-Japanese war. As a member of Mao's faction, he became a leading theorist. After 1942 he found his vocation in economic affairs.

In the early years of the People's Republic, holding positions at the highest levels of the Party and government, Chen Yun operated principally as chairperson of the very important Finance and Economic Committee. He directed the rehabilitation of China's industry, transport, and infrastructure and led the successful battle against hyperinflation. In the mid-1950s he was one of the promoters of the Russian-style Five Year Plan. Chen was a genial person without overweening ambition. He had a good mind for practical details and a grasp of what was realistically possible. In this respect he differed from Mao and some others, who sometimes saw what they wanted to see. Yet Chen Yun remained on good terms with everyone. Consequently, although sometimes shoved to the background, he was never purged.

Chen Boda (1904–   ): Theoretician

Chen Boda (pronounced "Chun Bwo Dah" and no relation to Chen Yun) came from poor peasant stock in southern coastal Fujian province. It is not entirely clear how he managed to get an education, but, according to most sources, he graduated from a normal school and then attended a university in Shanghai, where he became a leftist activist. Having joined the Party during the first Nationalist-Communist united front period, he escaped elimination at the time of the 1927 split only by signing a false confession. Soon afterward he went to Moscow, where he became one of the few Chinese deeply conversant with Marxist-Leninist theory.

He was a professor at China University in Beijing when, in 1937, Liu Shaoqi brought him to Yanan. His work in the Propaganda Department caught Mao's attention because he had a powerful writing style, a thorough command of Marxist texts, and a determination to Sinicize Communist theory. Soon Chen Boda found himself serving as Mao's political secretary. In the early 1940s, when Mao launched a drive for unchallenged supremacy within the Party, Chen Boda's pen led the attack against his enemies.

In 1949, Chen Boda became deputy director of the Party's Propaganda Department and vice president of the CCP's most important school. He actively participated in the formation of various mass societies and professional organizations, including those set up for philosophers, economists, artists, writers, social scientists, and natural scientists. Equally heavy was Chen Boda's responsibility as the chief promoter of Mao's thought and of the Chairman's claim to a high place in the pantheon of Marxist-Leninist thinkers. He participated in editing the first three volumes of Mao's selected works, which appeared in 1952.

The "short, stocky [Chen Boda] with thick glasses and a strong [southern] accent made all the more unintelligible by a pronounced stammer'' was probably not the most sought-after dinner guest, particularly as he was severe and puritanical and disdained idle conversation.[14] But he wielded an eloquent and prolific pen. He was, as it were, Mao's house intellectual, and under this powerful patron a steadily ascending career path opened up.

Lin Biao (1908–71): Battlefield Genius and Radical

Lin Biao (pronounced "Lin Beyow") got his start back in the 1920s as a military prodigy. Only twenty years old when the 1927 split erupted, he served under other Communist commanders, including Chen Yi (see later), when they took to the hills. They all linked up with Mao in 1928. That is when, as Lin told an American reporter in 1937, "I first made a name for myself."[15] A name indeed. Within months he emerged as one of China's most brilliant battlefield commanders and an authority on guerrilla tactics. He led his troops in numerous battles, distinguished himself during the Long March, and in 1937 treated the invading Japanese to one of their rare defeats. He received a serious battlefield wound in 1938, which kept him out of the field during most of the anti-Japanese war. During part of that time he served as president of the academy at Yanan and wrote on military questions. The years from 1939 to 1942 he spent in Moscow.

During the civil war the Party put him in command of battles in Manchuria and north China, now considered two of the three decisive military campaigns of the civil war. He secured Manchuria in 1948 and entered Beijing on the last day of January 1949. In the spring his troops moved south and soon took the central metropolis of Wuhan as well as Mao's old city, Changsha. By late 1949 and early 1950 he had taken Guangzhou (Canton) and other major southern cities. Thereupon he installed himself in Wuhan as head of the "Central-South" Party bureau and military region and as chairperson of the committee governing the 175 million residents of six provinces. He remained active in this role for a couple of years. His precise activities until about 1956 are not always clear. He was probably seriously ill during part of this period. A slight, sallow, bespectacled man, Lin withdrew from the forefront of events until the 1960s, when he returned with explosive effect.

Chen Yi (1901–72): Field Commander

Chen Yi (pronounced "Chun Yee" and no relation to the other Chens) came from a prosperous family in the western province of Sichuan. But he became a radical in the period following World War I. His career as a top Communist soldier began in the late 1920s, when he was part of Lin Biao's guerrilla band. They linked up with Mao in 1928. Later, having been left behind by the Long March as a rear guard, he excelled as the commander of the famous New Fourth Army. This force expanded vigorously during the anti-Japanese war and gave the Communists a strong presence in the southeast (although not so secure as their Yanan base). During these years Chen Yun worked closely with the army's political commissar, Liu Shaoqi. Then, rounding off his military career, he commanded the PLA forces that took the Shanghai region in May 1949. This was the third of the three decisive campaigns of the civil war.

Chen Yun stayed on in Shanghai, China's most important industrial city, to preside over the establishment of the regime in this key area. He was head of the East China Military Region and mayor of Shanghai. At this time he began to forge close links with Zhou Enlai, premier and foreign minister, and eventually replaced Zhou in the latter office. A U.S. diplomat described Chen Yi during the anti-Japanese war as "a man of commanding presence, evident vigor and determination." [16] Quite bald, he was outgoing, jovial, and blunt and also rather disdainful of strict ideological conformity.

Deng Xiaoping (1904–   ): Apparatchik Supreme

Deng Xiaoping (pronounced something like "Dung She-owping"), like Zhou Enlai and Chen Yi, began his revolutionary career when he was a work-study student in France in the early

1920s. Having joined the Communist party, he returned to China, via Moscow, in the late 1920s. He helped establish a short-lived guerrilla base in the southwest and then in 1930 made his way to Mao's Jiangxi Soviet. He was assigned military staff duties under Peng Dehuai (see later), the editorship of the Red Army's newspaper, and a lecturing post at the Red Army Academy. He soon became a member of Mao's faction. During the political infighting on the Long March, Deng rallied to Mao and thereafter climbed steadily higher in the Party hierarchy. He spent the anti-Japanese war as a political commissar in one of the three main armies in north China. During the civil war, these troops fought crucial campaigns against the Nationalists.

From late 1949 to mid-1952, Deng was one of the key officials in southwest China, headquartered in his home province of Sichuan. Not primarily a military man, he was the top Party secretary in the region. When he was recalled to Beijing in 1952, his career advanced still further. He was appointed one of five deputy premiers in 1952 and took charge of the Ministry of Finance in 1953. In 1954 he left the latter post to become the secretary general of the Party, a position of great importance. He went still higher in later years, emerging after Mao's death in 1976 as China's leader.

Although barely over five feet tall, Deng always made a powerful impression on people. Back in 1938 a U.S. military observer described him as "short, chunky and physically tough," mentally "as keen as mustard." [17] Colleagues commented on his encyclopedic knowledge, his decisiveness in making decisions, and a certain arrogance and argumentativeness. He was a fervent nationalist and convinced Marxist, but he retained a strong streak of pragmatism.

Peng Dehuai (1898–1974): General

Peng Dehuai's story (his name is pronounced something like "Pung Duh Why") is particularly arresting. He came from the same county as Mao Zedong and from similar rural roots. He apparently exceeded Mao in childhood rebelliousness, being expelled from home at nine years of age for disrespectful conduct (he had kicked over his grandmother's opium pan). He wandered through a succession of jobs until joining the army at sixteen. Among his later adventures was a month of torture at the hands of warlord troops. "I was hung from the roof with a rope round my wrists. Then big stones were piled on my back, while the gaolers stood round kicking me and demanding that I confess . . ."[18] He had found his calling and began to rise as a revolutionary leader.

In 1928, when Communists, hounded by Chiang Kai-shek, were taking to the hills, he linked up with Mao and his group. From that moment his life intertwined with theirs. He became, like Lin Biao, a brilliant battlefield general. He rose to occupy a military status inferior only to that of Zhu De, Mao's co-founder of the Red Army. He played a major role in the campaigns of the early 1930s and in the Long March. During the anti-Japanese war he became top field commander in the north. In the civil war he led an army that conquered the northwest and the far west. Then, like Lin Biao in the south, Chen Yi in the east, and Gao Gang in the northeast, he undertook the job of overseeing the establishment of regular administration in the Northwest Region. In 1950 the Korean War broke out. Peng commanded the Chinese "volunteers" sent to fight the United Nations troops. He remained engaged there until 1953. When he returned to Beijing, he became minister of defense and de facto chief of the PLA.

Jiang Qing (1914–   ): Rebel Actress

It is necessary here to introduce a different sort of person. Jiang Qing (pronounced "Jeeang Ching") exemplifies the special problems facing ambitious women as well as the readiness of many intellectuals to join the Communist movement. She was born in modest circumstances to an urban family in Shandong Province and was orphaned as a child. Raised by a grandfather, she ended her formal education with junior high school. From there she entered a drama school. Like many young women at the time, she admired Nora, the character in Ibsen's *A Doll's House*, who represented the awakened woman. Later Jiang Qing was to play this role on stage and was herself a Nora, striking out independently in defiance of Chinese norms.

At about nineteen she lived with a young Party member who introduced her to communism. When he deserted her, she gravitated to Shanghai's moving picture community. There she may have married a film critic (some say to advance her career), acted in plays and in minor film roles, and got a divorce. Her ambitious, aggressive, independent, and rebellious character was judged as rather scandalous by traditional standards of feminine behavior. She was neither happy nor successful.

The anti-Japanese war ended this phase of her life, for she left Shanghai. In the summer of 1937 she came to Yanan, following the path taken then and later by many leftist intellectuals. But her fate there was special because she happened to meet Mao. At that time his third marriage was either in the process of breaking up or had already done so. His wife, who had been wounded on the Long March, seems to have been suffering from depression or some nervous disorder brought on by the rigors of a revolutionary life. In any event, Mao was lonely and had already had a brief flirtation with a beautiful actress and interpreter. (It should be noted here that Mao married his first wife through a traditional, arranged match and never lived with her. His second wife, who bore him three sons, was beheaded by a Nationalist warlord in 1930.)

According to some, Jiang Qing made a calculated effort to attract the Chairman's interest. Before long the two had struck up a relationship, and she announced to his disapproving colleagues, "I have good news to report to you. The Chairman and I have started living together."[19] She had other news as well; she was pregnant (with a baby girl, as it turned out). With the reluctant consent of his colleagues, Mao married the young actress and gave her the name by which she is known to history (she had been using her stage name, Lan Ping). Through the anti-Japanese war and the civil war years she may have served to some extent as a personal secretary to Mao, especially in regard to artistic and literary affairs, her chief area of interest. She worked in the film section of the Party's Propaganda Department and began a long-term interest in reforming traditional theater.

As will be seen, Jiang Qing has not fared well in the public's esteem. She has become a prototype of the domineering, vain woman. A fair assessment of her life suggests that her sometimes abrasive personality did alienate people, eventually even Mao himself. On the other hand, it must be noted that she was probably forced to be pushy—or at least to seem pushy—by a culture that, even among supposedly liberated revolutionaries, discouraged independence and leadership in women.

Was China Ripe for Revolution?

As we look back at the events of the first half of the century, it all seems so inevitable: a fragmented, impoverished country buffeted by foreign exploitation and aggression; the collapse of the old dynasty followed by a succession of equally ineffectual regimes; the failure of a middle- and upper-class party (the KMT) to unite and reorganize the nation in the 1930s; the steady expansion of popular political participation, gradually even including the peasantry; the emergence of a radical, populist movement (the CCP); the triumph of the Communists based on mass peasant support. It is hard now to imagine another outcome.

Marxism

Was it all so foreordained? In particular, did China's poverty and unequal distribution of income create such a tinderbox of social discontent that the fires of revolution were bound to be ignited? This is one of those questions that it is important to ask—

and impossible to answer fully. One place to start is to ask about the significance of peasant poverty during the time of Mao's youth. Was the rural community so riven with class tensions that revolution was the necessary and inevitable solution to China's agrarian problems? For their part, Marxists have a ready answer to this question, and it deserves our attention because Marxists ultimately won out in the struggle for leadership.

Marxism rests on certain views about the forces really at work as any society changes over time. Karl Marx, living in an age that prized scientific, materialistic explanations, developed the idea that the nature of a society is determined by its technological or economic base (he called it the "mode of production"). The mode of production gives rise to certain "relations of production," that is, to a certain division of labor and a certain class system, for some people will own or control the technology while others will possess only their own labor power. As Marx put it, "The windmill gives you society with the feudal lord; the steam-mill, society with the industrial capitalist." [20]

As the mode of production gives rise to the relations of production, the ruling class (the ones who own the windmills or the steam-mills) will create law, politics, religion, philosophy, and artistic culture. Marx called these intangible phenomena the "superstructure," by analogy with the upper part of a ship, and he insisted that the superstructure is created by the ruling class in order to bolster its social dominance. Just as a ship's hull, not its superstructure, is its base, so a society's material base, not its high culture, is the fundamental determinant of the social structure. (It must be noted, however, that Marx and Engels realized that this matter is complicated and that sometimes the superstructure—especially politics—can affect the base.)

With time, the material base changes, owing to technological improvements. Such change, when great enough, creates a new division of labor, and new classes come into being, again comprising those who own the new means of production and those who provide labor. Also a new "superstructure" begins to emerge. But the old superstructure and the old ruling classes do not simply slink away. In fact, the old establishment resists change. What then emerges is a tension or, as Marxists say, a "contradiction," between the old class system and its superstructure on the one hand and the new system and its supporting culture on the other.

Marx saw the complex adjustments between the changing mode of production, relations of production, and superstructure as the engines of history. History is essentially humankind's progress through successive stages as one mode of production is displaced by another. He further felt that the transition from one type of society into another cannot be a smooth evolutionary process. The old guard defends its position, the new elite struggles for dominance, and the resulting "contradiction" is resolved by revolutionary upheaval.

How would a Marxist, using these concepts, describe the rural China of Mao's youth? The mode of production being peasant agriculture, the relations of production are primarily those between ruling landowning classes and those who possess only their own labor, the peasants. The superstructure consists of traditional authoritarian government and culture. Here is a more detailed description.

> The mode of production of late feudal China was one of land relationships in which state officials and their assistants, landlords, merchants, and moneylenders controlled the means of production, namely land. . . . The mass of poor farmers, artisans, and laborers claimed [only small scattered plots] and depended on their labor to earn a living. The powerful, wealthy feudal class extracted chiefly rent and taxes from the masses. . . . The surplus squeezed out of this economy by the feudal classes was expended partially for luxury consumption, but chiefly for supporting inefficient state organizations, the bureaucracy, and the military.[21]

Some groups, particularly the middle and rich peasants, seem to be in-between classes. But to the extent that they own land or expect to get some, they tend to side with the "feudal" establishment. In this view, the ills of the countryside at the turn of the century grew out of inequality and exploitation. Only redistribution of land and a new ruling class could solve the problem.

To return to Marx, his central purpose was not to expound on feudalism, but to analyze capitalism and to point the way to communism, the final phase of history. He saw that in the eighteenth and and nineteenth centuries a new mode of production had come into existence with the Industrial Revolution. The owners of the new industrial technology were the urban commercial and manufacturing classes. In terms of the relations of production, these are known as the capitalists. Socially they are also referred to as the bourgeoisie. They had sponsored a revolution that overthrew feudalism.

Capitalism is a new kind of exploitation. The value of manufactured products is created by laborers using the capitalists' machines. Out of the owners' receipts from sales of the product, the workers, who are referred to as the "proletariat," are paid just enough to survive. Competition drives the capitalists to appropriate the rest as profits and to reinvest these profits in still more capital. The internal dynamics of the capitalist system necessarily lead to the emergence of a few great capitalists and a wretched class of proletarians.

As the capitalists get richer and fewer and as the workers increase in number, a new historical stage is about to be born. Conditions emerge that will generate a new class of owners, the workers themselves. One day the crisis will erupt. The moment will come when "twenty years will be concentrated into a single day." The workers, made conscious of their plight and its causes, will make a revolution, dispossess the capitalists, take over the factories, and usher in a new final phase of history—communism. In this phase, exploitation is impossible because the workers themselves communally own the means of production.

What did all this have to do with China? By the World War I era, China's briskly expanding factories, mines, and railroads still constituted only the merest beginnings of industrialization. There were barely 2 million industrial workers in the entire population of hundreds of millions of people. Marx's vision of a few great capitalists exploiting a vast proletariat simply didn't fit. This is why Marxism failed to penetrate China before the war.

Marxist theory, however, was further developed by Lenin's concept of "imperialism." As Lenin guided the Russian Bolsheviks during the first quarter of the century, his theory made Marxism more applicable to backward countries like China. The new idea was essentially this: In a world where countries industrialize at varying rates, there will be some advanced and some backward peoples. The advanced nations are precisely those where the swollen proletariat is preparing to expropriate the capitalists. Faced with revolution, the latter stumble on a means of postponing their ruination.

Rather than continue plowing back all their profits domestically, they invest in the backward countries. Profits from overseas can be brought home. Some of these moneys may then be distributed as higher wages to a portion of the domestic proletariat, who will thereby be "bribed" into complacency. As a result, the revolutionary fever at home subsides. To save their necks, the capitalists have learned to exploit other nations, thereby transforming entire peoples into their proletariat.

Imperialism may be the shield that saves the capitalists, but it is also their Achilles' heel. If their colonies can drive them out, they will be unable to bribe the proletariat at home. With only their own fellow citizens to exploit, revolution will engulf them. The implication of this view is that the advanced countries are no longer the center of world history. The exploited backward countries have moved into the limelight. By defeating imperialism, they will bring on world revolution.

In China a century of bitter experience taught that the country was in the grip of some new force that the old traditions could not combat. In the beginning it was trade and missionary work carried on in the treaty ports. Then, after 1895, came ever larger investments in mills, mines, and railroads centering again on the treaty ports. Always these intrusions were secured by Western guns and arrogance.

In Marxist terms, China was partly feudal, with its traditional agrarian system, and partly colonial, thanks to the imperialist intrusions. The "people" in this "semifeudal, semicolonial" society consisted primarily of two classes: workers and peasants. Their historical mission, in cooperation perhaps with other classes, was to eject the foreigners and overthrow the old despotism. The leading role must fall, of course, to the industrial proletariat.

If all this is so, then what should Chinese do who want to save their country? First the workers must be made conscious of their condition. They must be called to action, perhaps in cooperation with peasants. And who will raise the workers' consciousness and lead the charge against the warlords and feudal elites? Naturally, the party of the proletariat, the Communist party. He who would save China must join the Party.

In addition to his theory of imperialism, Lenin also showed how to build a revolutionary party. He perfected the techniques of creating an organization fired with the proletarian cause and disciplined under a central leadership. Only such a powerful force would be equal to the task of battering down the walls of resistance that the exploiters had erected to defend their system.

Lenin's doctrine that the masses must be led by an elite of professional revolutionaries appealed to many young Chinese of Mao's generation. For many who burned inwardly because of foreign humiliation and Chinese retardation, for many who fantasized about becoming saviors of the nation, Marxism-Leninism provided not only an explanation but also a clearly defined role. Like a militant religion, it held out the prospect of salvation and summoned chosen soldiers to take up the bitter struggle. These true believers could be certain about the historical forces at work, the class struggle, and the final outcome.

Other Views

The fact that the Chinese Communists won out does not necessarily mean that their analysis was correct in all respects. There are other possible answers to questions of poverty, revolution, and historical inevitability. For example, it has been pointed out that poverty in China was general and that redistribution would only have spread the misery more evenly. The real solution was to increase production, and achieving this did not require overturning the social system.

Particularly in the first two decades of the century, reforms of existing arrangements could have put the peasantry on the road to greater abundance. This would have required a fiscally healthy government, which, in turn, implied a moderate, fairly apportioned land tax. To stimulate the farmers' efforts, the government would have had to improve land tenure arrangements, particularly rules to allow them to profit from improvements to the land. Technical assistance would have provided them with better seeds, more fertilizer, and pesticides. Cheaper transportation and communication and improved access to credit would have lowered farmers' costs and extended their markets. The thriving agriculture in Taiwan and southern Manchuria, both of which experienced such reforms under Japanese jurisdiction during the first half of the century, seems to support this view.[22] Thus, it has been argued that up through World War I, China's economic problems stemmed primarily from the inability or unwillingness of the government to undertake needed reforms. Of course, government paralysis was, in turn, affected by foreign military and political pressures. After about 1920 the economic crisis grew more acute, especially in the rural sector.

But when and how would the eruption occur? Would it necessarily be led by Communists? Would it necessarily succeed? The Marxist answers to these questions are clear enough. But there is another view that must be considered. In particular, there are those who emphasize the importance of anti-Japanese nationalism as a binding force in the crucial years of the Communists' rise to power. It may be that their success stemmed primarily from their leadership against foreign invaders and only incidentally from their political and social programs.

2

Revolutionaries Seize Power: 1949–52

By late 1949 the Communist movement was riding a wave of success. Chiang Kai-shek and other domestic enemies reeled backward in disarray, yielding up city after city, finding no refuge. Meanwhile, boatload after boatload of foreign businesspeople, missionaries, and the rest of the treaty port communities set sail from Shanghai and other ports. For the first time in more than half a century, China was about to be ruled by a single, legitimate authority unhampered by foreign domination. As Mao proudly proclaimed, China "will no longer be a nation subject to insult and humiliation. We have stood up."[1]

There was still an enormous agenda. Control over the entire nation, from Tibet to Taiwan, had to be consolidated, and China's position in the international community had to be defined. After years of upheaval it would be necessary to return life to normal, decide policies toward social groups such as landlords and capitalists, and begin to establish new institutions of government. A start would have to be made on economic development. As these daunting tasks got under way, there would be some unwelcome surprises and interruptions.

Establishing Sovereignty

Military Victory

In terms of population distribution and ethnic composition, China consists of two parts: a heartland and a great arc of large, sparsely settled border regions to the west and north. The heartland is based on the nine regions discussed in Chapter 1, and contains well over 90 percent of the population. The inhabitants are virtually all "Han," that is, people who speak Chinese dialects. Completing the conquest of this heartland was relatively uncomplicated for the Communists.

The peripheral regions are sparsely inhabited by ethnic minorities, supported primarily by pastoral economies. Their political ties to China had resulted from Qing dynasty conquests and had weakened from the time that the old regime collapsed. Tibet, vast and mountainous, is a strategically important buffer between China and India, whose people speak their own tongue. For centuries they been ruled by a Tantric Buddhist theocracy. A second region, Xinjiang (pronounced "Sin-jeeyang"), lies in the northwest. Its inhabitants include Turkic- and Mongol-speaking minorities of Islamic religion. Bordering on the Soviet Union, Xinjiang, too, has strategic importance and also contains rich mineral resources. The third region is Inner Mongolia, a 1,500-mile-long sweep of desert, steppe, and hills lying north of the Great Wall. It, too, has strategic importance for Manchuria, China's industrial heartland to the northeast.

By late 1950, Chinese armies penetrated Tibet, Xinjiang, and Inner Mongolia. Once again Tibetans, Uighurs, Kirghiz, Kazakhs, and Mongols found themselves subjects of Beijing. It was an uneasy conquest, one that required the development of a complex carrot-and-stick policy of control. Even then, naked force was occasionally needed in the years that followed. On the other hand, Outer Mongolia, situated north of Inner Mongolia and now known as the Mongolian People's Republic, was not recoverable. Once a part of the Qing Empire, it had declared its autonomy in 1911 and since 1924 has been the Soviet Republic of Mongolia, a satellite of Moscow.

To the east lay Taiwan and small coastal islands, particularly Jinmen and Mazu (frequently referred to as Quemoy and Matsu). Here the impediment was Chiang Kai-shek, whose forces had yet to be dislodged. Taiwan's importance extended beyond the Communists' desire to claim the entire country. The hostile Nationalist regime challenged the CCP's legitimacy. It constantly proclaimed its intention to retake the mainland and supported various forms of penetration and harassment. Nationalist planes even bombed some cities in early 1950. Conquest of these islands promised to be difficult, but Beijing intended to attempt it. Hainan Island in the extreme south was liberated In the spring of 1950, raising hopes for an early liberation of the others.

Leaning to One Side

A second important aspect of establishing the new regime's sovereignty was defining China's relationship to the rest of the world. Close ties with the Soviet Union were inevitable, given historical and ideological connections. Relations with the ''imperialist'' powers were more problematic and sparked debates. Economics was at the heart of the issue. After initial reconstruction, the People's Republic would need to expand its productive capacity. National power, popular support, and desired social policies all depended on this. Yet undeveloped countries like China require technological and financial aid to achieve rapid growth. Who would help?

The list of candidates was not long. The nation most capable of providing assistance was the world's economic colossus, the United States. The Marshall Plan in Europe and past American help for China suggested that this was a serious possibility. Zhou Enlai seems to have led a school of thought that wanted to explore it. In May 1949 he sent a startling communication to Colonel David Barrett, an American military attaché. He said that a split existed within the Communist leadership. His faction, which was opposed by Liu Shaoqi's group, wanted to mediate between the USSR and the United States and desired to talk about American economic assistance.[2] At almost the same time Chen Yi, whose troops had just taken Shanghai, was soliciting U.S. and British economic assistance.

Chinese-American relations had not gone completely sour, so there might be reason to suppose normalization possible. At the war's end both Mao and Zhou had offered to go to Washington to discuss relations. In 1946, General George Marshall had attempted to mediate between the Communists and the Nationalists. In Nanjing, as the 1949 victories unfolded, Ambassador John Leighton Stuart demonstrated a willingness to go up to Beijing to initiate a dialogue.

On the other side, Sino-Soviet relations were not as warm as many thought. There was some rancor against Stalin, who had not always acted generously or wisely toward the CCP. His early China strategy led the Chinese Communists to near annihilation at the hands of Chiang Kai-shek in 1927. More recently, Stalin had sometimes acted like an imperialist, as, for example, in the Yalta negotiations. Although Stalin entered the war against Japan at the eleventh hour, Russians plundered Manchurian factories as war booty. Then Stalin held back full support during the civil war, maintaining relations with the Nationalists until the very end (the Soviet ambassador, still wangling for concessions, was the last to abandon Chiang's government in 1949). He tried to stop Communist advances north of the Yangtze, apparently preferring to have a weak and divided China for a neighbor. There was also Stalin's condescension toward the Chinese Communists. "Cabbage communists," "radish communists," "margarine communists," he called them.[3] Later Mao said that:

the Chinese revolution won victory by acting contrary to Stalin's will. . . . If we had followed . . . Stalin's methods the Chinese

Revolution couldn't have succeeded. When our revolution succeeded, Stalin said it was a fake . . .[4]

Mao further claimed that only China's entry into the Korean War, by buffering Moscow against a direct U.S. confrontation, legitimized the PRC in Stalin's eyes.[5]

Still, China faced an American military threat and desired protection in order to begin demobilizing her huge armies and getting on with national development. This was probably the determining factor in China's decisive swing into the Soviet camp. As the Communists conquered China, Washington took steps to build a ring of containment in the Pacific. The motivation was the familiar domino theory, always much in favor on the banks of the Potomac.

The extension of communist authority in China represents a grievous political defeat for us. . . . If Southeast Asia is also swept by communism, we shall have suffered a major political rout the repercussions of which will be felt throughout the rest of the world, especially in the Middle East and in a then critically exposed Australia.[6]

American military assistance for South Korea, Japan, Okinawa, Taiwan, the Philippines, and Vietnam completed a ring around the People's Republic. Despite Mao's thesis that imperialistic atomic weapons were "paper tigers" to be respected tactically but despised strategically, China needed a powerful protector.

Events in 1948 and 1949 caused Mao to agree with Liu Shao-qi's hard-liners and align China strongly with the USSR. The United States contributed to the mutual alienation in various ways. For example, Washington refused to release the new Chinese government from preexisting treaty obligations. There were a series of incidents. American journalists in Beijing were smeared in the official press and, in effect, prevented from reporting. The U.S. consul-general in Manchuria and his staff were held hostage for nearly a year on an allegation of spying, jailed for a

month, and then expelled from the country. There were other
incidents as well. The Korean War only put the final touches on
this well-developed mutual antagonism. Two months after proclaiming the establishment of the new government, Mao paid his
first visit to Stalin.

Installing the New Order

As the new leaders extended their domestic sway and defined
their international position, many problems required immediate
attention. The country suffered from chaos and a vast array of
social ills. The new regime had to establish its governmental institutions: chains of command, specialized bureaucratic systems,
rules, and routines. In all these endeavors the Communists registered great success.

Restoring Normalcy

Inheriting a desperate situation, the new regime rapidly got things
under control and put the country on an orderly footing for the
first time in decades. Twelve years of war and civil war had
produced hyperinflation, stagnation in agriculture and industry,
a crippled transportation system, flight of capital and managerial
talent, massive unemployment and underemployment, refugees
and demobilized Nationalist soldiers, hunger and malnutrition,
social dislocation and festering evils of every sort, including opium
addiction, prostitution, gambling, criminality, and female infanticide.

The new rulers moved quickly. Many of their measures were
attempts to improve economic conditions, and here both Zhou
Enlai and Chen Yun played important roles. Chen got inflation
under control by a combination of austerity measures, balanced
budgets, currency reform, and price controls. By expropriating
major industries and the banks, Beijing achieved control over

the urban sector. Former capitalists and managers were induced to help get industry and commerce back into operation. Railways and roads were restored and expanded. Thousands of overseas Chinese returned to the motherland to help build the nation.

Virtually the entire remaining foreign community was summarily ejected; and its property, confiscated. For many Chinese this must have been a sweet revenge after a century of imperialism. An assault was launched on criminal gangs, opium use, and prostitution. The educational system was reorganized and expanded. Old, "feudal" social patterns and values came under attack, including the patriarchal clan, female subjugation, and infant marriages.

The Party

Drawing on Soviet models and twenty years of revolutionary experience, the new leaders built their regime around the Party. What follows is a brief description of the CCP's organizational structure (see Fig. 3). Speaking formally, the entity that defines and determines all structures is the Party Congress. This is a gathering of delegates representing the entire membership. But it meets too irregularly to function as an active component of government. There was a Party Congress in 1945, the seventh since the founding congress of 1921. The next one after liberation did not occur until 1956. This one held a "second session" two years later. The ninth, tenth, eleventh, and twelfth congresses occurred respectively in 1969, 1973, 1977, and 1982.

The Party Congress elects a Central Committee, containing from 100 to 300 regular and alternate members. The Seventh Central Committee, named in 1945, had 77 members and alternates. The Eighth Central Committee, elected in 1956, grew to 170 members; the Ninth, in 1969, to 279. The Central Committee convenes much oftener than Party Congresses and consequently constitutes a more active participant in policy-making. Its meetings, which often include outside officials and experts,

FIG. 3 Chinese Communist party structure (simplified).

are called "plenary sessions" or "plenums." Thus, the "Second Plenum of the Eighth Central Committee" refers to the second full meeting of the Central Committee elected by the Eighth Party Congress. Key turning points have frequently occurred as a result of decisions taken at these plenums.

The Central Committee is too large and meets too irregularly to direct day-to-day Party affairs. Consequently it elects a Polit-

MAO ZEDONG

ical Bureau or Politburo. Here is the real center of power. Although theoretically answerable to the Central Committee, the Politburo actually dominates the Party. It issues the orders, decisions, regulations, instructions, circulars, and notifications that govern the entire organization. It resembles an active board of directors whose members hold executive positions as heads of Party, government, and army.

Over the years it has contained between a dozen and two dozen members. All the leaders described earlier belonged at one time or another although some subsequently lost their positions. In 1949, besides Mao, there were eleven members, including Liu Shaoqi, Zhu De, Zhou Enlai, and Chen Yun. In the mid-1950s, Peng Dehuai, Lin Biao, Deng Xiaoping, and Chen Yi were added. Still later (in 1969), Chen Boda went on as Peng, Chen Yun, Liu, Deng, and Chen Yi were off. One constant was Chairman Mao. The Politburo was an extremely important vehicle for the exercise of power, and he insisted that all its documents cross his desk.

Even within the Politburo there are levels of authority. The highest possible power and prestige is vested in the Standing Committee of the Politburo (although this particular name did not come into use until 1956). This handful exercised a general oversight over central Party affairs whereas the other Politburo members had more limited, specialized responsibilities. The Standing Committee probably also had the power to act in place of the Politburo. In the 1950s it consisted of Mao, Liu, Zhu, Zhou, Chen Yun, and later Lin and Deng.

Because the Party controlled the state structure through its own hierarchy, certain other organs were very important, especially the Secretariat. This office communicated with and supervised all lower echelon Party committees. The director of the Secretariat was in a position to wield great influence and build up a constituency among lower Party leaders. In the early 1950s, Deng Xiaoping was appointed to this office.

There were other important bodies as well. Nearly as powerful as the Secretariat was the Control Committee. It exercised a police function within the Party, constantly monitoring the members and expelling those who failed to measure up. Repeatedly, the Party launched "rectification" movements to purify its membership and expel corrupt, lazy, or otherwise unsatisfactory cadres. There were also a handful of important Party departments, headquartered at Beijing, for rural work, propaganda, and other affairs. In addition, there were more than a dozen work departments and subordinate offices in charge of such activities as youth organizations, women's organizations, education, and health.

Party Center and Party Cadres

The Party center in Beijing might be likened to the head, a relatively small nerve center that gathers information and issues signals for action. The vast body of the Party was to be found in the provinces, connected to the head through a hierarchical structure. This hierarchy ran down from the center, through six regional and twenty-nine provincial committees, to about 2,500 city and county committees that supervised the Party committees in individual units.

Most members were not on the Party payroll; they were primarily leaders in factories, stores, schools, military units, and agricultural units, government offices, and mass organizations. They constituted the "Party fraction" within the leadership group in all units. They carried the dual burden of their specific jobs and Party work. The term *cadre* is frequently used to refer to persons in positions of authority whether or not they belong to the Party. Through this dovetailing of Party and other social institutions, the CCP achieved unprecedented control over China's political, economic, and cultural life. Every citizen belonged to at least one unit, if only to a street committee, and usually to several, most importantly the work unit. As each unit required a Party fraction, it was necessary to recruit millions of members. Party rolls grew from around 4.5 million in 1949 to about 10 million in 1955. China's population at that time was approaching 600 million, so that the Party made up between 2 and 3 percent of the people.

The Party member was part of China's new ruling elite. Despite the Yanan traditions of frugality and mass line, he or she enjoyed many privileges. These included career mobility, material benefits, access to education, and protection against police power. As the system jealously guarded and controlled information, the Party member also had access to privileged material, depending on his or her level in the hierarchy. But there was a price. The person who joined the CCP (which he or she could be invited to do only after demonstrating activism, as in the Communist Youth League) was expected to work tirelessly for the Party. Political study, meetings, criticism, and self-criticism were permanent features of Party life. Important campaigns frequently required extra effort. If a campaign should fail, the rank and file usually took much of the blame for having failed to carry out directives well.

The historian James Harrison characterizes this massive organization with its "techniques of self-criticism and endless meetings and discussions. Until the disruptions of the Cultural Revolution [in the late 1960s and early 1970s], China was among the most internally secure states in history. Police in the usual sense were hardly necessary, as all activists were policemen, monitoring themselves, their neighbors, and even their thoughts."[7]

Clearly, this party-dominated system departed radically from the principles of Western liberal democracy. Where was the separation of powers? What corresponded to the executive branch? The legislative branch? The judicial branch? What justification could there be for a polity in which every act of government comes under the Party's authority? The answer to these questions must be drawn from Marxist theory. The class destined to lead the way toward a classless utopia is the proletariat. The CCP is the party of this proletariat. However the present era is transitional in that the vestiges of feudalism and imperialism still survive, particularly in the form of certain classes. As Mao put it, the revolution was not in a "proletarian-socialist" phase, but rather in a "bourgeois-democratic" phase. But by "democratic," he did not mean the "old" democracy. This was a "new democratic revolution" in which the proletariat and its party, the CCP, joined with other classes (the peasantry, the petty bourgeoisie, and the "national" bourgeoisie) to shepherd the country through the transition. With the proletariat in control, this "new democratic" coalition justly exercised a dictatorship over reactionary classes and other bad elements.

The State Bureaucracy

As one writer says, "All government organizations in Communist China . . . function under very close Party direction; in fact they operate essentially as administrative agencies performing assigned tasks on behalf of the Communist Party."[8] The Party hierarchy was distinguished from the government organs through which to worked its will. It required ministries, agencies, and organizations to manage and tax agriculture, manufacture goods,

transport, communicate, educate, entertain, and carry out all the
other activities necessary to a national system. In the relationship between the two, the Party always asserted overriding authority.

In 1949 the new rulers discovered a diverse collection of left-
over bureaus and organizations that they needed in the short run
to keep the system functioning. Despite the authoritarian and
centralized character of the CCP, it was very important for the
new rulers to build their state through willing cooperation rather
than coercion. They knew that much of the country's expertise
belonged to non-Communists. Consequently, they took pains to
pay at least verbal allegiance to "new democratic," cooperative
methods. Of course, in the long run, they intended to create their
own government institutions staffed by their own personnel.

In September 1949 the Chinese People's Political Consultative Conference (CPPCC) was convened. This assembly contained members from many non-Communist parties and groups
although its deliberations were dominated by the Communists.
The CPPCC proclaimed the establishment of the People's Republic. It elected a National Committee to function continuously
and named Mao Zedong formal head of state. The CPPCC also
selected a Central People's Government Council as a kind of
legislature for the development of government decisions. This
temporary body actively deliberated on and issued all the major
legislation of the early 1950s.

Under the Central People's Government Council in a formal
sense, but even more powerful in reality, was the State Council,
a sort of cabinet that presided directly over the central government ministries. At the head of the State Council stood the premier, Zhou Enlai. He was concurrently head of the Foreign
Ministry. At the same time he was a member of the Party's Politburo and of its Standing Committee. Other leaders we have
met held major posts in the government. Peng Dehuai became
minister of defense until 1959, when Lin Biao succeeded him;
Chen Yun was named chairperson of the Finance and Economics Committee, which oversaw several economics ministries; and

Chen Yi took over the Foreign Ministry from Zhou in 1958. Like Zhou, they all held top posts in the Party hierarchy as well.

In 1954 a permanent government was established through the promulgation of a constitution. Elections were held to choose the 1,141 deputies to the First National People's Congress (NPC), which gathered in Beijing in September. They had been chosen through a multitiered process that began with 200,000 basic-level assemblies elected by some 275 million voters. These assemblies elected delegates to county assemblies, which, in turn, sent delegates to provincial and municipal assemblies, which elected the National People's Congress or NPC. The NPC and its Standing Committee then became the formal source of state authority and selected the head of state (Mao) as well as the premier and vice-premiers of the State Council.

Interestingly, the new system provided for other deliberative bodies in addition to the NPC. The National People's Congress itself was supposed to meet every year and be represented when not in session by its Standing Committee. It was the NPC that elected Mao president of the People's Republic, who in turn appointed Zhou premier of the State Council. Then the Chinese People's Political Consultative Conference continued to exist, no doubt because the presence of many non-Communist members made it a kind of united front organization, useful for co-opting prestigious individuals who were not members of the Party. Many CPPCC delegates were also NPC deputies, and the two bodies typically convened at the same time. Finally, the new constitution defined a Supreme State Conference, made up of eminent persons, which the president of the Republic could convene to consider issues and and make recommendations.

Despite this proliferation of assemblies, none exercised any real authority. As Mao put it, "Our constitution is of a new socialist type, different from any of the bourgeois type . . ."[9] This meant that the Party, rather than the electorate, was the ultimate authority for the "people's democratic dictatorship led by the proletariat and based on the worker-peasant alliance."[10] These bodies basically served to formalize, announce, and promote

FIG. 4 Government of the People's Republic of China (simplified).

policies decided on by the Politburo or, in some cases, by Mao himself. Subordinate to the ministries and bureaus in Beijing were the provincial governments. The provinces supervised municipal and county governments. These provincial and local governments, together with other bureaus reporting to the capital, administered the farms, factories, and other parts of the economic system (see Fig. 4).

The Military

The People's Liberation Army was established as the third major hierarchy. In its general structure it resembled the armed forces of other countries, with a ministry of defense, a general staff, and separate service arms. The Chinese followed their established practice of adding to this a strong element of Party control. To assure this control, the CCP had always maintained a Party-army linkage. Every military unit had its Party committee. The commander in chief, the chief of staff, the minister of defense, and all leading officers also occupied high Party positions. Subordinate to the Politburo was the important Military Affairs Committee, which set general defense policies and, through its General Political Department, supervised Party committees in all army units.

The Korean War

In a speech to the Central Committee, on June 6, 1950, Mao declared, "The present international situation is favorable to us." He enumerated some of the tasks ahead: land reform, centralization of the economy, demobilization of troops, educational reform, unemployment relief, cooperation with non-Communist groups, weeding out counterrevolutionaries, and expanding and consolidating the Party.[11] Although the Communist leaders probably knew that a North Korean initiative against the south was coming, more war was the last thing they wanted or expected.

On June 25 conflict did break out between North Korea and South Korea when troops from the north poured across the 38th parallel. Just who was responsible for starting it has been much debated. The Russians may have encouraged North Korea. Secretary of State Acheson's earlier statement that Washington did not consider Korea and Taiwan to lie within the U.S. "defensive perimeter" may have invited adventurism, and South Korean provocations may have played a role. Clearly, however, the Chinese were merely bystanders.

When the conflict started, Beijing gave vocal encouragement to North Korea but seemed to have no plans for direct involvement. Pyongyang's forces were doing well enough by themselves, having pushed the South Koreans and Americans back to Pusan in the southeast corner of the peninsula. In any case, China's concern was Taiwan. Two days after the invasion, President Truman ordered the Seventh Fleet to prevent attacks in either direction across the straits separating Taiwan from the mainland. This frustrated Communist plans to recover the island. Beijing also noted other signs of U.S.-Nationalist cooperation, in particular a visit to Taiwan by General Douglas MacArthur, commander of the UN forces.

The situation changed in the fall as MacArthur's counterattacks drove the North Koreans back to Seoul, then Pyongyang, and finally pell-mell toward the Manchurian border. The Chinese leaders had to decide whether to intervene. Some, like Chen Yun, urged caution. He called attention to the impact on economic modernization, pointing out that initial calculations for a five-year plan would have to be scrapped. Some generals worried that involvement would absorb energies required for the liberation of Taiwan. Stalin was against Chinese entry at that time. Probably a majority of the leadership favored restraint, and it was Mao, Zhu De, and Peng Dehuai who forced the decision to commit troops.

The Chinese did not enter the war before making repeated attempts to convince Washington that they could not tolerate a Korea dominated by the United States because that would threaten Manchuria. On September 30, Zhou Enlai warned

The Chinese people absolutely will not tolerate foreign aggression, nor will they supinely tolerate seeing their neighbors invaded by imperialists.[12]

Numerous other appeals, the massing of Chinese troops north of the Yalu River separating Manchuria from Korea, and even some firefights between Chinese and UN units failed to impress the more hawkish American leaders, especially General MacArthur, that Beijing would enter the war. Finally on October 8, in the teeth of Acheson's ominous warning that China would be risking a "tragedy of the most colossal nature"[13] and after pacing three sleepless days and nights, Mao issued the secret order. Chinese "volunteers" crossed the Yalu, as he put it, "to resist the attacks of U.S. imperialism and its running dogs."[14]

The intervention opened with a sensational Chinese success as 200,000 troops smashed the center of the UN line. MacArthur, who had engineered the brilliant Inchon landing just months earlier, now found himself in headlong retreat, complaining that China had committed "one of the most offensive acts of international lawlessness of historic record."[15] By January 1951, the front had swept back south of the 38th parallel. UN forces regrouped and counterattacked, restoring the front to approximately the 38th parallel. A cease-fire was agreed on in July 1951, but two years and 575 acrimonious meetings at Panmunjom would pass before an armistice was signed.

The war cost China dearly. According to American figures, the relatively lightly armed Chinese sustained a total of 900,000 killed, wounded, or missing. Economic reconstruction was set back. Hopes for the early recovery of Taiwan were ruined. A U.S-Taiwan alliance was forged that endured into the 1970s and beyond. The United States blocked Chinese admission to the United Nations until 1971. An American embargo further added to Beijing's isolation from the non-Communist world and its dependence on the USSR.

The war brought benefits, too, not the least of which was a boost to the country's self-esteem. The world had witnessed that Chinese soldiers with mortars could match, blow for blow, American heavy artillery. China had truly "stood up," and in the eyes of many citizens this further enhanced the Party's legitimacy. The war also seems finally to have won Stalin's respect. There were other gains as well. Aroused nationalism became an instrument for rooting out or silencing opponents of the regime. Land reform and other movements that had been proceeding with moderation suddenly intensified as the anticounterrevolutionary campaign was launched. Ironically, this hysteria was mirrored in America, although without the bloodshed, as

McCarthyism sought to hunt down the alleged traitors who had "lost" China.

Campaigns

Land Reform

Although the new rulers had to establish formal bureaucracies, as revolutionaries they favored mass upheavals where the people would come together in one voice to overthrow injustice. As Zhou Enlai expressed it in 1960

> The Party has always paid attention to combining its leadership with broad mass movements, guiding the masses to raise the level of their revolutionary consciousness constantly, and to organize their own strength to emancipate themselves step by step, instead of imposing revolution on the masses or bestowing victory on the masses as a favor.[16]

The techniques of organizing mass campaigns had been under development for many years and would continue to be used. At the time of liberation, the most important campaign was land reform. Moving from north to south between 1948 and 1952, it was one of the largest social upheavals in history. China's landlords were stripped of their wealth, and over one-third of the farmland changed hands.

To spearhead the movement, thousands of young volunteers trained to go to the villages as land reform teams. A team's first objective, on arrival in a given village, was to organize an Association of Poor and Middle Peasants. This would serve as the organizational base for the drama about to happen. The young activists explained the program to the peasants and learned which landlords or local toughs had been particularly oppressive. Mass meetings would be organized, featuring public denunciations of these bad elements. Peasants would gradually gather the courage to blurt out the humiliations and injustices they had suffered. The landlords' records would be examined for irregularities. All this would lead to the seizure and redistribution of their property and sometimes to their death. Although the land reform team generally orchestrated the events, the peasants' accumulated bitterness could not always be controlled.

Still, the number of executions is not thought to have been high through the middle of 1950, by which time about one-third of the peasantry, mostly in the north, had redistributed the land. Suddenly in late 1950 and in 1951, with the onset of the Korean War, the movement grew much bloodier. At this same time a fierce campaign against counterrevolutionaries was launched (see later). The toll of lives mounted as China began to taste true revolutionary terror. The total number of executions between 1949 and 1953 has been estimated at wildly different levels by various students of the subject. Many Western scholars have now accepted a range of between 2 and 5 million victims of all campaigns taken together.

Land reform changed the patterns of ownership and eliminated the landlords and rich peasant classes. In other respects, the villages remained little changed. The relationship between land and labor had not been fundamentally altered. Millions of households still worked their tiny scattered plots with hand tools. Although inequalities had been reduced, they had not been eliminated. Some peasant families remained richer than others, and some provinces and regions were relatively prosperous whereas others experienced endemic poverty. Even aspects of the old system reappeared as functions formerly performed by landlords, such as moneylending, were now done by rich peasants and even local cadres. This represented an incomplete solution to the problem. The leaders accepted it temporarily for the sake of production. But in the long run they intended to socialize agriculture like all other sectors. Mao said, "Without socialization of agriculture, there can be no complete consolidated socialism." [17]

Resist America, Aid Korea

Once the decision to fight America had been made in October 1950, China's leaders lost no time in organizing the people behind the war effort. They launched a series of campaigns collectively referred to as "Resist America, Aid Korea." These campaigns continued from late 1950 until Mao declared "a great victory in the war to resist U.S. aggression and aid Korea" in September 1953.[18]

The goals of these campaigns were to explain the nature of the conflict, to suppress any lingering pro-American feelings, and to collect funds to support the "volunteers" at the front. This last objective was particularly important because Soviet assistance did not become significant until around 1951. The propaganda system generated indictments against the United States, particularly charges of "germ warfare." There were campaigns to "comfort the Korean People's Army and Chinese Volunteers," to gather peace signatures, to collect donations, to sell Victory Bonds, to sign "patriotic pacts" for increased production, to pay taxes, and even to sever the links between Chinese Christian churches and their Western counterparts. There were many local variants. For example, Beijing college students were organized to trek to surrounding villages to explain the campaigns to the peasants.

Marriage Law

Women's liberation had long been promoted by the Communist movement and was particularly dear to Mao. So in May 1950 the new government enacted one of its first major pieces of legislation, the Marriage Law. It was decreed that henceforth a "New Democratic" form of marriage would prevail. Evil customs of the past, such as family marriage contracts against the individuals' consent, buying brides, polygamy, and child marriages were declared illegal. There were also important provisions relating to divorce. The principle of sexual equality was applied so that women could now apply for divorce under the same rules as men. They were no longer considered essentially chattels of the husband's family.

The Marriage Law did not automatically transform the status of women. Because traditional customs were deeply ingrained, it was necessary to publicize and promote the new regulations. Between 1950 and 1953 a series of national and local campaigns was launched for this purpose although in terms of intensity and expenditure these drives could not compare with the others discussed here. Traditional attitudes and practices survived, especially in the countryside. Indeed, the government proved to be unenthusiastic about free marriage and divorce. Some observers have felt that the primary intent was to weaken family and clan authority over the individual in order to facilitate totalitarian political control of every citizen. Nevertheless, after the new law was passed, the country witnessed a rash of divorces sought mainly by women. Gradually, new marriages and egalitarian values became more the norm, especially in the cities. As one writer recently put it, women in China have *risen* to second-class status.

Oppose Counterrevolutionaries

When China entered Korea, fear of external enemies and internal subversion intensified.[19] This brought about a change in the relatively restrained social policies. Mao must have felt considerable urgency about this because the fifth volume of his Selected Works contains several directives admonishing cadres and the people to "strike surely, accurately and relentlessly" against internal enemies.[20] Starting in February 1951, the Suppression of Counterrevolutionaries campaign got under way. It was purely political in its objectives and explicitly sanctioned violence although who all the targets were is not entirely clear. Generally speaking, the campaign aimed at bad elements who could be shown to be criminals or actively hostile to the regime.

A wave of arrests and mass trials swept the country. Millions of people were required to attend tens of thousands of accusation meetings. In Shanghai over 2,000 committees for the suppression of state enemies were organized and within a single two-day period 10,000 people were arrested. Altogether 3,000 accusation meetings disposed of 40,000 cases. In Guangdong Province during a ten-month period nearly 90,000 were arrested, of which over 28,000 were executed. In the end, between a half million and a million executions took place throughout the country, prompting observers to describe 1951 as a reign of terror.

Thought Reform

In December 1950 a privately produced film called *The Life of Wu Xun* (pronounced something like "Woo Shwun") premiered to favorable reviews. It told the story of a nineteenth-century philanthropist who rose from beggar to wealthy landlord. Wu Xun used his fortune to establish schools for the poor; he persuaded the imperial government to assist as well. His purpose was to give poor children a chance to rise through education. Suddenly, in the spring of 1951, this seemingly inoffensive and perhaps even touching film became the target of criticism from high places. The source of the criticism may well have been Jiang Qing, who had recently taken a position on the Film Steering Committee of the Ministry of Culture. She apparently converted Mao to her viewpoint. Before long newspapers were devoting as much as one quarter of their pages to denouncing the film. Wu Xun was unmasked as a wrongheaded, idealistic reformer who imagined that education and reform could save China. Marxism taught that only revolutionary class struggle could truly change society. Thus, the film violated proletarian thinking. There could be no defense of it as being apolitical. Filmmakers had no right to indulge in private expression. A person "is either progressive or reactionary--there is no third way." [21]

Soon many of the best-known writers were publishing confessions and self-criticisms, owning up to bourgeois thoughts, and thanking the Party for setting them straight. The filmmaker published his own confession in *People's Daily*. What was the meaning and purpose of this sudden campaign? The answer lies in the ambivalent attitudes of Mao and the Party toward intellectuals, a paradoxical mixture of hostility and support.

The hostility grew from the belief that the intelligentsia had sold out to the West. Many professors, writers, doctors, and scientists had studied abroad, assimilating foreign culture. The most famous one was Hu Shih (pronounced something like "Who Should" without the *d*). A philosopher and humanist, student of John Dewey, he believed in evolutionary social reform. The Communists saw this Western influence as "imperialist cultural aggression." Mao's feelings on this matter were unchanged since 1923, when he complained that "when one of our foreign masters farts, it's a lovely perfume."[22]

Another strike against the intellectuals was Mao's contempt for theoretical, ivory tower scholarship detached from the practice of revolution. For him "truth" meant applied truth.

> We do not study Marxism-Leninism because it is pleasing to the eye, or because it has mystical value, like the doctrines of the Taoist priests. . . . Marxism has no beauty, nor has it any mystical value. It is only extremely useful. . . . Dogma is less useful than excrement . . .[23]

Like everyone else, intellectuals should roll up their sleeves and work for the revolution. They must not only work in their respective fields but also respond to the needs of the people and the Party. Mao wanted them to cultivate both "spontaneity" and "discipline."[24] Nothing irritated him more than intellectuals who carped from the sidelines. In one outburst against a well-known "democratic personage" in 1953, he sneered, "What service did you do . . . ? In all your life what service have you ever done to the people? Not the slightest, not the least bit."[25]

Third, many intellectuals had straddled the political fence. Although critical of the Nationalists, they also rejected communism. They longed for a middle path of liberal reform. The Communists, Mao in particular, derided such timidity. As he put it, where are you going to "set your buttocks"?[26] Finally, the Party disliked intellectuals because of their traditional prestige in Chinese culture. Like the landlords and the business leaders, they were potential rivals for social leadership. The CCP could tolerate no rival. To the degree that intellectuals were not thoroughly Chinese and obediently "proletarian," Mao and the Party found them wanting.

On the other hand, many of the top Communist leaders were themselves intellectuals. Mao had received a higher education and wrote poetry as well as revolutionary theory. The same was true of Peng Dehuai and others. Chen Boda had been a professor. Moreover, in the preliberation years, many intellectuals did, in fact, rally to the left. Novelists exposed social injustices, supporting the Marxist critique of feudal society. And although many upper-class people left for Hong Kong and Taiwan in 1949 and 1950, many others stayed or returned from overseas to join in the building of a new China.

The talents of the educated were critically important for modernization, particularly because there were so few of them. Some appreciation for this can be gained by noting that in the countryside about half the cadres were illiterate or had less than two years of schooling. The situation was nearly as bad in the cities. In the short run, the country had no choice but to depend on the Western-educated intelligentsia for educators, engineers, geologists, and doctors despite their political shortcomings. Therefore, they had to be won over to the revolution—if not as true believers, at least as fellow travelers.

By 1949 the CCP already had a history of transforming intellectuals. At the famous "Forum on Art and Culture" held at Yanan in 1942, Mao lectured the participants on their duty toward the revolution. Individual expression must serve collective liberation. Literature and art must contribute to the cause, criticize the old, and inspire the audience through portrayals of the new socialist person. Writers and artists must drop Western styles. They must speak to the masses—through native folk idiom where possible. Above all, they must follow the Party line. "The science of Marxism-Leninism is a required course for all revolutionaries, not excepting artists and writers." [27]

In 1949 efforts to remold intellectuals got under way. "Revolutionary universities" were established in many cities. They were institutions to provide crash courses in Marxism-Leninism and Mao Zedong Thought. The students were mostly new cadres, either in the Party or government administration. In the second half of 1950, there was also a campaign to reform all intellectuals.

Then in the spring of 1951, with the Korean War, thought control intensified. The Party launched the campaign to criticize the Wu Xun film. Newspapers began to carry a series of quotations from Mao's *Selected Works*, the first volume of which appeared in October. In late 1951 the press began attacks on Hu Shih, who had moved to Taiwan. Soon the entire educational system was subjected to an intensive thought control campaign that lasted through 1952.

Thought control was a sophisticated program. Intellectuals were summoned to take part in mass meetings. Then they were assigned to small groups that met day after day. They discussed Marxist readings and engaged in criticism of others and in self-criticism. Everyone wrote his or her autobiography and repeatedly reworked it as the sordidness of his or her former bourgeois existence revealed itself. One feature of the program was the denunciation of one's father and family. As one writer puts it, "He had to write and rewrite until he satisfied the thought reformers with the thoroughness and sincerity of his confession." [28] When this grueling and often traumatic process was complete, the students could post their confessions. Large accusation meetings would then be organized. It all resembled a giant, coerced program of religious conversion.

Not only academics in universities, but also teachers and educated people of all sorts were put through the program. In the end it tamed this group just as land reform had crushed the landlords. Unlike the campaigns against landlords and counterrevolutionaries, this movement was not an effort to eliminate a class. Imprisonment and execution were not part of it. The object was to achieve conformity and, if possible, conversion. Just as with intra-Party purges and class struggle in general, the Party conceived of thought reform as an ongoing and recurrent process. Indeed, there were further campaigns in 1953. But there were also periods of relaxation when those leaders prevailed who worried about the numbing effects of brainwashing. In any case, the goals of thought reform remained unrealized as the dramatic events of the "Hundred Flowers" episode in 1957 were to demonstrate.

Oppose Bureaucracy

As the new rulers contrived to get the upper hand over landlords, counterrevolutionaries, and intellectuals, they scheduled two other groups for taming: deviant Party cadres and the business community. A pair of closely linked campaigns unfolded in the first half of 1952 to deal with these groups. The first one was called the "Oppose Bureaucracy" campaign. It was followed by a campaign to "Oppose Corruption" (see later).

A key ingredient in the Party's ability to mobilize people was the responsiveness of the the rank and file to the center. To ensure such responsiveness required monitoring of cadre performance and thought. In addition to routine measures such as regular study groups, personnel files, and yearly assessments, the Party launched recurring campaigns to weed out bad elements. The first major "rectification campaign" took place in the early 1940s. There was another in the years 1947–48 and yet another in 1950. In 1951 the leaders concluded that still a new rectification was needed. As one leader explained, there were three particular deficiencies that wanted correcting. Some cadres seemed to think that the revolution was over. They intended to relax rather than strive still harder for modernization, and they soft-pedaled "class struggle" now that the easy targets, the Japanese, landlords, and counterrevolutionaries, were eliminated. A second failing was "bourgeois individualism," which caused many cadres to concern themselves primarily with their personal careers. Third was the involvement of some cadres in business activities, both in the countryside and in the cities.

A major source of these problems was the rapid expansion of Party membership. Between 1945 and 1952, the rolls had doubled and redoubled to around 6 million. Some had joined less from idealism than to advance their personal fortunes and began to exploit their power and prestige. When rural cadres transferred from their villages to the cities, the temptations of urban life tended to corrupt them. There were also the cadres who ignored the approved leadership techniques. They committed "commandism" (ordering the people around) and "tailism" (doing what the people wanted), as well as "bureaucratism."

Consequently a "Three-Anti" campaign (anticorruption, antiwaste, and antibureaucratism) was launched. Party members studied prescribed documents, criticized their comrades, criticized themselves, and, in serious cases, went before mass "struggle" meetings where their failings were publicly exposed. Some severe punishments were meted out, especially for corruption, although most cases resulted in censure, demotion, or expulsion from the Party. By the summer of 1952 the campaign was terminated. About 10 percent of the membership had been expelled, resulting presumably in a tighter and more responsive organization.

Oppose Corruption

Businesspeople were the urban counterparts of landlords. But unlike the landlords, they were not to be immediately expropriated. For the time being, their skills were necessary to maintain production, and they were encouraged to continue operations. This conformed to Mao's theory of the New Democracy. Liu

Shaoqi, for example, spoke to the businesspeople of Tianjin (Tientsin) in the spring of 1949. He encouraged them to cooperate with the Party, increase output, and struggle against imperialists and backward classes. He reassured them that the transition to socialism and the elimination of private enterprise would take a long time.

Nevertheless, after little more than a year the Party abruptly changed its policy. In many cases, it seems that business community in the cities was "corrupting" the political system by influencing the cadres. The Party leaders may have believed that the bourgeoisie was blocking their efforts to control the cities. Labor union organizing was hampered by the close ties between small employers and their workers, who were often relatives or from the same native place. There were also financial considerations. The 1951 national budget was out of balance, and the government wanted to reduce the deficit to avoid reigniting inflation. In a situation where every bit of revenue was important, the tax evasion that businesses practiced was a serious concern. A campaign against this group could generate large amounts of back taxes and fines for the treasury.

Consequently, in the first half of 1952, a campaign to "Oppose Corruption" was set in motion. (Specifically, it was called the "Five-Anti" campaign, in reference to its five targets: bribery, tax evasion, stealing state property, cheating on government contracts, and stealing government economic data.) Just as poor peasants had been organized against the landlords, the workers were mobilized in the name of class struggle and soon found themselves confronting their capitalist masters. Everything was organized and coordinated by a high Party committee in each city. Even squads of repentant businesspeople and their relatives were used to pressure other capitalists to cooperate. Inspection brigades combed over each firm's books. There were letters of denunciation, confrontation meetings between businessmen and their workers, and public confessions. The press, public blackboards, posters, loudspeakers, newspaper reading teams, demonstrations with banners and kettledrums all played their part in informing the public and increasing the level of excitement.

It was a trying half year for businesspeople. Some committed suicide. Most made confessions and payed fines, reparations, and back taxes. In the end, the private sector was transformed. The financial penalties weakened businesses to the point where they became dependent on the government for loans and other assistance. A huge windfall, amounting to as much as 1.7 billion U.S. dollars from 450,000 disciplined businesses, poured into the national treasury. The once confident and influential bourgeoisie, the "tigers" as they were called during the campaign, had lost their teeth and claws. They remained thereafter a grateful and compliant class. As one writer put it:

> The combination of economic hardship and psychological demoralization so weakened the bourgeoisie that the Party leadership was able to set up, or reinforce, a variety of economic, political, social, and ideological control mechanisms and prevent any resurgence of bourgeois power.[29]

Disappointments, Ironies, and Contradictions

The Sweet and the Bitter

It may be that these initial three years of its existence were the regime's most successful period. They brought order to a disintegrated nation, consolidated political control, realigned foreign relations, and fought a formidable foe to stalemate. For a rustic band of insurgents, these were no small accomplishments. Still, the new rulers tasted some bitter disappointments.

The Korean conflict introduced an enemy that could not be defeated by Yanan-type warfare. The People's Liberation Army had built its early success on small units that equipped themselves with captured weapons, used primitive communications, and prevailed despite little coordination between armies. In Korea the PLA confronted an enemy that enjoyed a great advantage in firepower. Against such a foe, the lightly equipped Chinese won victories only at a dreadful cost in terms of casualties. Initial hopes of clearing the Americans out of the peninsula were completely frustrated.

Moreover, this experience presented the PLA with a fundamental choice: It could nourish its hallowed guerrilla traditions, or it could try to become a technologically advanced, professional army. But it couldn't very well do both. The roles that Peng Dehuai and Lin Biao played in Korea seem to have determined their stand on this dilemma. Peng commanded the Chinese "volunteers." Having experienced advanced warfare firsthand, he undertook to build a modern army when he became defense minister after the war. Lin Biao, on the other hand, took no part in the action, probably because of ill health. He remained strongly committed to the Yanan style. And the day eventually came when he displaced Peng at the head of the PLA.

Taiwan too was deeply disappointing. Not only did the Communists fall short of recovering all national territory. But they also saw the Nationalist regime revive and lead a successful program of economic modernization, even including a successful land reform. The Nationalists loudly proclaimed their right to rule the mainland and occupied China's seat at the United Nations. Taiwan became Beijing's most constantly annoying foreign policy problem.

A third disappointment also came in an area where greater success had been anticipated. Early in 1950, Mao went to Moscow to meet Stalin and seek Soviet assistance. Stalin did not throw out a warm welcome mat, and he proved to be a tough negotiator. The Chinese did come away with a Treaty of Friendship, Alliance and Mutual Assistance. And they received long-term credits for economic development and other concessions. But the amounts were disappointing, and there were strings attached, such as Soviet participation in joint stock companies to exploit Chinese mineral wealth and continued Russian occupation of the naval base at Port Arthur. Although for the moment it looked as though the Sino-Soviet alliance would be strong and permanent, there were already indications, whose significance would only become apparent later, that the Chinese expected far more out of the relationship than the Russians were prepared to provide.

Institutional Development Versus Revolutionary Transformation

Even as the new rulers successfully developed both political institutions and mass campaign techniques, they were creating a deep contradiction. It is simply this: Bureaucracy conflicts with mass mobilization. Regular, predictable hierarchies cannot easily coexist with irregular, unpredictable initiatives. A great modernized nation cannot at the same time continue to be a Yanan insurgency. It was a conflict between the head and the heart, between the rational requirements of national development and the emotional power of a revolutionary vision. Unfortunately, neither could be easily given over: institutionalization because there was no other way to run a country; revolutionary romanticism because that was the soul of the Chinese Communist movement and especially of its leader Mao Zedong.

In the early 1950s, however, this contradiction was not acute. Everything was in flux. So many urgent problems demanded attention that there was little time to consider whether important principles were being violated. The new regime was also understandably extremely optimistic. As Mao exclaimed in response to the possibility of an American economic blockade, "Let them blockade us! Let them blockade us for eight or ten years! By that time all of China's problems will have been solved."[30] So many insuperable difficulties had been overcome that there was no reason to suppose that institutional issues could not be ultimately worked out as well. Even in the mid-1950s, enthusiasm for building a mighty, Soviet-style socialist state obscured the contradiction lurking underneath.

In 1948 and 1949, the Communists organized victory parades in every city they captured. Possibly the largest took place in

Beijing in early February 1949. Thousands of students and workers, shouting slogans and dancing the popular peasant *yang ge* step, led a massive, hour-long parade of troops brandishing American and Japanese weapons. "Enormously impressive," thought one American observer.[31] This parade suggested something about the future. On that day Beijing's first big dust storm of the year blew in. Banners and posters were buffeted by the wind until they hung in tatters. At times it was difficult to see across the street. The elements seemed to be reminding that victory celebrations would soon give way to coping with great storms and blinding difficulties.

3

Socialist Transformation: 1953–57

The five years after initial consolidation were a period of successful institution building. It appeared that the new regime, however harsh toward its domestic enemies, had mapped out a clear direction, which it was following with determination and remarkable results. The 1954 state constitution defined a centralized administrative hierarchy. Industrialization, education, and public health all experienced dramatic improvements. But the clarity of direction was less sharp than it seemed. Achievements were offset by serious shortcomings. Debate flared on fundamental questions of policy. The struggle between the necessity of institution building and the cause of revolutionary transformation was not yet settled, particularly because the most formidable revolutionary of them all was determined to keep the flame burning.

Soviet influence dominated this period. In almost every sphere from governmental institutions to school curricula, from central economic planning to industrial management, from military uniforms to "wedding cake" architecture, the Chinese patterned their system on Russia's. Thousands of Russian advisers came to China, and thousands of Chinese went to study in the Soviet Union. Russian became the most popular foreign language as millions joined Sino-Soviet friendship associations. Little wonder, then, that the outside world perceived the People's Republic as another of Moscow's subservient satellites.

After Stalin died in 1953 and Nikita Khrushchev finally emerged as his successor, Sino-Soviet relations grew still closer. Khrushchev relinquished various concessions that Stalin had demanded. He negotiated more economic assistance. The new Soviet leader visited Beijing for talks with Mao on the occasion of the PRC's fifth anniversary in 1954. There were various other meetings where Chinese leaders flew to Moscow: Zhou in 1953, Liu in 1956, and both Zhou and Mao himself in 1957. Both sides frequently hailed their fraternal and indestructible relationship.

The First Five-Year Plan

With inflation tamed and key components of the economic system either owned or controlled by the state, specialists in the State Council, under the leadership of Chen Yun, worked out China's first Five-Year Plan for 1953 through 1957. Even though the plan was still very sketchy at the time (it was not even published until 1955), true to its Soviet inspiration, it laid out ambitious goals: to double industrial production and raise agricultural production by one-fourth.

Such goals required funneling about 20 percent of the nation's income to investment, a large share for a poor country. The necessary revenues would come from taxes and profits from state-owned enterprises. In the allocation of investment funds, "heavy industry" (steel, machine tools, and other producer goods) got the largest share, which reflected the determination to industrialize along Soviet lines. Lower priority went to industries making "light" or consumer goods. Finally, a very small portion of state investment was to go to agriculture. In fact, the agricultural sector was to be the main source of investment funds, meaning essentially that the farmers would "pay" for industrialization through taxes, low state prices for their crops, and high prices for the manufactured goods they bought.

Industrialization

Developing industries was not simply a matter of placing money into a magic box called "investment." The Chinese frequently lacked the expertise and equipment to design, build, and operate modern manufacturing plants. Consequently, they needed foreign experts, blueprints, machines, and materials. They needed credits in order to finance these purchases. The major source of both technology and aid was of course the Soviet Union. Agreements were negotiated in 1950 and again in 1953 and in the following years.

Soviet aid must be considered rather modest in view of China's great needs. The repayment terms were rather stringent. By 1955, China was already paying back to Moscow more than it was receiving in new credits. But China did benefit greatly from Russian technology. Moscow supplied the expertise to build 130 separate industrial projects by 1960. These enterprises constituted a very important contribution to China's modernization.

The result of these ambitious industrialization measures was a very rapid growth in heavy industry during the First Five-Year Plan. Consumer goods manufacturing also increased, but at a less rapid rate—a reflection of its lower priority.

Agriculture

In farming, Beijing had less to learn from Moscow. Stalin's brutal method of socializing agriculture had had catastrophic results and stood out as a negative model. China's Marxists shared the goal of eliminating private ownership of land and other vestiges of capitalism. But they knew that this transformation would be protracted and would have to be managed carefully. During the land reform, from 1948 through 1952, Mao urged moderation in the name of production. Landlords and rich peasants could be expropriated, but not middle peasants.

With land reform complete, the new regime was prepared to begin the gradual introduction of peasant socialism. As Liu Shaoqi put it,

For three solid years . . . we applied ourselves to awakening the class consciousness of the peasants. . . . [Consequently] the peasant masses stood up on their own feet, got themselves organized, closely followed the lead of the Communist Party and the People's Government, and took the reins of government and the armed forces in the villages firmly into their hands. . . . Conditions were thus created which were favorable to the subsequent socialist transformation of agriculture . . .[1]

The plan was a gradual one. First the peasants would be organized into mutual aid teams, four to ten families sharing production tasks. As mutual aid teams spread, the grass-roots Party apparatus would be expanding and preparing the way for the next step toward socialism: "lower" Agricultural Producers' Cooperatives (APCs). The "lower" or "semisocialist" APCs would encompass a small village or section of a village (twenty to forty households). Its members would derive income both from their their work in the fields and according to the land and tools they had contributed. Gradually, the lower APCs were supposed to develop into "higher" APCs (one hundred to three hundred households). The members would pool all their resources and allocate the collective income solely on the basis of labor contributions.

This social transformation was expected to succeed because it would make the peasants better off. As Mao said,

Output must not remain at the individual peasant or mutual-aid team level, for that would mean failure; what point, then, in having co-operatives at all? Still less can yields be allowed to fall.[2]

The reason that output was expected to rise, despite the the Five Year Plan's modest allocation of investment to this sector, was that socialism would be inherently superior to individual farms. The innumerable tiny plots would be joined into more efficient fields. Labor, including that of women, would be pooled and organized more rationally. Work gangs could be mobilized to dig irrigation canals, plant trees, reclaim land, and accomplish other capital formation projects without state investment funds. Also, social services could be better performed by the larger co-operatives.

Unfortunately, events did not follow this scenario. The transition from mutual aid teams to lower APCs, which began in 1952, did not always go smoothly. Peasant resistance, particularly from better-off households, was one problem. Cadre ineptitude was another (it must be remembered that many rural cadres were barely literate). Harvests did not increase as expected. The crops of 1953 and 1954 were disappointing. Grain output grew at between 1 percent and 2 percent. There were even smaller increases and even some declines in important industrial crops like soybeans, oilseeds, and cotton.

This sluggish growth was a serious problem because the growing population had to be fed and clothed. In addition, China had to export farm products to pay for the imports of Soviet technology. Light industry, which included the very important cotton textile industry, required increasing quantities of raw materials if it were going to grow according to plan. The fate of the entire program of economic development was being adversely affected.

It is no exaggeration to say that by mid-1955 agriculture's performance was beginning to undermine the credibility of all the industrial targets of the First Plan.[3]

This put the Party in the classic dilemma of rulers whose policies fail to produce expected results. Did they prescribe the wrong medicine, or was the dose too small? Should they go backward or forward? Just this sort of dispute arose in 1953 and intensified in 1954 and 1955.

Gradualists of more pragmatic leanings held that the disappointing results could be attributed to basic flaws in the program. APCs were being pushed too soon and too hard, which resulted in inefficiencies, dissatisfaction, and mismanagement. Furthermore, almost sole reliance on brute labor to create agricultural capital was unrealistic. Socialism in the countryside could be truly realized only when the economy could provide the farm sector with mechanized tools, chemical fertilizers, and other industrial inputs and support.

One of these gradualists was Deng Zihui (pronounced something like "Dung Dsuh-hway"; he was not related to Deng Xiaoping). He held important positions as director of the Party's Rural Work Department and director of the State Council's office in charge of agriculture. Although he had strong connections with Mao, the practical job of increasing farm output pushed him into agreement with Liu Shaoqi, Zhou Enlai, Chen Yun, and Chen Yi—all of whom advocated a slow socialization process in the interests of production. As Deng Zihui said in 1954,

> We [lack] the necessary conditions [for collectivization]. . . . Moreover, the Chinese peasants' conception of private ownership is relatively deep, while our rural task is heavy and we have not enough cadres.[4]

In 1953 and again in 1955 he presided over the dissolution of large numbers of APCs that were deemed premature. He favored the retention of private plots and some free markets to stimulate output.

There was another school of opinion that was led by Mao himself. To the handwringers who worried that the APC policy was too much, they answered that it was not enough. The Party should certainly not "get off the horse quickly." It should "get on the horse quickly."[5] Mao spoke these words at a 1953 conference on mutual aid and cooperation. Calling these efforts "a matter of vital importance," he declared that "if socialism does not occupy the rural positions, capitalism inevitably will."[6] Mao's kindred spirit in these views was Chen Boda, his longtime theoretical collaborator. They grew increasingly frustrated by the gradualists' inclination to moderate the APC program when difficulties surfaced. "We must guide the movement boldly and must not fear dragons ahead and tigers behind," urged Chairman Mao in 1955.[7] And further:

We must have faith, first, that the peasant masses are willing to take the road of socialism step by step under the leadership of the Party and, second, that the Party is capable of leading the peasants onto this road.[8]

During the first two years of the Five Year Plan, tugging and pulling between these two positions resulted in a seesaw APC policy. It began in the spring of 1953, when a decision was taken to push cooperatives. Late in the year Chen Yi (now the major Party leader in the Shanghai region) and others in east China felt that some APCs had been organized too hastily. They dissolved 15,000 of them. Mao disapproved strongly, and Chen Yi was obliged to criticize himself for his action. In the fall of 1954 and the spring of 1955, the call went out to push APCs. Because of disappointing harvests there was widespread reluctance to comply. In May, Liu Shaoqi chaired meetings in which Deng Zihui, with the support of Chen Yun, moved to dissolve 20,000 co-ops.

The like-minded minister of finance delivered the economic report to the National People's Congress soon thereafter. He stated that collectivization should proceed slowly, building up a solid core of well-organized and effective voluntary APCs. He anticipated that only one-third of the peasants would be in co-ops by 1957, and those would mostly be lower APCs. In the spring of 1955, the ''get off'' advocates seemed to have neutralized the ''get on'' enthusiasts even though they could not prevent repeated attempts to hasten rural socialism.

Education

In the First Five-Year Plan period, great strides were made in education. The system was brought under the control of central government ministries. New schools were established at all levels. Literacy increased. Primary school attendance shot up from 24 million in 1949 to 64 million in 1957. The numbers of those graduating from middle schools quadrupled, from technical middle schools doubled, and from universities more than doubled.

Still, problems lingered. As one scholar has said, "Revolutionary China's educational system presents a picture of tragedy and glory."[9] One major difficulty was that the country's needs were enormous and her resources meager. It was important to increase general literacy and education. It was also critical to produce large numbers of scientists, engineers, and other experts. Both of these needs could not be fully satisfied at once. Another source of difficulties was that the system aped the Soviet Union's to the disregard of China's special characteristics. There was too much stultifying central control. High standards, heavy demands on students, restrictive entrance policies, and elitism all conflicted with revolutionary ideals and with the need to spread education as widely as possible. The bureaucrats in charge of assigning graduates did a poor job of matching educational skills to China's manpower needs.

Toward the end of the Five-Year Plan, almost everyone had complaints. The Maoists criticized too much centralization and elitism and too little indoctrination. The more pragmatically minded were alarmed about poor manpower utilization. In early 1956, Zhou Enlai complained that many experts had been assigned to posts unrelated to their qualifications. Students themselves were dismayed by the narrow, difficult ladder of upward mobility. In 1957 two-thirds of primary school children completed that level of education. Only about 7 percent of the twelve-to-fourteen-year-olds graduated from junior middle schools. Less than 2 percent of fifteen-to-seventeen-year-olds completed senior middle schools. As for higher education, less than 1 percent of that age group received diplomas.

The graduates frequently received disappointing assignments. The system remained discriminatory against women. Males outnumbered females in primary schools by two to one and by progressively larger ratios at higher levels (in the universities, it was three to one). There was massive disadvantage for rural residents because the good middle schools and all the higher institutions were in cities.

Health

The general picture of public health improvement was highly positive during this period. Social order, an equalitarian distribution system, and improved medical care contributed to the results. Epidemic diseases were eliminated or brought under control. The mortality rate dropped. Here as well, however, difficulties persisted. One was the disparity between the relatively better health care and diets available in the cities and the more stringent health care and diets available in the rural villages. Another was the fact that as death rates dropped, birth rates declined more slowly. The result was an annual net population increase of around 2 percent. Given the huge population base, this pace of expansion put a severe burden on the economy. China had to run fast just to keep even.

The High Tide of 1955

Mao Counterattacks

By 1955 the dissolution of APCs and the cautious agricultural policies endorsed by the majority of Party leaders dismayed Mao and Chen Boda. The Chairman took steps to counter what he later derided as "the sad and dismal flatness and pessimism of the bourgeoisie." [10] Finding himself unable to prevail in the Politburo on this issue, he disregarded the normal procedures and mobilized his own support. He began with an extensive early summer tour of the provinces during which he no doubt pushed his views on the cadres who entertained him. In late July, when the National People's Congress met, he worked on the provincial Party leaders who came to Beijing.

With this base of support, he made his move. One day after the NPC had approved the cautious agricultural program of Deng Zihui, Chen Yun, and their colleagues, Mao summoned an ad hoc gathering of provincial and subprovincial Party secretaries.

His speech advocated policies utterly opposed to those just approved by China's supposed legislative body. "A new upsurge in the socialist mass movement is imminent throughout the countryside," he said. "But some of our comrades are tottering along like a woman with bound feet, and constantly complaining, 'you're going too fast' "[11] In measured and reasonable tones he warned against capitalist tendencies. He called for a "High Tide" of socialist transformation in the countryside, a careful and well-planned, but vigorous campaign to complete collectivization.

In a stroke Mao had regained the initiative. With Chen Boda he called upon each provincial Party apparatus to take the lead in forming APCs. The response was startling. Provincial officials, so sensitive to signals from Beijing that some of them kept restaurants in the capital as listening posts, decided that they did not want to be labeled rightists on this issue. Better to err in the leftward direction. Within weeks the stalled APC program took off. Across the country headlines like the following heralded the High Tide:[12]

STARTING A TIDAL WAVE CAMPAIGN FOR NATIONAL PROGRAM OF AGRICULTURAL DEVELOPMENT

MARCH BOLDLY ON THE GREAT DEVELOPMENT OF AGRICULTURAL PRODUCTION

Anxious to show not only that APCs should be formed but also that they could work well, Mao took great pains to strengthen his case. He solicited the cooperation of individual soldiers in his bodyguard detachment known as PLA Unit 8341. As most of them had been peasants, he sent them to their home villages to study local attitudes and views. Their reports, which they began to convey to him toward the end of the year, convinced him that he had a good feel for the situation in the countryside.

At this time Mao was assembling a collection of accounts of successful collectivization throughout the country, to be used as a guide for local cadres. He wrote enthusiastic editorial notes for the book, which was published late in the year. Typical of his commentaries was the following.

> This is an excellent article. . . . The party organization in this place never wavered on the question of cooperation. It stood four-square behind the destitute peasants in their demand for a coop and in their victorious competition with the well-to-do middle peasants; it firmly supported them as they grew from a small coop to a large one, increasing their output year by year, till by the third year the whole village was in cooperatives. The well-to-do middle peasants had jeered: "They've less money than an egg has hair, yet they think they can run a coop. Can a chicken feather fly up to heaven?" But that is just what this chicken feather did.[13]

During August and September thousands of APCs were formed. By the end of the year, two-thirds of all peasant households had been socialized. There were already thousands of higher APCs. The number of completely socialist cooperatives continued to increase until, by the end of 1956, 88 percent of peasant households were in them, with another 8 percent still in lower APCs.

Such an unexpected response was due in part to the fact that the Party had recruited large numbers of rural cadres. CCP membership had leveled off at around 6 million shortly after 1949. It began to grow rapidly again in 1954. By the end of that year, it reached 7.86 million. During the next year and a half, it burgeoned to 10.73 million. By mid-1957 there were over 12.5 million members, double the 1954 figure. These Party cadres were particularly responsive to the center at this time because of recent rectification campaigns. In the spring of 1955 the Party launched an internal purge and a tough campaign against non-Party intellectual dissidents and counterrevolutionaries. In the words of one historian

> The Party [carried out] a general campaign to liquidate all unorthodox thinking, hunt out counterrevolutionaries, and, most important, to purify political consciousness in accordance with the needs of the First Five Year Plan.[14]

With the Party thus enlarged, established in the villages, and disciplined, the center possessed a powerful instrument with which to mobilize the peasants.

Success also depended on the willingness of hundreds of millions of peasants to go along. Mao claimed that most farmers favored collectivization, especially poor peasants. Although he probably exaggerated, the formerly landless villagers were indeed a base on which cadres could build the APC movement. They remained a comparatively deprived group. Their attachment to the limited fields they had received through land reform may still have been weak. The tools, animals, and skills they possessed were often inferior to those of the middle peasants.

Starting with this core, the cadres used their repertory of pressures and blandishments to promote collectives. They painted a bountiful future. They said that the APC would assume all the risks of farming. Some promised free food. They mobilized group moral pressures against holdouts and even threatened to withhold community help, fertilizer, and other necessary things. The possibility also existed of labeling recalcitrant people as landlords, rich peasants, or even counterrevolutionaries.

The weather also aided the collectivization effort by contributing to good harvests. Mao said:

> In 1955 there was a bumper crop. Thus an increase in production coincided with a decrease in [government] purchasing, so that the peasants had 20,000 million extra catties of grain on their hands. All those peasants who had criticized us in the past now no longer criticized us. They all said, "The Communist Party is fine." [15]

The High Tide received what might be called its formal charter late in January 1956. For several weeks Mao's group had been developing a long term plan for agriculture, which they had circulated among the Party elite. It called for vigorous collectivization, use of off-season peasant labor for capital construction, and very rapid increases in output. Depending on the region, grain and cotton yields were to double or triple in twelve years. Mao

presented this Twelve Year Program to the Supreme State Conference that he had convened for the purpose of enlisting both
Party and non-Party support behind his bold vision.

The year 1955 ended, and 1956 began on a very positive note
for Mao Zedong. In February a renewed burst of APC formation
began. He had coined a slogan that in its defiant juxtaposition
of seemingly contradictory objectives, captured the optimism of
the moment. The slogan urged one and all to produce "*duo*
[more], *kuai* [faster], *hao* [better quality], *sheng* [and more
cheaply]." Mao also spoke about a "leap forward" in output.

High Tide in Industry and Commerce

From the beginning, the Communists planned to socialize the
entire nation and eliminate capitalism. But such a goal could not
be reached overnight. The scarcity of cadres competent to manage industrial and commercial enterprises, not to mention the
difficulty of organizing thousands of small-scale peddlers and
services into cooperatives, had persuaded the policymakers against
pushing socialism too fast. Even after the High Tide in agriculture began in July 1955, Guangzhou (Canton) businesspeople were
assured that they would continue to own their firms for years.

Then, in October, Mao turned his bold approach to the cities,
calling for wider collectivization. A former Shanghai business-
person told of being summoned to a meeting of manufacturers
and merchants. To the group's astonishment, none other than the
shuffling, slow-speaking, chain-smoking Mao Zedong had called
them together. With true Chinese indirection, he asked them for
their advice concerning the nationalization of private enterprises. Did they agree with those who wanted to hasten this process "lest the national bourgeoisie lag behind in the progress toward socialism?" Taking their cue, they all urged haste. But
Mao's idea of haste was to leave them breathless. A few weeks
later they received word that the transition to state ownership
would be accomplished within six days.[16]

As a result of the tremendous political pressures generated by these drives, the socialization of industry and commerce was complete by the end of 1956. Virtually the entire private sector had been taken over or reorganized into cooperatives. The capitalists now worked as salaried managers and received bonds for their expropriated properties (although they were not entirely free to spend the interest payments). Huge celebrations were staged in which businesspeople joyously greeted the transition to socialism.

Implications of Socialist Transformation

By the spring of 1956 the High Tide had introduced socialism to virtually every village, shop, and factory. Once again the Chairman's boldness seized victory where his more prudent colleagues had seen insuperable difficulties. It was hard to disagree when he said

> Provided [the workers, peasants, and working intellectuals] take their destination into their own hands, provided they have a Marxist-Leninist line and energetically tackle problems instead of evading them, they can overcome any difficulty on earth.[17]

Because of the High Tide's success, the People's Republic was entering a new era. The state had gained unprecedented (although far from absolute) control over the economy. Responsibility for the system's performance now rested squarely on the shoulders of those who controlled it. Central decisions, enforced by the Party apparatus, now had increased potential for huge successes—and massive blunders.

By early 1956, the leadership was already feeling out directions and strategies to fit this new situation. Mao's Twelve-Year Plan constituted a distinctive approach to agriculture. An analogous document for industry was under preparation. In March and April 1956, Mao presided over work reports and discussions involving thirty-four central departments and ministries. His summation of the principal findings were set out in a speech called "On the Ten Major Relationships." This address, which was intended for Party leaders only and remained unpublished for years, emphasized the complex relationships between the various parts of the economy. It suggested pragmatic, flexible modifications in the prevailing Soviet-style, heavy-industry-first approach to development.

A New Political Climate

Actually only the first half of the "Ten Major Relationships" speech dealt with the economy. The last five "relationships" discussed all had a political dimension, reflecting the fact that this period was marked by a search for new political approaches as well. The need to reexamine these relationships came from several sources. From the Soviet Union came an early and especially unsettling stimulus.

In 1955, Nikita Khrushchev had established himself as first secretary of the Soviet Union's Communist Party. His leadership marked a transition from Stalin's tyranny to more liberalized rule. Perhaps the most electrifying moment came at his secret speech to the Party's Twentieth Congress in February 1956. To party stalwarts who for many years had both adored and feared the departed leader, Khrushchev read a bone-chilling litany of Stalin's transgressions, which included self-glorification, paranoia, capricious despotism, mass arrests, torture, extracted confessions, punishments without trial, deportations, mass murder of military officers, and inaction against the Nazi invasion. Stalin's central flaw, said Khrushchev, was his cult of personality.

Khrushchev's sensational speech was communicated to other Communist parties. In China, as elsewhere, it had a stunning effect. Five weeks passed before the *People's Daily* took up the subject. When it did, it emphasized Stalin's achievements as well as his shortcomings. The main reason for this reaction was that Mao was the obvious center of a personality cult. Criticism of Stalin struck uncomfortably close to home. Yet it was hard to deny Stalin's excesses and the evil effects of deifying the leader.

There were other stimuli for rethinking the relationships between rulers and ruled. As the People's Republic matured, regular and predictable patterns emerged. What form would "mass line" now take in order to remain vital? This was extremely important to Mao, believing as he did that popular participation, through mass line, was the key to the success of the system. According to the Yanan ideal, Party cadres were supposed to be selfless, humble, and committed to mobilizing the workers and peasants against their class enemies. Other classes were supposed to transform themselves and join "the people." Unfortunately, bureaucratic behavior, excessive centralism, and bourgeois vestiges clouded this scenario.

The Party had developed a whole lexicon of terms to define undesirable cadre behavior. In addition to ordinary bureaucratism, there were also "commandism" (ordering the masses around rather than using persuasion), "sectarianism" (caring only about one own office or locality), and "subjectivism" (substituting wishful thinking for facts), in addition to corruption, and wastefulness. Many cadres acted increasingly like imperial mandarins: arrogant, arbitrary, slow to serve yet quick to pursue their own self-interests. How could such people lead the social and moral transformation of society? It was, of course, not a new problem, as evidenced by the repeated rectification campaigns since the 1940s.

Centralization was a more recent concern. As the Soviet model took hold, the ministries in Beijing increased their jurisdiction and functions, thereby creating an inefficient, unresponsive monolith. Mao complained thus in his "Ten Major Relationships" speech.

At present there are dozens of hands meddling in regional affairs, making them difficult to manage. Every day various ministries issue orders to the offices of provincial and municipal governments. These orders are supposed to come from the [Party] Centre, even though the Centre knows nothing about them and neither does the State Council. They put a great strain on the regions. Statistics and reports come rushing in like a torrent. This must change. We must discuss ways of correcting it.[18]

Fujian provincial leaders complained that construction of a much-needed paper factory dawdled along for six years while the ministry prepared plans and changed them. Because the most desirable posts were those at the top of the pyramid at Beijing, the ministries tended to become overstaffed. A consensus was growing that somehow this sluggish pyramid must be made more flexible and responsive. In his "Ten Major Relationships" speech, Mao went so far as to suggest that "the Party and government organs should be streamlined and that two thirds of their numbers should be axed."[19]

The fact that this newly socialized society must now intensify its development efforts also had implications for urban policy, especially in relation to the educated classes. Up to now, efforts had been directed mainly at transforming these people's consciousness, rooting out counterrevolutionaries, and suppressing dissent. The Party had perfected techniques of mobilization, education, propaganda, and brainwashing. Coercion was there as a last resort, but police power alone simply alienated people and cost a lot of money. Everything hinged on how well the people took Marxist values to heart.

Now it was time for more relaxed policies because the educated elite would play a key role in modernizing industry, technology, science, and education. As Mao acknowledged in May of 1957

> In China, the bourgeois elements and the intellectuals who served the old society number several million, and we need them to work for us; we must further improve our relations with them so that we can enable them to give better service to the cause of socialism and so that we can further remould them and help them gradually become part of the working class . . .[20]

By 1956 some were becoming convinced that the thought reform efforts since liberation had brought the intelligentsia around (although it was well understood that many mouthed tenets of Marxism-Leninism and Mao Zedong Thought without much conviction). It was now time to introduce a more predictable legal system and liberalization in art, literature, the press, and other cultural areas. Mao joined Zhou and others in calling for such changes. In the spring he raised two slogans. One was "Let a Hundred Flowers Bloom, Let a Hundred Schools of Thought Contend," meaning that diversity in culture and science should be encouraged. The second slogan was "Long-Term Coexistence and Mutual Supervision." This referred to the coexistence of Communist and non-Communist elements and to the need to have the latter "supervise," that is, criticize, the Party in order to keep it responsive.

Khrushchev's February speech and his recent actions contained other unsettling things for the Chinese to deal with. The Soviet leader had proposed things that Beijing received coolly. He said that in the nuclear era world war was not inevitable. Peaceful coexistence was possible. He argued further that socialism could win out through parliamentary means as well as through violent revolution. He took steps to reconcile the USSR with Yugoslavia's Tito, the arch "revisionist" whom the Chinese (and the Russians) had mercilessly criticized. And Khrushchev began moving away from Stalinist-style development of industry with its emphasis on steel, machinery, and other heavy manufacturing. He began to shift resources toward consumer goods and agriculture in order to improve living standards.

Retreat from the Reckless Advance

One other major disequilibrating force was the disruptions caused by the High Tide itself. Serious problems began to arise by late spring. This was especially true in agriculture. The expansion of APCs had gone so fast that troubling symptoms were appearing. It became clear that rural cadres were better at corralling the peasants into APCs than at managing the resulting organizations. The list of typical excesses included planting too much grain and cotton at the expense of other crops, mobilizing too much labor to the detriment of income-producing sideline handicrafts, distributing collective income improperly or unfairly, allowing livestock to sicken or perish through poor management, indulging extravagance and wastefulness, and setting overly ambitious targets. The cadres' difficulties were compounded by pressures from higher cadres to achieve spectacular results. For example, although the center had specified that Fujian Province should increase its grain production by 9 percent, the provincial authorities increased the goal to 16 percent, and the local leaders upped it to an impossible 40 percent.

The center, too, made mistakes and on a grand scale. Mao and his supporters became very enthusiastic about a Soviet double-wheeled, double-bladed plow, which they believed to be a technological breakthrough. On their approval and with little field testing, the implement was manufactured in huge quantities and sold to thousands of co-ops. Unfortunately, in most places it did not work at all well. Peasants dubbed it the "hanging plow" because the only thing it did was hang on the wall. In the end, 700,000 of these plows remained unsold, a massive waste of scarce steel.

Also, state revenues began to lag seriously behind expenditures, creating renewed inflationary pressures. Exacerbating these failures, nature took a bad turn. In August, Typhoon Wanda, the worst in fifty years, brought terrific winds and rain to many provinces. In the fall the harvest fell short of the expected bumper crop. Indeed, it only moderately surpassed the previous year. The peasants grew discontented. There were food shortages in some places. Many households clamored to get out of the APCs. Households slaughtered livestock rather than turn the animals over to the cooperative. In the cities, there were factory strikes and disturbances at the universities. Mao's High Tide seemed to have produced some very unfavorable results.

By the fall, Zhou Enlai, Chen Yun, Deng Zihui, and others were leading the retreat back to gradualism reminiscent of early 1955. An editorial appeared in the June 20, 1955, issue of *People's Daily* entitled, "Oppose Both Conservatism and Hastiness." Ostensibly an admonition against excess in either direction, this document was in actuality an attack on "reckless advance," that is, on Mao's brand of economic mobilization. The author advised "seeking truth from facts," that is, pragmatism over dogma in deciding on effective policies. When shown the draft of this document before its publication, Mao angrily scribbled, "Bu kan le" ["I won't read this"] in the margin.[21] Mao's ambitious Twelve-Year Program dropped quietly from discussion.

The Eighth Party Congress, September 1956

All these things were in the air at the September 15, 1956, Eighth Party Congress. Slightly over 1,000 delegates and 140 foreign guests representing 56 Communist parties assembled in Beijing for the first CCP congress since 1945. For 12 days the gathering heard well over 100 speakers and took action on a new Party constitution, the election of a new Central Committee, and various resolutions and proposals.

In terms of economic policy, the Congress heard provincial Party secretaries, one after another, complain about the High Tide and the Twelve Year Program. One of them added that rapid socialization had disrupted rural exchange patterns, thereby damaging production even more. Zhou Enlai's speech dealt with the economy. He, too, warned against impetuosity and criticized the Twelve-Year Program. His speech reflected retrenchment policies that had been put in effect a few days before the Congress opened.

Mao was not happy with these displays of vacillation. Even as the moderates were having their way prior to the Congress, he pleaded for speedy development:

> you are said to be building socialism, which is supposed to be superior; if after working at it for fifty or sixty years you are still unable to overtake the United States, what a sorry figure you will cut! . . .[22]

As the go-slow approach continued to prevail into 1957, he remained convinced that socialism was both necessary and workable. Hundreds of collectives had succeeded. If the Party would just remain bold and systematic and quickly rectify its errors, then success could be achieved in every county and province. His speeches and writings of the time contain many statements like the following:

> If [achieving big harvests in APCs] could be done here [in Zunhua County, Hebei Province], why can't it be done elsewhere? . . . I can see only one reason—unwillingness to take the trouble, or to put it more bluntly, Right-Opportunism.
> Why can't 600 million "paupers" create a prosperous and strong socialist country in several decades by their own efforts?[23]

Organizationally, the Party emerged from the Congress significantly altered. Collective leadership was the new watchword, thanks to Khrushchev's de-Stalinization speech and the recent problems with the High Tide. Consequently, the drafters of the new constitution did what would have seemed unthinkable a year earlier. They dropped references to Mao Zedong Thought as the Party's guiding doctrine. Mao himself decided to reduce his participation in day-to-day affairs. The "first line," as he called it, he left to Liu Shaoqi and Deng Xiaoping. He intended to occupy the "second line," considering broad policy directions. Time was to show that Mao did not find these new arrangements entirely congenial. The Congress also addressed the problem of overcentralization and bureaucratism and passed a resolution calling for more administrative efficiency.

Some significant power shifts occurred. At this time there was as yet no deep division between Maoists and moderates. Liu, for example, who differed with Mao on organizational questions, took his side on economic issues. Still, personal loyalties and the relative standing of various leaders were important matters. Deng Xiaoping was a supporter and spokesperson for Mao. That fact was not unconnected to his appointment to be Party

LIU SHAOQI

general secretary, in charge of the reorganized Secretariat, the Central Committee's powerful administrative arm. Lin Biao, another Mao loyalist, emerged with a higher relative standing within the Politburo, as did another former general, Chen Yi. Liu Shaoqi, widely considered Mao's successor, saw his standing slip slightly when Deng rose to more nearly Liu's level.

The most significant loser in the power game was the minister of defense, Peng Dehuai, now inferior to both Lin Biao and Chen Yi in the Politburo rankings. The reasons for this are not entirely clear. It is known that Peng was the person who moved to omit Mao Zedong Thought from the constitution. This would seem like a slim reason to demote him because others agreed to Peng's move. Perhaps a more substantive cause was the blunt general's resistance to military budget cuts, an important item in Mao's "Ten Major Relationships" speech. It is also said that Mao was unhappy with Peng's generalship in Korea, a grievance made personal by the battlefield death of Mao's eldest son in 1950. Finally, although there is no evidence for it, one wonders if Peng was not already grumbling about Mao's mobilizational strategies, as he was to do with disastrous consequences three years later (see further on).

The Hundred Flowers Campaign

The subject of Party-mass relationships had been vexing the entire Communist bloc ever since Khrushchev had denounced Stalin. It continued to be a live issue in China, especially for Mao, as his High Tide economic plans were being abandoned. As indicated earlier, his thinking on the relationship between intellectuals and the Party was encapsulated in two slogans: "Let a Hundred Flowers Bloom, Let a Hundred Schools of Thought Contend" and "Long-Term Coexistence and Mutual Supervision." The issue of Party-mass relationships became more insistent after October 23, 1956, when the people of Budapest revolted against their Communist government.

The Hungarian uprising was another symptom of de-Stalinization, but it presented agonizing questions to Marxist leaders. What did the insurgency mean? Who was to blame? Mao's initial answer was that overly repressive policies toward the intellectuals had alienated them. Although it was imperative that Moscow crush the revolt, all socialist countries should learn a lesson from it. In the last part of 1956, Mao turned his full energies to promoting Party rectification, involving "big democracy," that is, open criticism from non-Communists.

This open door to outside censure did not sit well with much of the Party establishment. There was every reason that cadres from the local levels up to the top should resist it. Although Zhou Enlai supported Mao, Liu Shaoqi and Peng Zhen led the opposition. Throughout the closing months of 1956 and the spring of 1957, the Chairman continued to press for his special brand of rectification while Liu and the others worked to dilute his efforts. The most striking episode in this contest occurred in late

February. As head of state, Mao had convened a meeting of the Supreme State Conference, which included many non-Communists. His audience was a very large one as he delivered one of his most famous speeches, "On the Correct Handling of Contradictions Among the People."

"Contradictions among the people" was a special term in Mao's thought. It referred to social conflicts that could be reconciled without the violent suppression of one class by another. Its opposite was "contradictions between ourselves and the enemy." In his speech Mao argued that even in socialist societies conflicts (contradictions) continue to exist, as for example between poorer and better-off peasants, between the peasants and the cities, and between the government and the citizens. But these "conflicts of interest," as a capitalist might call them, were all "contradictions among the people" and could be handled peacefully. (Incidentally the thesis of contradictions continuing in socialist society was always strongly rejected by the Soviet Union.)

One particularly important contradiction was the one between the Party and the intellectuals. China needs the intellectuals, and bureaucratic tendencies in the Party need exposure to the light of day. Once again Mao was promoting his program for allowing untrammeled criticism of the CCP. In presenting his case, Mao argued that the Party historically had been less harsh toward dissidents and opponents than was commonly believed. He claimed that the thought-control campaign of the early 1950s, far from claiming millions of victims, as had been charged, involved the execution of only 700,000 or so. In November 1956, Mao had made a similar apologia, pointing out that, although the campaign against counterrevolutionaries had involved investigation into 4 million cases, only 38,000 were convicted. It is to be wondered whether his audiences were reassured or terrified by these statistics.

Even at this Supreme State Conference, opposition to the proposal was evident. Several top leaders, including Liu Shaoqi, were conspicuous by their absence. Some accounts even speak of Politburo members leaving the hall while Mao was speaking. Nevertheless, by April 1957, Mao achieved grudging acquiescence from his colleagues on the understanding that the rectification campaign would not be a harsh one. There would be criticisms but no sweeping purge. It would be like "gentle breeze and fine rain." With the approval of the Politburo, Mao issued a directive on April 30 that was finally to bring his long-sought rectification to reality. But it was rather more than he bargained for.

There had actually been some scattered response to Mao's call for outside criticism as early as 1956. One case in particular was a short story by a young author named Wang Meng. Entitled "A New Young Man Arrives at the Organization Department," it depicted the disillusionment of an idealistic young Party cadre as he confronted bureaucratism and incompetence in his new unit. (The hero's faith was rekindled in the end, however.) But only in May after Mao's directive went out, did criticism pick up momentum. Then it threatened to spin out of control.

In various publications, in public meetings, and on posters put up at universities, the Hundred Flowers criticism came in startling profusion. The pro-Soviet "leaning to one side" was derided in view of Russia's lack of generosity toward China. Some argued that under socialist democracy officials ought to have limited terms of office, as in capitalist democracies. There were demands for the release of persecuted intellectuals, because they had done no more than express themselves freely as was now being promoted. Communism itself was questioned, and Mao Zedong was criticized for being "very confident about the false reports and dogmatic analysis presented him by his cadres." He was called "impetuous in making decisions without first making a careful study of the facts."[24] Students in Beijing went on a spree of pasting up thousands of posters expressing every conceivable view, often in provocative language. Near Wuhan a mob of peasants demonstrated violently and were suppressed with some loss of life. In Wuhan itself students rioted.

By mid-May, Mao was in a most embarrassing position. From

Party officials in all the provinces telegrams poured in complaining about the campaign. Liu Shaoqi and Peng Zhen could say, "I told you so." Toward the end of the month the Chairman had to backpedal. He began to signal that criticism that exceeded the proper boundaries was unacceptable. Because the Party was "the core of leadership of the whole Chinese people . . . any word or deed at variance with socialism is completely wrong."[25]

The beginning of the end came on June 8. *People's Daily* carried an editorial entitled "What Is This For?" It signaled that criticisms of the Party would no longer be tolerated. Ten days later Mao's speech on the "Correct Handling of Contradictions Among the People" was published for the first time. But there were "certain additions." A section was added distinguishing "poisonous weeds" from "fragrant flowers." Poisonous weeds included any statements against unity, socialism, people's democratic dictatorship, democratic centralism, the Party, and international socialism.

Although not formally disowned, the Hundred Flowers campaign was over. Henceforth those who put forth "poisonous weeds" would be subject to punishment, not to mention those who had already unwisely done so. One of the last anguished student posters at Beijing University said

Intelligent friends! Everybody has been cheated! . . . Even after the Emperor has ordered the Party to mend its ways, the mandarins of all degrees are nevertheless still in place, everything remains just as before . . .[26]

As spring turned to summer, Mao's hopes for "mutual supervision" were displaced by an anti-Rightist campaign. The instruments of repression swung back into action. Hundreds of thousands of intellectuals were arrested and punished in various ways. In the countryside the Party launched a "Socialist Education Campaign" to reinforce socialist thinking at the grass roots. From the atmosphere of heady freedom that had prevailed for a few spring weeks in May, the country was plunged back into the fog of ideological conformity.

Meanwhile, Mao was defending himself to the public and to various Party audiences around the country. It had all turned out just as planned. ''The purpose,'' he said, ''was to let demons and devils, ghosts and monsters 'air views freely' and let poisonous weeds sprout and grow in profusion so that the people, now shocked to find these ugly things still existing in the world, would take action to wipe them out. . . . The Communist Party foresaw this inevitable class struggle . . .''[27] Mao called for more frank airing of views in the future.

4

The Great Leap
Forward: 1958–60

In the last half of 1957 the leaders of China confronted some intractable problems. Could they sustain the high industrial growth rate, simultaneously spur agricultural output, and still move ahead with the social revolution? Or must they moderate some of these goals? The attempt to solve these problems led to a massive explosion of events that included the reorganization of the entire farm sector in a matter of weeks, the downward transfer of up to 2.5 million cadres, the mobilization of 90 million people to learn small-scale steel making, and the migration of as many as 20 million peasants to the cities. As revolutionary drama, this so-called Great Leap Forward was brilliant and exciting. The Chinese themselves and many outside commentators have credited the movement with shaking up old habits and attitudes. Nor did it entirely lack good sense. But on balance it failed badly as a modernizing effort. It caused calamitous economic setbacks, damaged foreign relations, and opened serious political wounds that did not heal for years.

Initial Stages of the Great Leap

The Summer of 1957

In June 1957, Premier Zhou Enlai addressed the fourth session of the National People's Congress. His long speech covered the whole spectrum of government, society, and culture. Acknowledging numerous criticisms, he minimized shortcomings and painted a picture of solid achievement and optimism. There was indeed cause to be pleased with the progress in the eight years since liberation. National consolidation (except for Taiwan) was complete, the Korean War had been successfully weathered, and China had become an important member of the socialist bloc. Domestic modernization efforts had created the constitution of 1954, an expanded educational system, and improved public health.

The first five-year plan, based on Soviet-style planning and Russian assistance, was concluding. Despite serious concerns, the overall results were very good. Especially impressive was heavy industry, where priority investment had produced an 18 percent annual growth rate. The overall economy had grown at a very respectable 10 percent per year. Figure 5, which graphs estimates of national income, adjusted for price changes, illustrates the relatively rapid growth in the economy as a whole.[1] Massive structural changes (the establishment of agricultural co-operatives and the nationalization of industry) had been smoothly accomplished by comparison with the historical experience of the Soviet Union. Even though statistics, pricing, and resource allocation were still inadequate to manage China's size and backwardness, central planning capabilities had greatly increased. Premier Zhou concluded his speech with the following words:

> Fellow deputies! The international situation is favorable for our
> socialist construction. Basing ourselves on the brilliant directives
> of Chairman Mao Tse-tung on the correct handling of contradic-
> tions among the people, we Chinese people are forging an even

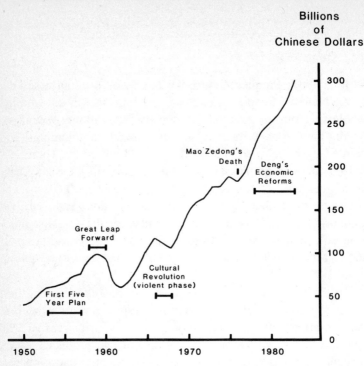

FIG. 5 Chinese national income estimates: 1950–83 (in 1952 prices).

stronger unity. . . . So long as we continue to exert efforts to strengthen national and international unity and carry through the policy of increasing production and practicing economy and building our country by hard work and thrift, no force on earth can block the victorious advance of our great socialist cause.[2]

On the other hand, as Zhou's acknowledgment of shortcomings attested, the overall picture in 1957 was not completely rosy. Politically, the Hundred Flowers Campaign had ended badly in a fierce persecution of rightists. Communists had been stung by the outside disapprobation. Mao resented the intellectuals' reluctance to give their hearts to the new regime. For their part, the frightened intellectuals could react only with cynicism and resignation at having been lured into criticizing the Party only to be sternly punished for what they said. This did not bode well for future cooperation.

The Hundred Flowers campaign had also created a rift among the CCP leadership. Mao's Yanan idealism was opposed by Liu Shaoqi and by Peng Zhen. Peng was a tall, bald, vigorous man whose genial countenance belied the fact that he was a tough, ambitious revolutionary veteran, capable of presiding over mass trials and executions in 1950. Born to a northern peasant family, he got involved in leftist labor organizing as a young man. The Nationalists imprisoned him for six years in the early 1930s, after which he joined the Party and began a long-standing connection with Liu Shaoqi.

Although not a Long March veteran, Peng rose rapidly in the CCP hierarchy in the anti-Japanese struggle and the civil war years. Soon after liberation, he was appointed mayor of Beijing, and here he built his political base. At the peak of his career in the 1960s, he was, among other things, head of the Beijing Municipal Party Committee, a member of the Politburo, and deputy director of the Party Secretariat, responsible for political and legal affairs. Having been a member of several delegations overseas, he had an international standing and was widely regarded as one of three or four possible successors to Mao. Even in June, when cultivating ''flowers'' gave way to rooting out ''poisonous weeds,'' Liu and Peng remained at arm's length with Mao. The Beijing press, which Liu and Peng controlled, evidenced this divisiveness. It permitted veiled but bitter criticisms of Mao to be published under the guise of rightist confessions. One rightist even admitted to having said, ''The peasants are cursing Chairman Mao.''[3]

In foreign relations there were problems, not only with imperialists but also with other socialist powers. Taiwan continued to elude China's grasp. In early 1957, Beijing was trying to coax the Nationalists toward reunification. Suddenly anti-American riots erupted in Taipei. This welcome development seemed to promise a more favorable turn. But the Chiang Kai-shek regime quickly suppressed the disorders and proclaimed itself more fiercely anti-Communist and pro-American than ever. Worse yet, a U.S.-Taiwan accord was signed to install Matador missiles on the island, missiles that could hit many parts of the People's Republic. In the other diplomatic direction, relations within the socialist block showed strains. Although Sino-Soviet friendship apparently continued to flourish and the Chinese press admired everything Russian, an undercurrent of deep displeasure was growing over Khrushchev's de-Stalinization efforts, his thesis on the peaceful transition to socialism, and what the Chinese saw as his responsibility for unrest in Eastern Europe. The Hungarian uprising strengthened Mao's conviction that Communist parties in socialist countries must exert the utmost effort to keep in touch with the masses.

Among the many concerns of the day, perhaps the thorniest problem was agriculture. Despite Mao's glowing expectations, bad weather and the High Tide produced a disappointing 1956 harvest, and the government had to dip into its grain reserves. This also threw the national budget out of balance, causing inflationary pressures. Alarmed moderates, particularly Zhou Enlai and Chen Yun, spoke out against "reckless advance," and by the summer of 1956 Mao had to suspend his High Tide.

Unfortunately, forswearing radicalism did not achieve quick results. On the contrary, the 1957 harvest was even worse than the one of 1956. Grain production increased only 1 percent, just half the rate of population growth. In the demoralized co-ops, many cadres underreported the crops to evade taxes and forced sales to the state. They looked the other way as peasants produced vegetables, livestock, and handicrafts for sale on the free market. Inadequate staffing below the county level made it difficult to monitor these cadres. If this kind of slack leadership continued, socialized agriculture would be in serious trouble. In the cities, food rationing had to be tightened up. But it was more than merely a question of food because, as noted earlier, the agricultural sector produced exports, government revenues, and raw materials for light industry. If output did not improve, China's whole economic modernization effort, even its industrialization program, would be in jeopardy. Ironically, Zhou Enlai and Chen Yun, who had put the brakes on the High Tide, collected some of the blame for this crisis.

There were problems in overall management of the economy as well. Heavy industry had gobbled up so much investment that consumer goods and housing supply lagged far behind demand. The central planning bureaucracy was inefficient and cumbersome, especially in providing consumer goods. Many advocated decentralizing the management of factories and other enterprises, turning them over to the provinces. Uncertainty about Soviet aid arose. By 1957 the Chinese had exhausted all their credits and needed more. But Soviet willingness to satisfy their needs did not keep pace. One reason for this was the unexpected expenses incurred by Moscow in connection with with the uprisings in Hungary and Poland, which forced the Kremlin to scale down its own five-year plan. Thus starved for funds, Beijing's planners found it difficult to resist creative initiatives in both agriculture and industry.

Truly, the Chinese faced difficult economic choices. Skewed investment had created lopsided growth to the detriment of agriculture. To rectify this, some suggested more investment in the farm sector and less in industry. Others retorted that that would slow down industrial growth, a view that Liu Shaoqi aptly represented in his 1956 speech to the Party Congress.

> In order to develop our national economy according to plan, we must carry through the policy of giving priority to the development of heavy industry. Some comrades want to lower the rate of development of heavy industry. This line of thinking is wrong. . . . If we do not very quickly establish our own . . . heavy industry, how are we going to equip our light industry, transport, building industry and agriculture?[4]

Added to this was the question of the agricultural cooperatives: Should they be tightened up or relaxed? And how would harvests be affected?

Revival of the Radical Agricultural Program

The conditions just described opened the door for Mao to revive his agricultural plan and Party rectification as well. During July and August 1957, even as thousands of intellectuals were experiencing persecution under the anti-Rightist campaign, Mao was inching toward a reconciliation with Liu Shaoqi and Peng Zhen. Their eventual understanding had both a political and an economic aspect. They agreed that ideological strengthening of rural cadres was a prerequisite for a prosperous socialist agriculture.

The first signs of reconciliation appeared in July, when Mao spoke to a conference of provincial officials. The surviving fragments of this speech reveal his concern for both politics and production.

> Our objective is to create a political climate in which there is both centralism and democracy, discipline and freedom, unity of purpose and personal ease of mind and liveliness, in order to benefit the socialist revolution and socialist construction, make it easier to overcome difficulties and to construct a modern industry and agriculture for our nation more quickly, and in order to consolidate further the party and the country to enable us better to weather the storms.[5]

In short, one for all and all for one, under the guidance of the Party, can solve all the problems at the same time. The solution of economic problems through political mobilization had always been the central strength of the CCP, especially in the glorious Yanan days. If it worked then, why not now?

During August, Mao and Liu came together still more in promoting ideological conformity. The Central Committee issued a directive launching a Socialist Education Campaign among the rural population. In particular, this prescribed a rectification movement to bring the rural cadres into line. About a week later, to facilitate economic control over the peasantry, the State Council ordered rural free markets closed. In early September the Party announced that the anti-Rightist movement would change into an "all-people's" rectification movement. That they were quite serious about conformity was clear from the announcement that the leaders of the Wuhan student demonstration had been executed.

But at the same time, other policymakers were promoting contradictory policies. In June word had come down to the rural cadres that private plots could be expanded from 5 percent to 10 percent of the land. In September a Politburo meeting that Mao did not attend promulgated a moderate agricultural policy of dissolving some APCs and administratively strengthening the rest. At this time, rural cadres were reassured that, once these adjustments were complete, they could expect no more changes for ten years.

Which of these two approaches would prevail was decided in September and October at the Third Plenum of the Eighth Central Committee. The Central Committee appeared to favor the central planners' second five year plan proposal. But then (shades of July 1955) late in the session, Mao, Liu, and Deng turned the meeting completely around toward their all-out agricultural mobilization. How they accomplished this is not clear. Perhaps they took advantage of the euphoria over Moscow's announcement of the launching of Sputnik, humankind's first artificial earth satellite. No doubt, Mao exercised his unmatched political wiles. When the meeting adjourned, the planners had been shoved aside again. "The Third Plenum gave . . . a clearer direction," Mao later said. "After[wards] we had the Great Leap Forward."[6]

Having prevailed at the Plenum, the Mao group now began to push their program. To give it more legitimacy, Mao convened the Supreme State Conference and the standing committees of the National People's Congress and the Chinese People's Political Consultative Conference. These bodies "basically" approved the Twelve-Year Program. Although such formal declarations were important, the Maoists needed more than that. Who would dare openly oppose the Chairman's policy? On the other hand, would everyone carry it out? The Maoists had to blunt silent opposition at Beijing and in the provinces. They had to persuade as many as possible and silence the skeptics. Consequently the anti-Rightist campaign was extended to the Party to combat pessimistic and retrograde views. Party leaders came under pressure, causing some of whom, even Zhou Enlai, to criticize themselves for having opposed the High Tide. The Party was expanded while cadres were transferred downward to lead the mobilization efforts. Mao promoted the decentralization of industry in order to weaken the central bureaucracies. These initiatives were increasingly successful. They were punctuated—and probably aided—by Mao's trip to Moscow in November 1957.

Mao's Trip to Moscow

The fortieth anniversary of the Russian Revolution drew Communist leaders from all over the world. It was Mao's second trip to Moscow. This time, however, he came not as a fresh revolutionary waiting in Stalin's antechamber but as the canny old Marxist whose country commanded increasing influence and prestige. His performance in Moscow was uninhibited and bold. The Chinese were very excited about Soviet military progress. Russia's successful test of an intercontinental ballistic missile in August 1957 and Sputnik I in October had cheered the Maoists. The day after Mao arrived in Moscow, a second Sputnik rocketed into space, this one carrying a dog. Mao bubbled with optimism. Coining one of his more memorable slogans, he urged the Communist bloc to determined action.

> The wind has changed direction in the world. The struggle between the socialist camp and the capitalist camp is marked either by the West wind prevailing over the East wind or the East wind prevailing over the West wind. . . . At present it is not the West wind prevailing over the East wind, but the East wind prevailing over the West wind.[7]

He even went so far as to make light of nuclear war, arguing that the surviving populations of the socialist countries would soon be stronger than ever, relative to the rest of the world. This shocked most of the other participants.

Mao brought his own agenda. In the present situation, the triumph of socialism and China's needs could be simultaneously achieved. Soviet strength, the worldwide people's struggles, and the weaknesses inherent in the imperialist camp justified great optimism. Beijing argued that the principal "contradiction" in the world was now the struggle between imperialism and national liberation movements. To promote the collapse of the imperialists, the socialist bloc must foster revolutionary movements and exploit Soviet strength. In the process China could achieve the liberation of Taiwan.

But others, particularly the Russians, did not share Mao's easy optimism. Moscow emphasized the horrors of thermonuclear war and argued that peaceful transition to socialism was possible. To the Chinese, these views smacked of "revisionism." There was another doctrinal disagreement. As Mao said in his "On the Correct Handling of Contradictions Among the People," even a socialist society can have "contradictions," including conflicts of interest between the Party and the people. Bureaucratism and elitism do not vanish with capitalism and feudalism; they can persist within the Party itself. These contradictions were mostly nonviolent or "nonantagonistic contradictions among the people." Rectification could cleanse the Party. The Russians, however, disagreed. Perish the thought that contradictions, antagonistic or nonantagonistic, could exist between the Communist party of the Soviet Union and the Soviet people!

There were other irritants as well, one of them being economic aid. In Moscow, Mao began to realize that Soviet help would not come up to Beijing's expectations. There was also Chinese disenchantment with Russian influence. Mao even complained that his doctors wouldn't let him eat chicken soup for three years because they had read that the Russians considered it unhealthy. In literature and art, the leaders in Beijing began to worry about Russia's corrupting influence on Chinese writers. Mao returned from Moscow buoyed by Sputnik and his East wind theory and yet dissatisfied with the Soviet Union. More determined than ever to strike out in a new, revolutionary, Chinese direction, he immediately threw himself into the struggle already in progress.

The Great Leap in the Ascendant

The First Phase: December 1957–May 1958

In the next six months, Mao and his supporters mobilized the country for a frontal assault on economic backwardness. For them to succeed, it was important to convert or silence balky cadres and intellectuals at all levels so that the entire nation could pull together. Many provincial leaders harbored bitter memories of 1955 and 1956. In the winter, Mao and some of his lieutenants visited various provinces to help put friendly supporters in charge. Henan Province was the first to have a purge of moderates. The Chairman himself was in Zhejiang Province where the first secretary succeeded in ousting the governor on grounds of corruption, immorality, anti-Party activities, and provincial and sectarian views. Within months similar confrontations affected every province. The political casualties included "four Central Committee alternates, a provincial first secretary, five other provincial secretaries, eighteen members of provincial committee standing committees, four governors, ten vice-governors, and about twenty-five other provincial leaders . . ."[8]

The Socialist Education Campaign in the villages put similar pressures for conformity on the local levels. Basic level elections during the spring were used to eliminate "Rightists." Propaganda campaigns featured exemplars such as Liu Jiemei, whose life was the subject of a pictorial exhibition. A poor peasant, he had joined the Communists in 1949 and acquired some fields during land reform. By 1953 capitalistic ideas got into his head, and he lost interest in the collective. Demoralized after the High Tide retreat, he began hoarding grain. But his comrades "struggled" against him in 1957, causing him to see his selfishness. As a result he rededicated himself to the collective.[9]

In January, February, and March 1958, Mao convened three conferences of central and provincial Party leaders as well as a Supreme State Conference and the National People's Congress. His rambling speeches make interesting reading.[10] One of his themes was dislike for bureaucratic planners and managers. He disapproved of unquestioning mimicry of Russia. The Soviets taught us many things, he admitted, but we must learn from them creatively and avoid "dogmatism." He recalled the days when artists used to paint him shorter than Stalin. Mao also urged that the time was right for China to launch an all-out effort.

> Our nation is like an atom. . . . When this atom's nucleus is smashed the thermal energy released will have really tremendous power. We should be able to do things which we could not do before.

Rejecting the charge that he craved excessively for greatness and success, he retorted, "Well then, should we seek pettiness and failure?"

> There are two lines for building socialism: is it better to go about it coldly and deliberately, or boldly and joyfully? . . . If, in eighteen years, we can equal what [the Soviet Union has] done in the past forty years . . . we should do precisely that. For there are more of us and the political conditions are different, too: we are livelier, and there is more Leninism here. They, on the other hand, have let part of Leninism go by the boards, they are lifeless and without vitality.

He did recognize that movements can build up too much steam and run off the track. He cautioned against rashly publishing reports of the achievements in one province that would challenge others rashly to match or surpass them. But although the leaders must not nourish false illusions among themselves, the masses should not be publicly discouraged from forging ahead. "Pessimism is wrong."

> Right now there is a gust of wind amounting to a force 10 typhoon. We must not impede this publicly, but within our own ranks we must speak clearly, and damp down the atmosphere a little. We must get rid of the empty reports and foolish boasting, we must not compete for reputation, but serve reality.

Mao even admitted that only a minority of leaders were enthusiastic and that the others, although they were going along, would have to be shown concrete results. Again and again he reverted to airy optimism. He extolled creativity and youth against book learning and stale institutions. He said, "If you are too realistic you can't write poetry." As the poet of revolution, he had no intention of bogging down in reality.

In these meetings and dozens of others at the provincial level, the new strategy for development emerged. China must "walk on two legs," which meant building a capital-intensive modern sector while relying on less sophisticated technology in agriculture and small-scale manufacturing. At the same time, the social revolution must continue: The economic and social gap between village and city, between mental and manual labor, between bosses and workers, and between school and production must be closed. Slogans from the High Tide period reemerged. Everyone was urged to produce "more, faster, better, and more economically." China was carrying out a Great Leap Forward. The Party asked Chen Boda to set up a new theoretical journal, *Red Flag*. It became the clarion for the new developments.

These conferences heard reports of dramatic increases in output. Starting in December 1957, the upward adjustment of both agricultural and industrial targets began. It soon escalated to the claim that the goals of Mao's ambitious plan for agricultural development would be reached far ahead of schedule and that in industry China would surpass Great Britain in fifteen years. (But these claims were still modest compared with later ones.)

Rural mobilization took the form of off-season water control projects. As many as 60 million peasants were involved, being fed in communal mess halls. A movement was launched to spur technological innovations, such as the effort to ''cartize'' the south, that is, to replace carrying poles with wheeled carts. (This initiative failed to recognize that adequate roads and paths did not yet exist.) There was a campaign to eliminate the ''four pests'': flies, mosquitoes, rats, and sparrows. (When it was recognized that sparrows actually controlled other pests, they were replaced on the list of four by bedbugs.) There were mass mobilizations to gather fertilizer, reclaim land, and improve soil.

The modern sector was not neglected. In December the propaganda apparatus began to promote a Great Leap Forward in industry: not merely increased output but also the thorough decentralization of this sector. Starting in December 1957 and with further pushes in January and March 1958, ministries in charge of consumer goods were ordered to hand over their enterprises to provincial, municipal, or county governments. In addition, it was decided that every locality should establish small-scale industries by using its own financial resources and local labor power. This use of both large-scale and small-scale technologies was called ''walking on two legs.'' Concurrently, there was a movement to revolutionize industrial relations and management. Reviving one of Mao's favorite themes, the Party began to attack the worship of technicians and experts and the social gulf between managers and workers. Cadres were expected to join in production work, and laborers were supposed to participate in management.

Because decentralization and mobilization required large numbers of supervisory personnel, the Party began a massive downward assignment of cadres: from the central government to the provinces, from the provinces to the counties, from the counties to the production line in agriculture or industry. In all, well over 2 million cadres were transferred down. They were joined by a million students sent to do manual labor and by large numbers of People's Liberation Army soldiers. Many demobilized soldiers were assigned as local cadres on their release from the army. At the same time, large numbers of male peasants were transferred to industrial work, which created, of all things, a labor shortage in the countryside.

By spring, results appeared to be excellent. Many water control projects had been completed and may have contributed to the abundant summer harvest of 1958. There was great hope for the flexibility and creativity of the decentralized and local industries. During April, Mao and his supporters traveled the provinces to inspect progress and to make sure of political support in the important upcoming Party meeting.

Exerting Our Utmost Efforts: June 1958–November 1958

From summer to early winter, the Maoist program of revolutionary modernization reached its climax, punctuated by announcements of ever higher targets and achievements. Agricultural collectivization culminated in the formation of the Rural People's Communes. In virtually every other field there were vigorous initiatives inspired by the new line. Military confrontation added extra tension and excitement, particularly during the brief bombardment of the Nationalist-held island of Jinmen (Quemoy).

The stage was set by the meeting of the Eighth Party Congress (second session) in early May 1958. Mao and his allies had been pushing the radical program for six months, and, as early as February 1958, the National People's Congress had endorsed the Great Leap Forward. The May Party Congress was convened in an urgent and secret session to consolidate the Party behind the new movement. Mao and Liu were the dominant figures at this meeting, and they gained the support of a number of hitherto cautious leaders. Zhou Enlai receded into the background while Chen Yun, the chief spokesperson for a gradualist economic program, was not even in attendance. He had been on assignment to Moscow.

Liu Shaoqi delivered the major address at the Party Congress. Many have discerned a certain reserve underneath his enthusiasm, but Liu left no doubt about his commitment to the Great Leap. Hurling a challenge at the remaining doubters, he said

> But some [comrades] have not yet learnt anything. They say: "We'll settle accounts with you after the autumn harvest." Well let them wait to settle accounts. They will lose out in the end![11]

He announced that the Party had adopted a new "General Line," one of those statements of overall goals that the Party issues at important transitions and that govern all policies. Back in 1952, with consolidation completed, the General Line became

> to bring about, step by step, socialist industrialization and to accomplish, step by step, the socialist transformation of agriculture, handicrafts and capitalist industry and commerce over a fairly long period.[12]

This emphasis on "step by step" and "a fairly long period," was briefly abandoned in the High Tide of 1955 with the introduction of "more, faster, better, and more economically," then reinstated in 1956 as the country backed away from the High Tide. Now the new General Line revived the urgent overtones

> to build socialism by exerting our utmost efforts, and pressing ahead consistently to achieve greater, faster, better, and more economical results.[13]

Liu also spoke of a "leap forward on every front in our socialist construction,"[14] another revival of a High Tide slogan. Although Liu did not call it a "Great Leap Forward," the man who delivered the important agricultural report did use these words, and the Party Congress officially approved the movement under this heroic designation.

The Party Congress and the Central Committee Plenum that followed effected some significant political reshuffling at the top of the pyramid. Zhou Enlai and Chen Yun lost influence. Lin Biao, moving up the ladder, was elected to the powerful Standing Committee of the Politburo. This promotion weakened the minister of defense, Peng Dehuai, whose position had already begun so slip in 1956.

Then Mao called an important meeting of the Military Affairs Committee. More than a thousand officers were in attendance from late May to July 22, 1958, and heard speeches by the highest Party luminaries, including Lin Biao, Deng Xiaoping, Peng Dehuai, and Mao himself. This meeting abandoned Peng Dehuai's approach. Rather than continue building a Soviet-style army dependent on Russian aid, the Military Affairs Committee mapped a course of complete independence, including the development of China's own nuclear weapons. This new policy spelled fewer advanced conventional weapons and a greater reliance on guerrilla strategy.

Another outcome of this military conference was renewed belligerency toward Taiwan. The Chinese leaders seemed to be acting on their view that the "East wind" could overcome the "West wind" and to be putting their Soviet support as well as American resolve to the test. Beijing may have acted to forestall anticipated action against the mainland from Taiwan. An additional motive (possibly the main one) was the emotional charge that a national military crisis would add to the Great Leap Forward.

At the end of July, Nationalist and Communist Chinese aircraft clashed in the Taiwan straits. This made the Russians extremely nervous, and on July 31, Khrushchev came secretly to Beijing with his minister of defense. He may well have tried to persuade the Chinese to dampen the Taiwan crisis. As inducements he offered several deals, including construction in China of a radio station for the Russian fleet, a joint Sino-Russian naval command in the Far East, joint air defenses, and perhaps even Soviet missiles in China. But what Khrushchev considered inducements the Chinese viewed suspiciously. They had no illusions about who would dominate joint ventures. Consequently, the first secretary returned to Moscow empty-handed. The Chinese began a campaign to increase steel production for a possible war over Taiwan. On August 24 the People's Liberation Army began heavy bombardment of the offshore island of Jinmen (Quemoy).

The Party launched a stepped-up and harsher rectification campaign in which all cadres examined their thoughts in small-group meetings. Although CCP membership was expanding rapidly at this time, as many as a million cadres were rebuked, put on probation, or expelled during the year. This further dampened potential dissent and predisposed Party members to embrace directives from the center with utmost enthusiasm.

The most spectacular of all the Great Leap Forward developments was the Rural People's Communes. Already in the winter of 1957–58 the massive water control projects demonstrated the need for a large organizational unit. This need converged with two notions dear to Mao and other Chinese Marxists. One was the memory of Yanan when distinctions of rank and status were at a minimum. Everyone did everything: Peasants fought, soldiers spun cotton, and Mao even grew his own tobacco. The second was the ever-present inspiration of the 1871 Paris Commune, when the lower classes briefly established an egalitarian dictatorship.

In the early summer of 1958 supercooperatives appeared, especially in Henan Province, which had become a hotbed of Maoism. The first and most famous was the "Sputnik Commune" established in July. Also in July, Chen Boda wrote major articles in the new Party journal *Red Flag*, outlining the theory of the commune. It was to be an all-purpose organization.

Our direction is to combine, step by step and in an orderly manner, workers (industry), peasants (agriculture), businessmen (exchange), students (culture and education), and soldiers (military) into a large commune, which is to constitute our nation's basic social unit. In this kind of commune, industry, agriculture and exchange are the people's material life; culture and education are the people's spiritual life which reflects their material life. The total arming of the people is to protect this material and spiritual life.[15]

As Chen Boda was known to be Mao's ideological collaborator, this article was bound to have great influence.

Soon the Chairman himself got into the act by touring some of the new communes. On August 12, the *People's Daily* carried a headline story entitled "Chairman Mao Inspects Henan Farm Villages," in which he praised their productivity and said, "If there is this kind of commune [here] then there can be many communes [everywhere]." [16] In September he called for extending the movement to the entire country. Coming just when the fulminations against American imperialism and its Taiwan lackeys were at their fiercest, this gave the commune movement a mighty push. Communes formed at an incredible pace. By the end of August, when the Party formally announced its approval, already 30 percent of peasant families were in communes. In all, it took only two months to reorganize virtually the entire peasantry of China in approximately 24,000 communes.

These new units attempted to mobilize the rural labor force to achieve many things at once. Bumper harvests were expected while at the same time a variety of other enterprises went rapidly forward. Most prominent was the movement to build "backyard furnaces" to make iron and steel in the belief that production of these basic industrial materials could be increased by adding thousands of simpler local operations to China's modern mills and foundries. Here again was the "walking on two legs" strategy in operation. Mao later said that 90 million were mobilized to construct and operate furnaces. An eyewitness described them as follows.

Furnace fields are everywhere in Lushan county, southern Henan province—plots of hundreds of small earthen furnaces were "growing," in late autumn when I was there, alongside fields of sweet potatoes and tobacco. From a distance the leaping flames and columns of smoke look like some new construction site accidentally ablaze. On the scene the atmosphere is like a fairground, with scores of people bustling in and out of the rows of furnaces.

Small red flags fly overhead indicating the sections belonging to the various companies and squads of farmer-steelworkers, who are organized like militia units. The air is filled with the high-pitched melodies of local operas pouring through an amplifier above the site and accompanied by the hum of blowers, the panting of gasoline engines, the honking of heavily-laden lorries, and the bellowing of oxen hauling ore and coal.

At one of the ten-foot-high furnaces, a man climbs a wooden ladder to dump coke and firewood through the top. After a few minutes beside the 1,000-degree heat, he descends and another worker goes up to tamp the fuel down with his rake. A third man follows to pull the hot rake away from the blast of the fire. Beside the furnace another crew is pushing the handle of the huge homemade wooden bellows. With all his might one of them pulls the handle, half as tall as himself, and pushes it back with the weight of his body. Three other men standing by to take their turns jokingly cheer him on.[17]

One striking feature of the Great Leap Forward was the massive entry of women into the work force. Millions of female peasants entered the fields as all those backyard furnaces and expanded operations in established plants drained men from the farm. One estimate suggests that between 1957 and 1958 the numbers of clerical and industrial workers increased by over 20 million. Demographic statistics show a sharp increase in urban population between 1957 and 1960 and a corresponding slight decline in rural population. To replace this labor, the communes had to mobilize women and free them from their household tasks. This required mess halls and nurseries to take over cooking and child care. Estimates differ, but by early 1959 there were possibly as many as 3 million of these commune canteens feeding perhaps 90 percent of the rural population.

Observers and participants have reacted variously to this massive infusion of women into the production front. Lamenting the disruptive effects of the changes, Peng Dehuai, the key critic of the Great Leap Forward, wrote the following verses.

Grain scattered on the ground, potato leaves withered;
Strong young people have left to smelt iron, only children and
old women reaped the crops;
How can they pass the coming year?
Allow me to appeal for the people.[18]

On the other hand, many saw these changes as a further step in
the liberation and equalization of women.

Another striking feature of the Great Leap was its effect on
education. Mao had ambivalent feelings about book learning. He
had been trained as a teacher and in his last years claimed that
he wanted to be remembered only as the Great Teacher. On the
other hand, he had been bitterly disappointed by the criticisms
of intellectuals during the Hundred Flowers campaign and hoped
to create a new intelligentsia out of the peasants and workers.
He was suspicious of stuffy, uncreative academics and convinced that true education must combine both theory and practice, study and labor. Nothing pleased him more than reports of
ordinary people making important discoveries and innovations.

It was not surprising that the Great Leap included an assault
on the existing school system and bold strides toward revolutionary, egalitarian education. Mao was adamant that China scrap
foreign models, especially the Soviet Union, and chart its own
course. She should revive the Yanan tradition, where study and
propaganda had been an integral part of social revolt and guerrilla war. In January 1958, he instituted a work-and-study curriculum, combining labor and education. This approach de-em-
phasized classroom academics, memorization, and teacher
authority. In the name of equity, Mao preferred to increase
peasants' and workers' access to basic schooling rather than to
extend expensive advanced training to the educationally advan-
taged in the name of economic development. Even in the elite
track, he pushed for worker-peasant quotas, remedial classes, and
decentralized admissions.

The administrative decentralization of the Great Leap Forward also hit the Ministry of Higher Education. The Beijing bu-

reaucrats who had controlled over fifty institutions of higher education were absorbed by the Ministry of Education, and the new combined ministry lost control of all but fourteen of these schools. Mao also promoted local preparation of educational materials and committees of Party members, teachers, and students to determine curriculum and methods. Prior to 1958, educational opportunities had been contracting, but the Great Leap created thousands of new work-and-study schools and many new places in the ordinary secondary schools and universities. For a euphoric moment it seemed that ''more, faster, better, and more economically'' was a slogan for education, too, and that China could have it both ways: universal mass education and expanding secondary schools and colleges.

In the summer and fall of 1958 the ''Three Red Banners'' (the General Line, the Great Leap Forward, and the People's Communes) were being carried by the masses toward a great victory. In the cities there were boom conditions. The sense of a great people's crusade pervaded everywhere. Martial music and exhortations pouring from millions of loudspeakers were matched by slogans painted on every wall: ''PUSH OUT THE WITHERED, TAKE IN THE NEW. . . . WALK ON TWO LEGS. . . . TURN OVER YOUR LIFE. . . . DON'T CRAWL BEHIND OTHERS AT A SNAIL'S PACE. . . . DOWN WITH ALL FOREIGN FRAMEWORKS. . . . SELF-RELIANCE. . . . STRIKE THE IRON WHILE HOT. . . . BETTER GET IT DONE IN ONE STROKE THAN DRAG ON.'' [19] Reports coming in from factories and communes indicated heroic increases in production. In late October the 1958 harvest was announced as virtually double the output of 1957. Steel output reportedly doubled as did the production of other commodities. Similar increases were anticipated for 1959.

Not only was there euphoria over quantitative leaps. The belief began to spread that the Great Leap Forward was leading to an early establishment of true communism. In factories, the new management-worker relations and the abandonment of the piece-rate payment fostered egalitarianism. The communes seemed to be even more advanced. Many of them had socialized virtually all property under communal ownership. Some inaugurated a free supply system for food and other commodities and services, thereby approaching the Marxist ideal of "from each according to his abilities, to each according to his needs." As an enthusiastic editorial in the *People's Daily* for September 3, 1958, said

> the people's commune is the most appropriate organizational form in China for accelerating socialist construction and the transition to communism. It will become the basic social unit in the future communist society as thinkers—from many outstanding utopian socialists to Marx, Engels, and Lenin—had predicted on many occasions.[20]

However, underneath the glittering surface all was not well. No doubt, the soundness of the Great Leap principles will continue to be debated, but clearly in 1958 they were pushed too far, too fast. The massive reallocation of labor and resources during this period ranks as one of the largest peacetime disturbances ever and caused massive disruptions in the economic system. Many of the initiatives were ill-conceived, the most blatant example being the backyard steel furnaces, which Mao himself later declared to be a great mistake. Other examples include deep plowing, close planting, and other inappropriate innovations. The tendency of commune managers to force socialized ownership and equal compensation and the disruptions in family life caused by mess halls, labor gangs, and long working days lowered worker incentives. By the winter of 1958, China's buoyant leaders began to realize that something had gone seriously amiss.

The Great Leap in Decline

Readjustment: November 1958–June 1959

In the winter and spring, signs of trouble multiplied. The summer harvest had been excellent, and the fall crop was hailed as no less outstanding according to glowing government statistics. How could it be then that grain rations in the cities were actually reduced? Later in 1959, Peng Dehuai claimed to have learned that average rice consumption fell below levels of the 1930s and 1940s. Even Mao himself later acknowledged that state procurement of grain from the peasants declined.

Other sectors experienced equally serious problems. During their brief heyday, the backyard furnaces produced 3 million tons of nearly useless steel while draining off resources that could have been used productively elsewhere. Forests had been chopped down to fuel the furnaces, causing long-term environmental degradation. Efforts to expand manufacturing output at all costs led to serious deterioration of quality and to the neglect of plant maintenance. With economic consequences beginning to affect the already pinched circumstances of most people, both in the city and the countryside, rumblings of restiveness and dissatisfaction began to surface (although it must be observed that probably nowhere in peacetime have the lives of so many people been so deeply altered with so little overt protest).

Foreign relations also deteriorated during the period of the Great Leap. Tension with the United States increased over the shelling of Jinmen. Moscow strongly disapproved of China's audacity both in foreign and in domestic affairs. And in March a new crisis arose in Tibet when Khambu rebels revolted and briefly threatened Lhasa, the capital city. The Tibet troubles, together with deep disagreement over the Sino-Indian border, began to put serious strain on relations with New Delhi.

Mao and the other leaders were not slow to notice these difficulties. High-level meetings, culminating in a Central Committee Plenum, punctuate this period and tell the story of how the leaders attempted to define and cope with the problems. They tended to explain the difficulties by blaming lower cadres for improperly carrying out central intentions. The Great Leap Forward, the Rural People's Communes, and the General Line remained correct, but implementation was too hasty and extreme. Therefore, the Party readjusted the inflated production claims and passed resolutions to dampen the excesses. Some have interpreted these meetings as the beginning of a retreat from the Great Leap. But this view may be too simple. Mao and his supporters shared with millions of regional and local cadres a heavy personal investment in the Great Leap. To repudiate it was out of the question. This was equally true of the Party organization. Having committed so much authority and prestige to radical modernization, the Party could not reverse itself without calling its vaunted judgment into question. In these circumstances, the proper course of action was, not to retreat, but to save the Great Leap Forward through judicious trimming and to vindicate it by launching more all-out efforts as soon as possible.

More conferences were convened between January and March. These included both Party and non-Party gatherings, capped by a Central Committee Plenum and a Supreme State Conference and National People's Congress. They carried on the task of assessing the damage and moderating the policies of the Great Leap. Mao took the lead in this retrenchment effort. In one meeting he went so far as to refer to himself as a "right opportunist" struggling against "left adventurists" on behalf of millions of local cadres and hundreds of millions of peasants.[21] As these remarks of Mao's suggest, there were now sharp differences of opinion about the success of the Great Leap Forward and whether or not to continue it. Advocates of retrenchment argued that excesses had to be reversed. By contrast, the directors of Party rural work departments at all levels, who attended a conference in January, 1959, had lost none of their confidence in the movement. They extolled the enthusiasm of the masses and called for a new "Leap" in 1959.

The general inclination during the spring and early summer of 1959 was to correct the mistakes of the Great Leap Forward, consolidate its achievements, and prepare for a new surge. This advance-and-retreat was a familiar pattern. Long experience had told the CCP leaders that campaigns led to excesses that then required readjustment. Even as the Great Leap was getting under way, they spoke of "saddlelike" development. They did not anticipate having to retreat so far that the advance would be virtually negated.

By June it appeared that the country could expect more relaxation. The top leaders were continuing to tour the provinces to assess developments. Various moderating resolutions and statements issued from the Party center. Mao's speeches emphasized going slowly, combining a practical spirit with revolutionary fervor, and setting realistic targets. The Party and government issued corrections of previously reported figures. Some of the more pragmatic leaders promoted this slogan, "The Whole Nation Is a Single Chessboard," in an effort to restore centralized economic coordination. Directives went down telling local Party cadres to quit monopolizing all governmental authority. Commune leaders were now directed to turn back land ownership, production decisions, and income allocations to the production brigades, which, in most cases, meant the former cooperatives. Agriculture was declared in need of a larger share of national investment.

A political change of uncertain significance also took place. Mao Zedong had been both the Chairman of the Party and formal head of state since 1949. He now decided that when his term expired in 1959, he would not stand for reelection to the latter office by the National People's Congress. This decision had been taken in early 1958 for the purpose of relieving him of ceremonial chores and allowing him to concentrate his energies on overall policy. Coming, however, during the contraction phase, Mao's replacement by Liu Shaoqi as head of state could be construed as a demotion. The center took great pains to reassure the Party rank and file and the public that this was not the case. But despite the appearance that political affairs were under control, a ferment was working beneath the surface. Deep dissatisfaction among some Party leaders and Russian opposition to the Great Leap Forward were the main ingredients in this leadership crisis, which erupted in July and August 1958. The key figure was Peng Dehuai.

Showdown at Lushan: July 1958–August 1958

Peng Dehuai seems to have been an early critic of the Great Leap Forward, as his poem, cited earlier, attests. His dissatisfaction must have been compounded by Lin Biao's May 1959 promotion, over Peng's head, to the Standing Committee of the Politburo and by the summer Military Affairs Committee meeting that gutted his long-standing policies in national defense. There was also personal friction between him and Mao. The two men had a history of disagreements dating back to the war years. By contrast, Lin Biao struck an adoring posture toward Mao. During Mao's June 1958 speech at the Military Affairs Committee, for example, Lin interrupted the Chairman several times with fawning praise and echoes, such as the following comments when Mao said China must be more selective in learning from the USSR:

> Chief Lin said: "In political matters, such as Party leadership and in political work, our army has a fine tradition of its own. Our Party's Marxist-Leninist level is very high, not to speak of the Chairman's. The Chairman has said that our editorials are at a higher level than those of *Pravda* . . ." [22]

Peng Dehuai, who at this stage in his life had become gruff and testy, may perhaps be forgiven if he felt not only professionally but also personally afflicted.

In the course of an April 1958 Politburo meeting, Peng criticized Mao for conducting the Great Leap Forward on his own authority and circumventing the other members of the Politburo Standing Committee. Mao, in return, criticized Peng. This exchange had no apparent immediate effects. But, in fact, the subsequent events suggest that on both sides personal and policy differences were pushing the two men to a confrontation. Peng, in his capacity as minister of defense, left China later in April for a tour of the Soviet Union and Eastern Europe. While he was gone, personnel changes in the armed forces removed some of his supporters. For his part, Peng appears to have tried in some way to enlist the help—or at least the sympathy—of the Russians in his disagreements with Mao. When he was in Albania, he met the Soviet premier and, as a hostile Maoist attack of several years later expressed it, he "informed baldheaded Khrushchev of the shortcomings of the Great Leap Forward, and the latter encouraged the former to go home and oppose Chairman Mao."[23]

Just how Peng hoped to use the USSR is not clear. Both he and Khrushchev may have believed that a Russian threat to withdraw military assistance would put irresistible pressure on Mao. If that was Peng's thinking, he miscalculated because, by colluding with foreigners, he was committing a cardinal sin of the CCP. This was the transgression for which Gao Gang had been purged in 1953. Just one week after Peng's return, the Russians abrogated their agreement to supply China nuclear military technology. We may assume that, upon his return, Peng advocated restoring the Russian assistance and that this involved some Chinese concessions.

Thus the stage was set for trouble. In July 1958 the Politburo met at Lushan for more discussion of Great Leap problems and countermeasures. The conference began on the generally positive note sounded by Mao:

> The achievements are tremendous, the problems are numerous, the experience is rich, and the future is bright.[24]

But in small-group discussions Peng and others were outspokenly critical of the hectic campaign and the communes. They also seem to have done some personal lobbying for their position. Peng wrote and circulated a letter to Mao. Although the letter was temperate in its criticisms of the Great Leap Forward and explicitly exonerated the Chairman, it was read, probably correctly, as an attack on Mao's leadership. There was at least one other letter circulated, and there were several verbal expressions of agreement with Peng. The day after Mao received the letter, his Great Leap was the object of another attack, this one by Nikita Khrushchev writing in the pages of *Pravda*. The issue had now escalated to the question of the basic correctness of the Great Leap and to Mao's style of leadership. Peng was treading on dangerous ground.

A week after receiving Peng's letter, Mao counterattacked. In at least two different talks, he responded, not to the substantive issues, but to the challenge to his leadership. He charged the dissidents with anti-Party activity, conspiring in secret, and colluding with a foreign power. Mao played his trump card: that, above all, the Party must stay united behind him. Certainly, unity would collapse if Mao chose to oppose a majority of the Politburo, and more than once the Chairman threatened to break with his colleagues.

Probably Peng was looking for Mao to shoulder some of the blame for China's troubles and to relinquish active leadership to others. This would allow the pre-1958 policies to be reinstated, particularly Peng's military policies. But once the Chairman began to frame the issue in terms of Party unity and patriotism, Peng and his supporters were lost. During the next few weeks Peng and several supporters were isolated and attacked. In a vain attempt to salvage his position, he publicly criticized himself and also wrote a penitent letter to Mao.

Thus ended the career of one of the CCP's more colorful and capable leaders. Peng was dismissed as minister of defense, to be replaced by Lin Biao. Henceforth he received only minor assignments. Actually, he was treated rather gently, which reflected a widely held, if unspoken, belief that his criticism of Mao was just. In 1962 he attempted an unsuccessful political comeback. In 1974 he died in detention through cruel neglect.

End of the Great Leap: 1960

Peng Dehuai's challenge at the Lushan meeting disrupted the normal wavelike pattern of the movement. Although a moderating phase had set in, Mao counterattacked politically to protect his position. Cadres in the ministries of defense and foreign affairs were organized to criticize Peng and the "anti-Party" clique. In the provinces, meetings were held to expose "rightist thinking, rightist sentiments, and rightist activities."[25] Many were purged. It appears that the rapid growth in Party membership of the preceding years reversed, as up to a million cadres were expelled. An anti-Rightist media campaign grew increasingly strident and began to suggest an insidious connection between the USSR, Peng, and anti-Party Rightist subversion.

A revival of the Great Leap Forward accompanied this political crackdown. Maoist credibility was linked with revolutionary modernization. When Peng challenged the program, Maoists reacted by reaffirming its correctness. Moderate commune policies were partially countermanded and abandoned as local cadres, fearful of appearing to be Rightist opportunists, swung back to radicalism. More mess halls and more mobilization were called for as devolution of management to production brigades was denounced. There was a push to establish urban communes, mainly among workers in light industry. By the summer of 1960, for example, virtually all the residents of Canton were organized into such communes.

This backlash was accompanied by increasingly bad feelings toward Moscow. The mutual irritation between the two sides over such issues as East-West policy, Taiwan, and the Great Leap was deepened when Mao perceived a Russian shadow behind Peng's challenge. Protests to the Soviet Union were presumably rebuffed. And then, as China's differences with India over the Tibet crisis and border issues grew sharper, *Tass* published an editorial that, far from backing the Chinese, struck an even-handed posture between the two sides. This amounted to a disavowal of China and has been considered by some to be "the first broadside in the Sino-Soviet dispute."[26]

Differences widened further in the wake of Khrushchev's visit to the United States. Although the Chinese cautiously supported the trip in the beginning, by late September 1959, Mao was extremely upset about Khrushchev. On the very day of the latter's arrival in Beijing to participate in the celebrations marking the tenth anniversary of the People's Republic, a vituperative criticism of Peng Dehuai appeared in the *People's Daily*. The Soviet leader returned this slap by lecturing the Chinese leaders on the subject of peaceful coexistence at their formal National Day reception.

Mao later complained that at this time high Party discussions were so preoccupied with foreign relations that domestic policy suffered. In April 1960, *Red Flag* published a long attack on Yugoslav revisionism. It was an open secret that the real target was the USSR. The passage of time only exacerbated the conflict. By the summer, Peng Zhen and Khrushchev were to be found trading insults at a conference of Communist powers. The culmination came in July, when Khrushchev recalled all Soviet technical advisers in China. No doubt, he thought that this would bring Mao around, but the effect was to alienate the Chinese even more. This split profoundly affected China's development. However inadequate Moscow's assistance may have been, it was now withdrawn completely. Beijing burned an important bridge at a time when no alternate support was at hand. That China would pay such a price for autonomy reflects the depth of Chinese nationalism.

The revived Great Leap Forward could not last. It was cut short by the same economic difficulties that had forced the earlier policy reversals. Weather conditions in 1960 were even worse than in 1959. The innumerable dislocations further hobbled production. So, by the summer of 1960, the Party was again adopting moderate policies. But the Great Leap came to an end without ever being explicitly repudiated. Indeed, the press continued to trumpet the correctness of Chairman Mao and the Three Red Banners more fervently than ever. Within the Party at all levels there persisted a current of pro-Great Leap opinion. The central icon for these elements was, of course, Mao, and their strongest organizational base was the PLA under Lin Biao. But these enthusiasts were opposed by many who, like Peng, were dismayed at the actual results of the Maoist policies.

The Great Leap Forward has had its apologists, who argued that its harm was exaggerated. They countered that, despite temporary economic problems, revolutionary gains were achieved. Old ways were shaken up. Market economies have setbacks, too, they said, and without the communes China would have experienced even greater difficulties in coping with the adverse weather conditions of the years 1959 through 1961. These arguments were most often heard in the late 1960s and through much of the 1970s. Since Mao's death, both the official Chinese view and the prevailing outside opinion have emphasized the damage caused by the movement.

While taking cognizance of this apologetic view, our own summary is that the Great Leap Forward, like the 1955 High Tide, of which it was essentially a massive revival, resulted in a short-term economic disaster, comparable in scale to a major depression. The years 1960 and 1961 were particularly trying for the entire nation, almost everyone struggling just to get food to eat. The aftereffects of this effort to carry out revolutionary principles in the economic sphere were felt for several years, especially in agriculture. Politically, the Great Leap produced fallout in the form of increasing strife and disagreement within the Chinese Communist Party and in the form of ruined relationships with the Soviet Union, relationships that had greatly benefited China. Moreover, domestically, these serious difficulties gave the CCP no choice but to bolster its damaged prestige through intensified indoctrination and coercion, thereby weakening the legitimacy of the regime. All the same, it must be admitted that the Great Leap Forward was a heroic failure, a colossal revolutionary drama that may have produced some intangible results favorable to modernization. If Maoist policies did not create a socialist utopia, it was not for want of trying.

5

Depression, Recovery, and Struggle at the Top: 1960–65

The Great Leap Forward plunged the whole country into hunger, unemployment, despair, and lawlessness. Alarmed Party leaders had to abandon the radical policies. As a result, the hard times bottomed out in 1962, and the economy improved each year thereafter. But recovery also caused disagreements. Was the revolution being sold out in the name of economic production? Some, like Mao, said yes. Although he conceded that the Great Leap had flaws, he still embraced its central vision: achieving wonders through the determination of militant cadres and mobilized masses.

In late 1962, Mao insisted that the relaxation had gone too far and pushed for steps to revitalize the revolution. Consequently the Party launched a series of campaigns in the countryside collectively known as the Socialist Education movement. There were parallel campaigns in industry, education, and cultural life. But three years of developing and adjusting these programs produced deepening disagreements between a disgruntled Mao and his recalcitrant colleagues. By 1966 consensus among the Party elite fragmented into a great falling out.

The Immediate Repercussions of the Great Leap

Depression

The years 1960 and 1961 were a terrible ordeal. As one economist concludes, "The scale of fluctuation in this trough was almost unprecedented in the history of any country in peace time."[1] Grain production dropped to a level where the national reserves were being exhausted. China, which had recently exported grain, now had to purchase Australian and Canadian wheat to feed the cities. Across the land, people went hungry. Nor was the industrial sector spared. First consumer goods and then heavy industry followed into a steep decline. Fig. 5 in Chap. 4 dramatically illustrates the drop in in overall national income during the difficult years starting in 1959.

Millions who had poured into the cities during the Great Leap Forward and more millions of young people finishing school were thrown out of work. The birth rate slumped. The death rate surged. From recently released statistics it is estimated that for the period 1958–1962 abnormal mortalities totaled around 16 million persons. China's population actually declined by 1.5 percent in 1960 and 0.5 percent in 1961. There are scattered accounts of popular unrest and even some armed uprisings.

Adjustment

In 1960 a Chinese mountain climbing team scaled Mt. Everest. Drawing a lesson from their achievement, the Chairperson of the State Planning Committee hailed not only their daring but also their careful calculation. They

> cherished the high ambition . . . [yet] they conducted scientific analysis . . . adopting decisions on the basis of seeking truth from facts. . . . [By contrast, although the Chinese people recently] . . . created many miracles unknown before in history, [there were nevertheless] shortcomings, . . . acting blindly, . . . and indis-

criminately starting more and more projects [mistakes that re-
quired] certain sensible adjustments.[2]

This soberly optimistic note, so restrained by comparison with
the tone of just a few months earlier, reflected a dawning realization of very serious economic trouble. The Party held a
succession of top-level meetings starting in the summer of 1960
and culminating in a February 1962 conference attended by 7,000
Party officials. In the course of these eighteen months the consensus moved toward an increasingly sober and even alarmed
appraisal. In response, the components of the Great Leap Forward were abandoned or modified. Posters still trumpeted, "Long
Live the People's Communes," but the unspoken operative rule
was this utterance of Deng Xiaoping, "Black cats, white cats,
what does it matter? So long as they can catch rats, they are
good cats!" Fig. 6 is a schematic representation of the modified
commune system as it existed from the early 1960s into the late
1970s.

Two *People's Daily* editorials illustrate how successive adjustments in agricultural policy responded to the deepening concern. The editorial for November 20, 1960 advocated transfer-
ring decision making from the central commune administration
to the smaller production brigades. Five days later the paper went
even further. It argued for devolving authority onto the smallest
subdivisions, the production teams. "Production teams . . . are
the key in perfecting the people's commune system . . ."[3] They
should have more cadres assigned to them and land and tools
permanently turned over to them. As inducements to higher production, the teams should be offered contracts for fixed quantities of grain, with bonuses for overfulfillment. Individual team
members should be compensated according to their labor. In addition, they should be permitted to make and sell handicrafts on
open markets. The fact that some families would do better than
others under these arrangements must be accepted. Such proposals read like a list of Great Leap heresies.

These measures were progressively implemented under the

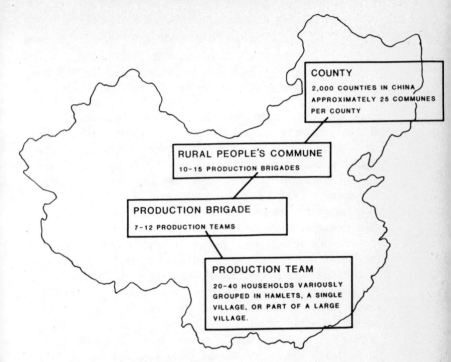

COUNTY
2,000 COUNTIES IN CHINA
APPROXIMATELY 25 COMMUNES
PER COUNTY

RURAL PEOPLE'S COMMUNE
10-15 PRODUCTION BRIGADES

PRODUCTION BRIGADE
7-12 PRODUCTION TEAMS

PRODUCTION TEAM
20-40 HOUSEHOLDS VARIOUSLY
GROUPED IN HAMLETS, A SINGLE
VILLAGE, OR PART OF A LARGE
VILLAGE.

FIG. 6 The rural People's commune system: 1960–80.

leadership of some of the more pragmatic leaders, particularly
Chen Yun, whom Liu Shaoqi raised again to a position of authority. A Party directive made production teams the basic ac-
counting unit by March 1961. Chen Yun and Deng Xiaoping
pushed an extension of private plots, free markets, and—by early
1962—even the "Anhwei responsibility system," a family-based
farming arrangement organized according to production teams.
It was getting very close to private farming. (This system was
later widely adopted in the 1980s.) For the economy as a whole,
Chen Yun undertook to lead the effort back toward more planning, more coordination, and even some reliance on private enterprise.

One urgent need was to get the unemployed out of the cities.

Programs to return these people to the villages began in late 1960 and continued into 1962. In 1961 alone upwards of 10 million people were moved away; and still more millions, in 1962. A Swedish observer who was then in Beijing gave the following account of how those who "went down" were chosen.

> Each firm has to report a certain number of people moving out. But no one can be compelled to go; the decision must be voluntary. Meetings are held evening after evening to consider these conflicting obligations. Everybody knows that the list of those who are to leave has already been drawn up. Everybody knows that the meetings will not end until those whose names are on the list have volunteered to go. This list is never mentioned. People all talk about patriotic duty and the welfare of the individual. But they all look at each other and wonder whose names are on the list. Those who feel safe volunteer—and are then told that they cannot leave. One by one they take the plunge, until the only ones left are those who know they have been chosen. Evening after evening the pressure is increased. Eventually it is impossible to refuse, but some people manage to find a loophole. Everybody notices this and knows what it means; someone else will have to go instead to fill the quota. Evening after evening these people sit facing each other, torn between conscience and self-interest, choosing the victims of the Chinese crisis.[4]

On the other hand, the heavy-handed treatment of the intelligentsia eased up. Khrushchev's withdrawal of Soviet advisers made China's own experts all the more critical. Their contribution could not be maximized in a repressive atmosphere. Consequently, not only technical, but also cultural areas were allowed to push Marxism into the background. Plays, articles, books, and films appeared that obliquely criticized the Great Leap Forward and, by implication its author, Mao. The year 1961 saw the staging of one particularly interesting historical drama about a Ming dynasty official named Hai Rui, of which more will be said later. There was also talk of strengthening the democratic parties. The National People's Congress and the Chinese People's Political Consultative Conference became more active.

Meanwhile, in the countryside it was necessary to consider both sanctions against cadres who had unscrupulously used the Great Leap to advance their own careers and restitution for their victims. Rectification of rural cadres began in late 1960. Even some provincial officials were dismissed. An overlapping campaign to "reverse verdicts" (i.e., rectify past injustices) culminated in early 1961 with a sweeping campaign of apologies, rehabilitation, and even compensation.

At such a critical time it was also prudent to minimize hostility in foreign relations. Consequently, criticism of the USSR abated. In June 1961, Liu Shaoqi gave a speech in which he paid "high tribute to the great Soviet people and the Communist Party of the Soviet Union."[5] Mao himself advocated solidarity with the USSR at a January 1961 Plenum. Even toward the United States a softer line was taken.

These policies enjoyed broad support. Although many leaders, including Mao, denied that the Great Leap was a mistake, they conceded excesses and accepted criticism. In June 1961 and again before 7,000 cadres at a conference in February of 1962, Mao admitted responsibility. He called for free discussion within the Party, including criticism of himself.

No matter. Let everybody criticize us. As for me, I will not go out during the day; I will not go to the theatre at night. Please come and criticize me day and night (laughter).[6]

He told the lower cadres they could not duck responsibility: "You think that nobody will really dare to touch the arse of tigers like you? They damn well will!"[7] Opinions differed on just how much to blame the Party center. Some, like Liu, were prepared to suggest that 70 percent of the failure was attributable to human error and thus by implication to central policy. Many shared this view and even made veiled criticisms of the Chairman. At this time Peng Dehuai, the ousted minister of defense and archcritic of the Great Leap Forward, was hoping to make a comeback, and some Party leaders supported his rehabilitation. Not everyone joined the retreat. Lin Biao, the newly installed minister of defense, and Jiang Qing, the Chairman's wife, were prominent among those who continued to hymn the ideals and symbols of the revolution. Lin launched a vigorous program of making the PLA a revolutionary force. His military doctrine emphasized people over weapons in preference to Peng Dehuai's weapons-oriented professionalism. (The major exception was the new nuclear program, which produced a test bomb by 1964.) Lin gave ideological study and practice the top priority. At every echelon down to the company level, he installed a political officer or committee. To staff these positions, he recruited a quarter of a million new Party members within the army. Other programs complemented these efforts, including a rectification campaign among the officer corps.

Jiang Qing was virtually unknown in 1959. Because of lengthy illnesses and Mao's earlier commitment to keep her out of politics, she had stayed in the background, raising her daughter by Mao and Mao's daughter from his previous marriage. But during the retreat from the Great Leap Forward the ex-actress's interest in the performing arts began to converge with her political zeal. Attending the theater at Shanghai, she was appalled at the slack, satirical, degenerate quality of plays that were then being produced. She began a personal crusade to revolutionize the arts and to drive out all traditional, foreign, and bourgeois themes. She began to prevail on Mao to purify the arts, acting as his personal cultural watchdog. In 1960 she found young radical teachers and students at Beijing University who were anxious to subject plays, operas, and books to Marxist criticism and thus began to form her circle.

Lest one idealize either the left or the right as disinterested champions of rational views, it must be stressed that power, too, was at stake. The Great Leap had damaged Mao's authority. Although still Chairman, he retreated from the "first line" and resigned as head of state. He made only one public appearance in 1962. Mao was still peerless in his capacity to influence general policy. But the only way for him to implement his wishes was through the bureaucrats, and he could not help but chafe at the difficulty of getting them to carry out both the letter and the spirit of his policies. Also, in 1963, Mao would be seventy years old. Far from being invalided, he swam and rode horseback. But he wheezed from decades of chain smoking and gave signs of fading health. When he would go, no one could tell, but his passing would surely initiate some rearrangement of power. Against this day everyone was concerned to shore up the best possible position.

Liu Shaoqi moved into the opening created by Mao's semi-retirement. As head of state and CCP vice-chairperson, Liu assumed responsibility for the overall direction of Party affairs. He was widely considered to be Mao's successor. Deng Xiaoping, the Party's general secretary, and Peng Zhen, deputy general secretary and the Beijing Party boss, also assumed increased power and authority. These men favored policies that would enhance their position. As they performed their Party and state duties, they were daily strengthening their own bastions of power—"independent kingdoms," as Mao sometimes growled. For example, in 1960, Deng tightened the Secretariat's control over the provinces by establishing six regional bureaus. On the other hand, Lin Biao, who had little strength in the Party bureaucracy; Jiang Qing, who had no political network; and other persons whose ambitions outran their political connections embraced Maoism as a vehicle to advancement. They were paralleled on lower levels by cadres who had bettered themselves during the Great Leap Forward and who now were being undone by "reversals of verdicts."

Recovery

Beginning in 1962 the economy steadily improved. In agriculture this was the result of good weather and changes in commune policy. It also came about as a result of the decision to invest more in agriculture and improve farm technology. The slogan used was this: "Take agriculture as the foundation and industry as the leading factor." Conferences were convened, such as the national agricultural science and technology conference held in the spring of 1963. Extension stations were set up. In 1963 and 1964 improved plows, seeders, land levelers, fertilizer sowers, and walking tractors were developed. Between 1962 and 1965, China imported several complete factories to produce chemical fertilizers and other agricultural inputs.

There was a dramatic increase in the production and use of irrigation pumps. Mechanical irrigation increased sixfold between 1961 and 1965 to 6.6 million hectares, mostly around Shanghai, Guangzhou (Canton), and Beijing. Several very successful high-yield areas were established in these three regions as well as in the central and the upper Yangzi. A rapid increase in petroleum production in the mid-1960s made this mechanization possible.

The result of all this was that from 1964 to 1967 grain production increased from 5 percent to 6 percent annually. Per capita availability of grain rose from a low of about 220 kilograms in 1960 to nearly 300 by 1966. (This was, however, still slightly below the pre-Great Leap levels.) The population growth rate, after its decline in the famine years, surged to 3.5 percent in 1963 and then dropped off toward 2 percent. In industry the picture was roughly the same. Indeed manufacturing assumed a typical rate of growth much higher than that of agriculture. Because of this industrial growth, the per capita gross national product in 1965 stood at 220 U.S. dollars in 1965 as compared with 190 U.S. dollars in 1957. Figure 5 in Chapter 4 illustrates the recovery of overall national income adjusted for prices.

Political Crisis

By mid-1962 the worst days of deprivation seemed to be behind. The crops were better, and, with a new rationing system for consumer goods, the industrial situation improved. However, China was still poor as the rehabilitated Chen Yun was acutely aware. In the early months of that year he strongly urged holding to a steady, pragmatic, long-term course in order to achieve full recovery. "How many years are required for the recovery stage? In my personal opinion it requires about five years, starting from 1960."[8] But some economic planners with a bias for heavy industry did not accept Chen's willingness to downgrade investment in heavy industry for an extended period. Mao agreed. Moreover, he saw dangers that were just as urgent as food and fiber. He disapproved of the political price being paid for economic recovery and grew alarmed that his colleagues were happy to drift indefinitely with "peaceful coexistence in politics, the attitude of muddling through in organization, and the attitude of superficiality in economics."[9]

Mao was also alarmed about the deterioration of the Yanan ideal, which he believed to be the only truly revolutionary path. This ideal, it will be remembered, featured cadres whose commitment, ideology and self-sacrifice could mobilize the masses to storm all obstacles. But since liberation and especially since 1960, the cadres had all too often lost their Marxist-Leninist backbone and sometimes their basic honesty. This gloomy assessment was not groundless. Although the millions of cadres differed individually, they had come to constitute a many-layered elite. They had become modern equivalents of the mandarins of old, who valued their procedures and political connections more that the welfare of the people. Because almost everything in China was terribly scarce, many cadres habitually exploited their influence to obtain goods and special advantages for themselves and their families.

The Tenth Plenum

In late July 1962, Mao summoned the entire Central Committee and several other central and provincial Party heads, more than two hundred in all, to a work conference at the seaside resort of Beidaihe. The agenda included agriculture and the economy, the government budget, class struggle, and other major questions.

The business of hearing reports, airing views, listening to speeches by Mao and other luminaries, and hammering out policy decisions lasted many weeks into September. Immediately thereafter, this same body constituted itself as the Tenth Plenum of the Central Committee to put the Party's official stamp on the various decisions. These deliberations launched a three-year effort to integrate Mao's revolutionary views into the recovery program.

Chen Yun, Liu Shaoqi, and others spoke up for the recovery adjustments. But the Chairman had not called this meeting to be given lessons in pragmatism. He shot back, heaping scorn on the Ministry of Finance, raising the great issues of revolution. Where is all this private farming leading? Is China not slipping back toward the restoration of capitalism and feudalism? Toward revisionism, like the Soviet Union? Mao coined another of his slogans: "Never forget class struggle." He admonished, "From now on we must talk about this every year, every month, every day." [10] The debates at Beidaihe may have grown heated. But when the Plenum convened, differences had been reconciled into a united Party voice. Although Mao conceded the importance of fostering production, cadre morale, and Party discipline, he forced the others to accept his conditions. In promoting these things, they should "never forget class struggle." They must take concrete steps lest China slide into revisionism.

Trouble was built into this compromise. Although the moderates recognized Mao's concerns, they were not prepared to push class struggle hard. They feared disruption that could plunge the country once more into economic crisis. Because they held the administrative levers and were prepared to hobble the very initiatives they were ostensibly promoting, Mao was bound to lose patience. Compromise was hindered by the situation in the countryside. Communes, production brigades, and production teams were laced with conflicts between demoralized cadres, corrupt cadres, ousted cadres, disgusted peasants, and freewheeling private producers and traders. These tensions intertwined so tightly that to touch one affected them all. To placate peasant resentment would probably ruin cadre morale. To restore old cadres would embitter the new. To attack corruption and spontaneous capitalism would endanger production.

The Socialist Education Movement

The Tenth Plenum launched the new movement to rekindle the socialist flame in the countryside. It had several phases and campaigns, but it has come to be known collectively as the Socialist Education movement. It ran its course for more than three years. The movement began in the winter of 1962–63. The first step called for careful examination of rural conditions and experimental solutions. Investigations confirmed widespread shortcomings among rural cadres. Logically, then, improvement of the commune system would depend on reforming these rural cadres. There were some pilot programs to clean up the local leadership through criticism, self-criticism, propaganda, and other measures. The phases through which the Socialist Education movement passed, marked by the succession of central documents, illustrate the growing difficulties encountered in attempting to make a society at once revolutionary and orderly.

The First Ten Points. In February 1963 the Party held a top-level conference to study progress to date. Mao praised the results in certain places. "Once we grasp class struggle, miracles are possible," he enthused.[11] These efforts led to the formulation of a central directive on the Socialist Education movement. This document, which turned out to be the first of four, is called the First Ten Points. To rectify the local cadres, it called for the formation of "Associations of Poor and Lower Middle Peasants" to help identify and correct cadre problems. This would require auditing the accounts and correcting irregularities. Cadres were also asked to spend some time working in production for the good of their proletarian consciousness. The campaign also included propaganda against landlords, exploiters, and other bad elements. The leaders, especially Peng Zhen, closely monitored the progress.

Unfortunately by the summer of 1963, the Socialist Education movement as a whole was falling short of the expectations. Local cadres were uncooperative. Some could not find the time to participate in labor. Others failed to publicize the rules on auditing accounts. Still others represented the Socialist Education movement as a campaign to promote production. No doubt the results were modest primarily because Party leaders on all levels hesitated to push too vigorously.

The Second Ten Points. Peng Zhen, whose star in the Party was rising rapidly, was chosen to draft another set of guidelines. The product of his labors came to be called "the Second Ten Points." He introduced work teams, a technique used in land reform, to guide the cleanup of local cadres. Squads of reliable, trained provincial and county cadres would go to selected production teams and brigades, "link up" with the peasants, and gain detailed knowledge of the local situation. In the early months of 1964 the Second Ten Points were implemented with moderation. The work teams walked a fine line between undermining the local cadres and mobilizing the peasants. Consequently, cadres with something to hide could still avoid exposure.

But this did not apply to cadres and rural entrepreneurs of Peach Blossom Brigade, located near the capital, for they came under the sharp eye of Wang Guangmei, wife of Liu Shaoqi. Wang took an active part in monitoring the Socialist Education movement, as did her husband and other members of the top elite. Her identity unknown, she joined a work team assigned to Peach Garden Brigade, where they investigated and rectified for many weeks. Wang was appalled by the extent of cadre corruption and rampant capitalism among the peasants. Her findings seem to have been considered representative and argued for a get-tough approach. In the summer, Liu, who had carried out his own investigations, and Mao, who seemed to share the alarm of Liu and his wife, agreed that stricter efforts were needed. They decided that local cadres and even provincial-level officials must be subjected to the criticism of the Associations of Poor and Lower Middle Peasants, led by the Party. At this juncture Liu took over the movement from Peng Zhen.

The result was a vigorous assault on local cadres in the second half of 1964. This phase of the Socialist Education movement was part of a year of heightened political conformity in all spheres of life. The Mao cult was being pushed as millions of copies of *Quotations of Chairman Mao* were published, and many cultural and educational figures came under attack. ''Let politics take command!'' was the operative motto.

The Revised Second Ten Points. The document ruling this phase of the movement was the third to be promulgated. It was drafted in September by Liu, and because it changed some of the points of its predecessor, it was known as the Revised Second Ten Points. This no-nonsense program to root out bad cadres rested on the premise that the movement under Peng Zhen had failed miserably. Liu's new approach called for large and aggressive work teams. No more tiptoeing around to protect local cadres. ''Human sea'' work teams would move in and take over a unit from its leaders. They would mobilize the peasants to struggle against the cadres.

The result was a sweeping purge of local Party personnel. Estimates vary, but the toll could have exceeded a million despite the fact that human resources only permitted the program to be carried out in about one-third of rural areas. This may have been the largest rural purge ever undertaken. Thus, Liu Shaoqi, ever the hard-boiled Party chief, sought to smash the problem of bad cadres.

The Revised Second Ten Points created an uproar, and Mao was not pleased. When he had agreed to a new approach, he meant that the Associations of Poor and Lower Middle Peasants would be free to criticize the cadres. But Liu's method was to control the peasants through the work teams. The big work teams also disturbed the peasants who wondered what new heaven-sent calamity was on its way. The cadres were even more upset and frequently refused to serve any more. This program threatened to weaken the newly recovering rural system once again.

Liu's case was further weakened by the fact that the work teams occasionally threatened people connected with other high leaders. One team moved in on Beijing University and mobilized students against the school administrators—who had close ties with Peng Zhen. Another attacked the agricultural unit that was fast becoming the model for all of China, the famed Dazhai Brigade in Shanxi Province. Investigators claimed that the vaunted self-reliance of this unit was a sham and that numerous irregularities had occurred. In desperation, Dazhai's leader wangled an audience with Mao, who had recently taken to praising him. He won Mao over completely, and the work team at Dazhai soon withdrew.

The Twenty-Three Points. The Chairman was thoroughly alarmed over this turn of events. Subsequently, a fourth and final phase of the Socialist Education movement began. In late 1964 and early 1965, Mao himself oversaw the drafting of yet another set of guidelines, the so-called Twenty-Three Points. This new document called for a more truly populist approach. "We must boldly unleash the masses." [12] Peng Zhen again took primary responsibility. Immediately, the aggressive rectification work teams were recalled to receive new instructions. But in the end Peng did not come much closer to Mao's intent than Liu. In fact, the peasants were not unleashed. Although the Twenty-Three Points called for county-level cadres to be criticized by the masses, this did not happen widely.

Thus, by mid-1965, after almost three years of pushing for a socialist revival in the countryside, Mao felt thoroughly frustrated. He was appalled by Liu's tough approach, which created fear and increased bureaucratism. His Twenty-Three Points dealt Liu a stiff—and certainly resented—rebuff, seriously affecting the relationship of the two men. On the other hand, Mao was disappointed with Peng's approach, which generated mostly words and motion without tangible results. To make matters worse, Mao's pique over the way his colleagues had handled the Socialist Education movement intermingled with other sources of discontent.

Education

When Mao preached, "Never forget class struggle," he was concerned that forty years of revolution could be negated by the "ogres" of capitalist restoration.

> We must acknowledge that classes and class struggles still exist for a long time to come, and that the reactionary classes may stage a comeback. We must heighten our vigilance and successfully educate the young people, the cadres and the masses . . .[13]

This explains why the Tenth Plenum's agricultural program would include a "Socialist *Education* movement" and why Mao intended to radicalize the educational system as well. But what, specifically, troubled him?

In the post-Great Leap Forward crisis years, the policy for education paralleled the retreat in agriculture. Radical innovations were abandoned. Many of the work-and-study schools simply ceased to function. The Ministry of Education began to regain its grip. In July the labor requirement was eliminated for regular students. In December 1962 the Education Ministry identified a network of "key schools" ("little treasure pagodas," as their detractors called them) to educate China's brightest, from primary school to university. Deng Xiaoping and Liu Shaoqi oversaw these changes.

This marked a retreat from universal education. By 1962 the number of middle school students had declined to less than 15 percent of its earlier level. Not much more than half of all primary age children were in school. To address this problem, Liu began to develop two separate systems: a college and a vocational track. The renewed emphasis on expertise meant that the choicest opportunities went to those best equipped to pass the entrance exams and excel in class: urban youth, in particular children of intelligentsia and cadre families. It worked to the disadvantage of rural children and even offspring of factory workers, Marxism's cherished proletariat. There was a marked ideological relaxation as well. In late 1962, the blunt-talking foreign minister, Chen Yi, addressed graduating college students in Beijing. He downplayed political study and emphasized the need for technical expertise.

Mei Lanfeng was a great artist, and as such had won honor for our country. Did he have to study political books thoroughly? No, he did not have to. But he had to perform for the people under the leadership of the Party.[14]

Upset by all this, Mao launched an attempt to reverse the liberalization in education following the Tenth Plenum. This effort enjoyed some success but, like the Socialist Education movement, was repeatedly watered down by established leaders who were prepared to beat the Maoist drum and march their own merry way. Admissions policies favorable to workers and peasants were reintroduced. Students met to "remember the bitterness [of the past] and think of the sweetness [of what the Party had achieved]." A new breed of PLA hero, the sincere, unassuming servant of others, was publicized for students to emulate. (See the next section.) Now secondary schools and colleges experienced an epidemic of students' sweeping the halls or secretly washing their comrades' bedsheets in an attempt to turn the difficult trick of standing out unobtrusively.

In 1964, Mao pushed for a reduction in college-preparatory emphasis and for wider access. As a consequence, there was soon more recruitment of worker and peasant students and even expulsions of students from "bad" (e.g., middle class or landlord) backgrounds. From 1964 on, students constantly heard of themselves referred to as the successor generation whose duty was to become true revolutionaries. There was pressure for greater equality between student and teacher, problem solving rather than recitation, and open-book exams. In interviews with his nephew and his niece, Mao scoffed at book learning and extolled independent, action-oriented thought. Students should sleep through boring lectures, he said, and rebel against school authority.

But although Mao's colleagues and the educational establishment acceded to some changes, they worked steadily to strengthen contrary policies. Their general approach was to expend most of the educational budget on secondary and higher education, that is, to train those who could contribute most to modernization. Universal primary schooling and irregular adult classes received lower priority and local financing. Aside from nourishing an elite system of "key schools," the Ministry of Education promoted conventional goals, methods, and materials. In the spring of 1964 the director of propaganda blocked a Maoist effort to reduce class time and cautioned against innovations that had not been tested out. In 1964 the old Ministry of Higher Education was reestablished. Liu Shaoqi, despite Mao's great interest in this sphere, became the leader most influential in educational policy.

The students themselves were not aware that these struggles were going on at the top or what political issues were at stake. Some responded fervently to the ideological appeals; others focused on getting ahead within this unpredictable system. But all lived under the shadow of the very restricted opportunities. Despite their relative advantages over peasant children, admitted students could not look forward to a steady climb up the ladder of success. Indeed, chances were against them. Not only were the places in secondary and higher education limited, but also the modern sector was not growing fast enough to provide jobs for all the graduates.

Consequently, only around 20 or 30 percent of high school graduates were accepted for further education. The rest were "sent down" to labor in the countryside. As they left, they were told that it was for a glorious, transforming purpose.

Going to share the bitter and the sweet with the laboring people in the countryside, educated youths can gradually cultivate the habit of doing labor eagerly, establish a correct attitude towards physical labor, [and] reform their nonproletarian thoughts . . . an important guarantee for preventing themselves forever from being corrupted.[15]

One can imagine the uneasy mix of idealism and disappointment felt by the students. But their parents, while the Party official was thus preaching, were lamenting to one another, "Don't let this bright pearl of yours drop into a heap of ashes."[16]

Culture

Mao's intention after the Tenth Plenum was to shake up writers, artists, and scholars, too. As usual, the Party responded but in a measured and controlled way. When Mao then pushed for a full-fledged cultural purge in late 1963, the response again failed to satisfy him. So in early 1965 he determined to circumvent the cultural establishment. This turned out to be the opening salvo of the Cultural Revolution.

After 1960, as the Great Leap Forward faded, two rival cultural camps emerged: radical and establishment intellectuals. The former have already been noted, particularly Jiang Qing with her faith in revolutionary transformation. The radicals seized eagerly on Mao's Tenth Plenum effort to tighten up the cultural realm. Most notably, Jiang Qing's circle took steps to reform the theater. Companies were encouraged to abandon traditional and foreign plays in favor of revolutionary themes. In 1963 the Party boss of Shanghai, a Mao supporter, appointed Zhang Chunqiao as head of the Shanghai Party Propaganda Department. Zhang, in turn, recruited Yao Wenyuan. The destinies of these two men were about to intertwine with Jiang Qing's as they constituted the avant guard against bourgeois culture.

Zhang Chunqiao (pronounced something like "Jang Chuncheeow") was in his early fifties, a thin-faced, bespectacled commissar. An active leftist since the 1930s, he had risen to become, in effect, Shanghai's "cultural czar" as head of the municipal Party's Propaganda Department and publisher of *Liber-*

ation Daily. His name had long been associated with the left, as he had strongly attacked "rightists" in the 1957 backlash following the Hundred Flowers campaign. During the Great Leap, he published an article advocating radical economic ideas, which caught Mao's attention.

Whereas Zhang was primarily a cultural bureaucrat, the younger Yao Wenyuan (pronounced "Yow One-you-an") was a talented polemicist, a leftist literary hatchet man. He too had taken an active role against "rightists" in 1957 even though his own father, an old-line leftist intellectual, had been stigmatized with the dreaded rightist label. One of Yao's articles that came to Mao's favorable attention attacked a newspaper for not placing the Chairman's words in boldface with banner headlines. Yao was one of several young writers recruited by Zhang Chunqiao. Round-faced with prominent eyes, he was later commonly rumored to have married the daughter of Mao and Jiang Qing.

The other camp, the establishment intellectuals, were scholars, writers, and cultural workers who occupied positions in the major schools and propaganda departments. Some of them became polemicists in a kind of high-level debate over the Great Leap Forward, Mao's leadership, and Peng Dehuai's dismissal. Because of the treatment Peng received, high-level airing of views on these issued was risky. Criticism then disguised itself in hints and allusions in the essays, fiction, theater, and academic debates of intellectuals who were patronized and protected by high Party officials.

One of these people was Wu Han, author of the play *Hai Rui Dismissed from Office.* He was not only a well-known member of the Chinese Academy of Sciences, but also a public figure with connections. He was a deputy mayor of Beijing, and his eminent friends included fellow bridge enthusiast Deng Xiaoping. Wu Han's direct patron was Peng Zhen, the Beijing Party chief and associate of Liu Shaoqi and Deng Xiaoping and of the director and deputy directors of the Party's Propaganda Department. These men sponsored scholars like Wu Han and controlled the major newspapers and periodicals in the capital.

Thus, when Wu Han dramatized a sixteenth-century official, he was not merely dabbling in theater. He was joining in the debate over the policies of the past three years. There were many other such Aesopian attacks on the Great Leap. Wu Han himself collaborated with two other writers in Peng Zhen's orbit to publish a series of short essays, some of which could be read as satires against the recent radical policies. In addition, a large number of films, novels, plays, and other artistic expressions, if they did not carry a hidden political message, at least avoided the heightened politics of the Great Leap and presented a more complex reality.

While the radical intellectuals hailed Mao's 1963 call to "never forget class struggle," the cultural establishment gave it a cooler reception. Some of the satirists sniffed danger and ceased publishing on the eve of the Tenth Plenum, and Peng Zhen's Beijing machine complied with a rather low-keyed program of criticism in the arts. But they undertook no thorough housecleaning. Moreover, in various forums and meetings, they encouraged the expression of moderate views and counterarguments.

By the end of 1963 it seemed as though Peng Zhen's cultural bureaucrats had made a fairly comfortable adjustment. A certain amount of tightening up had occurred. Some liberalization had been suppressed. At the same time, in the interests of fostering a creative environment, some diversity was tolerated. Perhaps representative of this were letters to the editor in which readers expressed their view of happiness, rejecting extreme self-sacrifice. As one of them wrote

> I think that happiness means leading a peaceful, pleasant life, not a life of struggle amid hardship . . . It is strange logic to equate hardship with happiness and enjoyment of creature comforts with bourgeois thought.[17]

Mao indulged this. But gradually, perhaps under his wife's influence and because of his growing hatred of Soviet revisionism, he lost patience with cultural laxity. From the winter of 1963 through the summer of 1964, he repeatedly nagged his colleagues about excessive liberalization. For example, traditional operas drew his fire. "Operas abound in feudal emperors, kings, generals, ministers, scholars, and beautiful women, but the Ministry of Culture doesn't care a bit." [18] In December he lashed out at "problems" in all forms of art: "Hence we should proceed with investigation and study and attend to this matter in earnest." [19]

In January 1964 ten of Mao's poems were published for the first time to great fanfare. Like almost all of his poetry, these selections were highly allusive and metaphorical, inviting diverse interpretations. But he may well have had liberal artists and writers in mind when he wrote:

> Away with all pests!
> Our force is irresistible. [20]

In the spring of 1965, Mao again expressed his impatience. He lashed out against the cultural bureaucrats, charging that they had "slid right down to the brink of revisionism." [21] And to leave no doubt about the seriousness of his intent, he linked liberalization to the bourgeois revisionism of the Soviet Union. In his polemic "On Khrushchev's Phony Communism and Its Historical Lessons for the World," published in July, he warned:

In socialist society, the overthrown bourgeoisie and other reactionary classes . . . sneak into the . . . cultural and educational institutions so as to resist or usurp the leadership of the proletariat. . . . In the ideological, cultural and educational fields, they counterpose the bourgeois world outlook to the proletarian world outlook and try to corrupt the proletariat and other working people with bourgeois ideology . . . [22]

Meanwhile Jiang Qing and the other radicals were at work. In December, under her urging, the Shanghai Propaganda Department organized an East China District Drama Competition to encourage the creation of new plays on revolutionary themes.

This was Jiang Qing's first big breakthrough. It was followed in
June by a still greater triumph, the Beijing Opera Festival on
Contemporary Themes. Thirty-seven new works were pre-
sented, along with numerous speeches by Party luminaries. Jiang
Qing gave her first speech.

> Our operatic stage is occupied by emperors, princes, generals,
> ministers, scholars, and beauties, and on top of these ghosts and
> monsters. . . . The grain we eat is grown by the peasants, the
> clothes we wear and the houses we live in are all made by the
> workers, and the People's Liberation Army stands guard at the
> fronts of national defense for us and yet we do not portray them
> on stage . . .[23]

In December 1964 her stature rose another notch when she acquired her first formal position, delegate to the National People's Congress.

Mao's Party colleagues had little choice but to concur with
his sentiments on culture. Over this period they responded with
several efforts to implement his wishes. Most significant perhaps, the Secretariat, in May or June, formed a "Five-Person
Group" to supervise a "cultural revolution." It was led by Peng
Zhen. There were efforts to reform the arts and dispatch intellectuals to farms and factories for political "tempering." Several prominent writers and thinkers became the targets of criticism campaigns. There was a rectification campaign targeting
cultural bureaucrats from the summer of 1964 to the spring of
the following year.

But these efforts were decidedly less enthusiastic than those
of Jiang Qing's circle. The Party leaders expressed reservations
and attempted to keep reform firmly under the control of the established system. Peng Zhen's Five-Person Group contained only
one Mao supporter. In December, although conceding that new
dramas were needed, Liu Shaoqi suggested that feudal plays must
continue to be staged because recent works were simply not as
good yet. The cultural establishment kept the Jiang Qing's Bei-

jing Opera Festival under its control as much as possible, omitting, for example, to publish her speech. The 1964 rectification was both sluggish and gentle by comparison with earlier antecedents. Its victims were selected from the second rank and escaped serious punishment. Wu Han was not attacked at all. In April 1965, the minister of culture declared the cultural rectification a success and terminated the movement. Not surprisingly, Mao took little pleasure in this result. He now responded to Jiang Qing's urgent suggestion to attack Wu Han.

The PLA and Foreign Policy

Even in the period of retreat from the Great Leap Forward, Mao had good reason to be pleased with Lin Biao and the People's Liberation Army. In his demeanor toward Mao, Lin was the diametric opposite of Liu Shaoqi, Deng Xiaoping, and Peng Zhen. Whereas they dismantled the Great Leap and treated the Chairman as first among equals, Lin continued to defend the movement and glorify its author. He strengthened indoctrination and political structures in the army. So by the time of the Tenth Plenum in September 1962, the PLA's organization, morale, and commitment to Mao Zedong Thought were all strong. Lin became part of a radical faction around the Chairman. As Mao relinquished routine administration to Party headquarters, he gathered his own circle, some of high Party rank such as Chen Boda, some with little standing at all, like Jiang Qing. Lin Biao was a prized member of this camp as leader of the one powerful institution truly responsive to Mao.

As the Tenth Plenum met, military conflict was erupting on the Indian border over a rugged region called Aksai-Chin. Chinese generals considered it strategically vital because through it passed the one road between western Xinjiang Province and Tibet. Conflicting Chinese and Indian claims were stalemated although some believe that diplomacy might yet have won through. When fighting erupted during October and November 1962 the PLA troops sent Indian forces reeling backward and then withdrew to

LIN BIAO

defensive positions. Thus was another proud page added to the achievements of the armed forces and Lin Biao.

After 1962, Lin's PLA continued to stand out. There were tangible successes such as the testing of China's first atomic weapon in 1964. There were endless ideological campaigns featuring exhortations like the following.

Respond to Chairman Mao's Call to Learn Resolutely from Comrade Lei Feng. (1963)

Anti-Chemical Warfare Company in Canton [Guangzhou] Trains Successors in Hard and Meticulous Way. (1964)

Be Good and Do Good by Learning From Good People and Good Deeds; Look to Wang Chieh for Inspiration. (1965)[24]

The army published special materials, in particular the famous "Little Red Book," *Quotations of Chairman Mao*, and sponsored arts festivals on revolutionary themes. Political commissars were added and strengthened at every level. As the most revolutionary gesture of all, the PLA in 1965 abolished all military ranks and replaced Soviet-style uniforms with khaki fatigues for all.

The army also functioned as a model for society. Drawing on the Yanan days, when the troops intermingled with the people like fish in the sea, the PLA revived its role as exemplar. In addition to PLA literature and arts festivals, there were the emulation campaigns. The most famous model hero was Lei Feng, a young soldier whose family had suffered terribly before liberation. His boundless gratitude to the Party was such that he dedicated himself to "serving the people" in quiet humble ways. When he died in a freak accident (a telephone pole fell on him), the army published his diary as a paragon of quiet service to Chairman Mao. Lei Feng emulation campaigns were organized by the Communist Youth League and the Chinese Trade Union, with Mao personally scripting the slogan "Learn From Lei Feng."

By late 1963 Chairman Mao was calling for the whole country to learn from the PLA, by which he meant more than study groups. The idea was to replicate in the civil administration the ideological tautness of the army. To this end Lin and Mao wanted various ministries, especially those related to the economy, to have special political commissars assigned to them who would report to the PLA's General Political Department. This was in addition to the regular Party branch in every unit. The Party leaders complied with this plan, but they weakened it by insisting that the new "political departments," as they were called, should report to the Central Committee rather than to the PLA. There were other PLA intrusions into the civilian sector. In 1965 some army personnel were being used in Socialist Education movement work teams in the countryside. The PLA also involved itself to a limited degree in education.

The army played a role in foreign policy as well because important strategic issues had to be addressed. China was learning, as the French had learned in 1789 and the Russians in 1917, that great revolutions arouse great enemies. In this case, it was both of the superpowers. Would there be war with the United States over Vietnam? If so, should China commit massed armies as in Korea? Or should she prepare for invasion and Yanan-style guerrilla tactics? Was there an imminent Soviet threat as well?

Decisions on these questions had implications well beyond battlefield training. A guerrilla war strategy would not require heavy expenditures on sophisticated weapons and would thus permit sustained economic investment and independence from the USSR. It would require, however, some dispersal of industry to reduce vulnerability. On the other hand, a strategy of conventional war against the United States would require more investment in armaments, more concentration of industry, and better relations with Moscow, the source of military technology. It would also require the army to concentrate on defense and reduce its political role.

Perhaps the deciding factor in these deliberations was Mao's growing alienation from the USSR and his holy war against revisionism. As if to confound all the Western observers who considered the People's Republic another docile satellite of Moscow, China was in the process of fashioning a defiant new independence. By 1962 the great revolutionary friendship that was supposed to endure forever was rapidly disintegrating. China got little Soviet support in its dispute with India and criticized Moscow for backing down to Kennedy during the Cuban missile crisis. Nothing seemed to stem the tide: not the visit to Moscow by Deng Xiaoping and Peng Zhen, not Khrushchev's letter to Mao suggesting cooperation against imperialism (both in 1963), not efforts by Vietnamese and Japanese Communists to intercede, not Khrushchev's ouster in 1964. Not even imperialist U.S. bombs raining on Vietnam in 1965 reversed the downward trend.

Mao failed to see anything but revisionism in Moscow. As he said in his July 1964 diatribe "On Khrushchev's Phony Communism and Its Historical Lessons for the World,"

The questions of whether revolution . . . and . . . the dictatorship of the proletariat should be upheld or opposed . . . are now the focus of struggle between Marxist-Leninists the world over and the revisionist Khrushchev clique.[25]

Soviet leaders had betrayed Marxism-Leninism and their disease was communicable. Thus, Mao's battle with the Russian monster abroad and with capitalist ogres at home fed on one another—were in fact one and the same struggle. As he said rather poignantly to Zhou Enlai the year before they both died,

> You and I, old friends, can we just
> watch our efforts be washed away?[26]

In response to the military threat on two fronts, Beijing defined a new global policy. In 1963, China began to issue calls to the nonaligned countries, portraying herself as the model of a self-reliant people's liberation struggle. All peoples must join in resolutely rejecting Russian revisionism and defeating U.S. imperialism.

China launched a diplomatic offensive aimed at supplanting Russian influence in Asia and Africa. Although the Aksai-Chin conflict alienated India and damaged China's image elsewhere and although China's resources were limited, this new independent policy enjoyed considerable success. Between 1960 and 1965 diplomatic relations were established with fifteen new countries. Border issues were settled with five countries, from Burma to Mongolia.

In Asia, China participated in the settlement of the Laos conflict in 1962 and assisted the growth of an extremely powerful Communist party in Indonesia. In early 1965, China was joined by the parties of North Vietnam, North Korea, Japan, and Indonesia, as well as of Albania and Romania, in boycotting a Soviet-sponsored Communist conference. In Africa the effort to challenge Soviet influence led to extending nearly 300 million U.S. dollars in foreign aid between 1960 and 1965 to black nations. China began training guerrillas of several African states, most importantly the Congo, and participated actively in meetings of the Afro-Asian People's Solidarity Committee in 1960,

1963, and 1965. In 1965, Zhou Enlai and Chen Yi led an ambitious diplomatic mission to eleven African nations.

This new diplomatic thrust was not without its problems. Many African leaders resented Chinese efforts to export revolution. In 1964 the Beijing-supported Congolese rebels were defeated, and Burundi broke off diplomatic relations. Also damaging to Beijing's stature was its caution in Vietnam. Despite anti-American rhetoric, the Chinese offered little assistance to Hanoi. Only when the Tonkin Incident of August 1964 led to a widening U.S. involvement in the north did China begin to send military assistance. Even then a definite policy on Vietnam did not emerge until the fall of 1965. Despite these difficulties, the Chinese could compliment themselves on a successful new thrust in foreign policy. However, 1965 brought a number of serious setbacks, involving Vietnam, Indonesia, Africa, and Cuba, which helped worsen tensions among the leaders.

The Crisis of 1965

In the summer of 1965 the average person had no inkling that there was trouble brewing at the commanding heights. The fact that on August 1 the PLA's *Quotations of Chairman Mao* was published for study in both rural and urban units did not seem particularly ominous. *People's Daily* readers saw a photograph of Mao and Liu out for a swim together, talking to children. Peng Zhen had recently been declared "Chairman Mao's Close Comrade-in-Arms." And there were many signs of normalcy. The economy had continued to grow since 1962, supplying markets with adequate food and consumer goods, at least by a poor nation's standards. In the countryside, cadres could relax as the Socialist Education movement moderated. A new rectification began in the fall for cadres at the county level, but it was superficial, resulting in very few dismissals. Such was the calm before the storm. Meanwhile, cut off from public view, a handful of critical disagreements were about to boil over, heated by the radicals' and Mao's dissatisfaction. These disagreements over defense, economic policy, education, and culture eventually stimulated a chain of events called "the Great Proletarian Cultural Revolution."

Vietnam suddenly became an important issue. In February 1965, President Johnson, authorized by the U.S. Congress's Tonkin Gulf Resolution to use military force against North Vietnam, ordered operation "Rolling Thunder," a program of sustained bombing. In 1965, American troop strength in the south stood at 70,000, then climbed to 125,000 with further increases on the way. Up to this time the Chinese had supposed that the United States would get tired and go home. But China now had to make decisions. The Americans, who had frequently charged that China was the source of the Vietnamese revolution, were assaulting a fraternal Marxist state. Parallels with Korea were too obvious to miss. Comradely instinct impelled Beijing to aid Hanoi. Indeed, when bombing of the north started, China sent a squadron of MIG-17s. By fall construction and engineering troops were being sent, eventually to total as many as 50,000.

This was a relatively modest contribution, for there were considerations pushing in the other direction. Washington did not want the war to spread to China and repeatedly signaled this in 1965 and 1966. Secondly, to the extent that embroilment would mean cooperation with Moscow, the Chinese hesitated because relations had become strained to the breaking point. Even the minimal cooperation required to send Russian aid through China succeeded only after prolonged wrangling. This created a third restraint on Chinese involvement: Alienated from Russia, China had no protection against U.S. nuclear weapons.

Still, a controversy did arise because Vietnam intertwined with domestic politics. The Maoists, led by Lin Biao, promoted a people's war thesis in order to keep the PLA off the battlefield and fully deployed in politics. Arguing that the anti-imperialist fight was a worldwide people's struggle, they held that every national liberation movement must rely on its own masses, a thesis that allowed China to remain relatively disengaged. The contrary view, too, had its supporters. They argued that China must actively aid Hanoi and prepare for American retaliation and that this required healing the breach with Moscow. The most prominent hawk was Luo Ruiqing, who had been named PLA chief of staff in 1959, when Lin became defense minister. He spoke for many PLA professionals who opposed some of Lin's policies. They wearied of Lin's Mao cult. They disliked the abolition of ranks, not merely because it removed their prestige, but also because it made them vulnerable; for, without ranks, they lacked any standing once deprived of a command. As professionals, they considered Lin's nostalgic guerrilla strategy a recipe for technological backwardness. Although their views sounded a little like the ousted Peng Dehuai's heresy, they received support from Liu Shaoqi and others bothered by Lin's growing prominence.

This issue came to a climax in September 1965. Lin Biao published an essay entitled "Long Live the Victory of People's War," which remained the classic Chinese statement on anti-imperialist struggles.

> . . . to make a revolution and to fight a people's war and be victorious, it is imperative to adhere to the policy of self-reliance, rely on the strength of the masses in one's own country, and prepare to carry on the fight independently even when all material aid from outside is cut off . . .[27]

At this same time, Luo Ruiqing delivered a contrary speech, arguing for a more positive policy and suggesting reconciliation with the Soviet Union.

> It is possible that U.S. imperialism may go mad in trying to save itself from its doom; we must take this into full account and make preparations against its expansion of the war of aggression in Viet Nam and against any war it may impose on us.[28]

This debate played itself out mainly behind closed doors, perhaps in the Politburo meeting that convened at this time. Details about this important meeting are extremely scarce, and observers differ about the participants' exact positions. However, it is clear that Lin Biao won the argument. China did not undertake massive defense preparations, reconcile with the Soviet Union, or extrude the PLA from politics. In December 1965, Luo Ruiqing was removed from office. He made a self-criticism but later retracted it and attempted suicide by jumping from a window. Thus, Luo became in a sense the first victim of the Cultural Revolution.

This Politburo meeting in September 1965, had to deal with other foreign setbacks. The Indonesian Communist party failed in an attempted coup d'état, which the Chinese had encouraged. Suppression of the attempt virtually obliterated the Indonesian party. Thousands of its members were massacred. In Jakarta, the generals who assumed control broke off relations with the People's Republic. A further fiasco was Zhou Enlai's unsuccessful effort to head up a second Afro-Asian conference in Algeria while excluding the Soviet Union from participation. In the end, China was unable to prevail and, to avoid rubbing shoulders with the USSR, insisted on scuttling the entire conference. At this same time, there were other setbacks in connection with the India-Pakistan conflict and in relations with Cuba. These setbacks in China's new Third World diplomacy cannot but have exacerbated an atmosphere of anger and frustration.

The Socialist Education movement, too, was a disappointment. After three years and numerous twists and turns, Mao's dream of the rural masses mobilized to help rectify the Party failed to come true. This source of friction was compounded by disputes over industrial policy. The economic planners considered the industrial decentralization of the Great Leap period extreme and counterproductive. Soon, under Liu Shaoqi's direction, they reversed the trend by setting up large, centralized, integrated industrial enterprises called "trusts." Several of these organizations had been created or were under development in 1965. This blatantly contradicted the radical slogan then being pushed: "In Industry, Learn from Daqing," Daqing being the name of the successful Manchurian oil field recently developed in a Maoist, mobilizational, self-reliant fashion. Education was another bone of contention. Mao and the radicals wanted to extend the work-and-study principle to all institutions. Liu was determined to continue two parallel systems. By late 1965, Mao was carping at this limited progress.

But the issue that triggered the catastrophe of 1966 was the politics of culture and, in particular, Wu Han's play, *Hai Rui Dismissed from Office*. It is impossible to be sure whether Mao equated Hai Rui with Peng Dehuai when the play was first published, but he had certainly come to that conclusion by the spring of 1965. Jiang Qing had long been pushing that view and asking permission to develop a Marxist criticism of Wu Han. Now, exasperated with the cultural establishment and its feeble feints at rectification, Mao acceded. He allowed her to have Yao Wenyuan, the aggressive Shanghai radical, write the article. But lest Peng Zhen's culture machine get wind of this and head it off, the project was kept confidential.

Little happened in the summer to soften the Chairman's feelings on this subject. Indeed, time only brought new confirmation of the Party leaders' balkiness in cultural renovation. They soft-pedaled the campaign to study Mao Zedong Thought and obstructed efforts to radicalize the arts. Consequently, Mao resolved to pressure them and decided to use an attack on Wu Han's play as the opening gambit. At the September 1965 Politburo meeting, Mao blasted the Party leaders' obstruction of the cultural revolution. Ominously he raised the question, "What are we to do about revisionism that crops up at the Party center?" [29] He insisted that Wu Han be criticized, and he gave the assignment to none other than Peng Zhen.

This was a favorite tactic of Mao's. By ordering Peng to criticize Wu Han, he put him in a ticklish position. If Peng condemned the play, he would have to discipline his own subordinate and weaken his Beijing political machine. Yet to exonerate Wu would be to risk criticism for whitewashing the affair. However, the issue did not seem to be too serious at that moment.

Deng Xiaoping continued to play bridge with Wu Han. Peng Zhen did essentially nothing.

Then in November 1965, Mao dropped a bombshell. He ordered a Shanghai paper to publish Yao Wenyuan's polemic on *Hai Rui Dismissed from Office*" Unaware of Mao's connection, Peng was furious over not having been consulted. Did he not head the Five-Person Cultural Revolution Group specially assigned to examine the Wu Han play? How dare a regional committee take liberties over a writer directly linked to the Party center! He got on the phone with Shanghai, but his protestations had little effect. In contrast to Peng's spleen, other leaders sensed the need for caution. Certainly, Deng Xiaoping seems to have smelled trouble, for he cut off social relationships with Wu Han. But Peng, through desperation or foolhardiness, set out to protect his organization.

There followed four months of tactical moves. From November 1965 through February 1966, Peng tried to reassert Beijing's jurisdiction over the affair and to have the Shanghai group disciplined for breach of Party procedure. He blocked and countered Shanghai's efforts to proclaim Wu Han's guilt, arguing that the historian was participating in a purely academic debate. When he did permit the *People's Daily* to publish Yao's article on November 28, he added an introduction explaining that

Our policy is to allow freedom of criticism and countercriticism; as for mistaken views we shall adopt the method of reason and persuasion, seeking truth from facts.[30]

Other papers throughout the country also carried this explanation, thereby demonstrating the hold Peng Zhen's group had over the propaganda apparatus.

In the course of his maneuvers, Peng summoned several meetings of his Five-Person Group and initiated two private audiences with Mao to explain his position and seek Mao's acquiescence. Mao remained out of Beijing, remote and difficult to figure out. Peng's specific object was to put the matter to rest with an official document that could be disseminated as Party policy. This document, called the February Outline Report, did receive Politburo approval and was sent down to Party committees. It called for open debate, equality before the truth (without appeals to Mao's authority), maintaining academic standards, and emphasizing construction over destruction.

But during these weeks, the radicals, too, were busy. Sniffing blood, they undertook to counter Peng's moves. Their greatest asset was, of course, Mao himself, who alone could proclaim holy writ. At a meeting in December 1965, the Chairman assailed Peng Zhen on the subject of Wu Han. Then in February Lin Biao commissioned Jiang Qing to convene a "Forum on the Work in Literature and Art for the Armed Forces." This meeting drafted a document, personally edited by Mao, frontally contradicting Peng's February Outline Report. It emphasized the importance of class struggle, the rejection of literature from the past, and the misdeeds of Wu Han and company. Finally, it advocated a "Great Socialist Cultural Revolution," a name that, with one alteration, was about to blaze across the pages of China's history.

Thus, into March 1966 the issue seemed to be at dead center, with Peng's report officially sanctioned and a rival document being promoted by the PLA. But then Mao intensified his attack by directly criticizing Peng and his Beijing machine at a Politburo meeting. It may not have been wholly coincidental that just at this time Chief of Staff Luo Ruiqing, a Peng Zhen ally, was being accused, interrogated, and dismissed. Nor did it help Peng's situation that at the crucial moment Liu Shaoqi departed on a diplomatic mission to Pakistan, Afghanistan, and Burma.

Politically, Peng was now mortally wounded. He tried to justify himself, but at a Secretariat meeting in early April 1966 Mao's men pummeled him with criticism. Deng Xiaoping and Zhou Enlai, who were present, sided with the radicals. Barely was this ordeal over when Mao personally convened the Politburo on Peng's case. He announced his intention of having the Five-Person Group disbanded. The final blow to Peng's career came in mid-May, as will be described in the next chapter.

Thus did several years of struggle and maneuver come to an end. But much is still unclear. Did all these grievances (USSR, agriculture, education, medicine, culture) vex Mao equally? Or were one or more of them decisive? Or did he simply espy behind all of them the great evil, revisionism? Did he at a particular moment, perhaps in early 1965 or September 1965 or January 1966, concoct a full-blown plan to decimate the Party center? Or did the sorry line of victims accumulate in an unanticipated way as events unfolded? And why was so much blood, both figuratively and literally, about to flow? Was it truly over policy issues, or were they just a smoke screen behind which loomed the great question, Who would succeed Mao?

6

The Cultural Revolution:
1966–69

Participants

The Great Proletarian Cultural Revolution took the whole world by surprise. Suddenly, China was at war with itself and at odds with just about everyone else. Nobody could quite understand what was going on or why, partly because systematic reporting was impossible. Millions of students were on the march; entire cities were festooned with wall posters; mighty leaders were wearing dunce caps; thousands of victims were dying in pitched battles; foreign embassies were being mobbed, even burned to the ground. And always words, a Niagara of rhetoric, slogans, accusations, denials, directives, and, above all, Mao Zedong Thought. Clearly, it was a power struggle. The fight seemed to be over ideological differences. Why did it drag on for so long, roughly from the spring of 1966 to the spring of 1969? What could explain the irrational extremism?

Mao Zedong occupied the center of this maelstrom. It was declared to be his personal revolution. The participants waved their Little Red Books and chanted his name while they savaged his own Party. This confirmed his foreign critics' view that he was mad or evil. Only gradually did it become clear that he had a rational purpose, albeit an audacious one, and pursued his goals with skill though he did not foresee all the consequences.

It has also become clear that one cannot understand the Cultural Revolution solely in terms of Mao's actions. He interacted with three distinct organizations: (1) the People's Liberation Army under Lin Biao, (2) the so-called Cultural Revolution Small Group under Chen Boda and Jiang Qing, and (3) the State Council with its central ministries under Premier Zhou Enlai. We may consider them as three factions protecting and promoting their own interests, sometimes cooperating and sometimes competing with one another in unstable coalitions. They reflected the personalities and objectives of their leaders.

Lin Biao had labored unremittingly to indoctrinate the armed forces and to promote the cult of Mao throughout society. This adulation of the leader was his unwavering theme and coincidentally enhanced his own stature as Mao's closest comrade in arms. The backing of Lin's disciplined military was an absolute prerequisite for Mao's attack on Party authority. The success of that attack, in turn, made the PLA the principal governing institution, causing many observers to speak of a military takeover.

Jiang Qing's faction was also notable for its dogmatism. One exasperated official remarked, "When the old hen begins to crow at sunrise, the honorable farmyard is in danger."[1] Her obduracy was, no doubt, the product of many causes: long, painful illnesses; the unwillingness of powers like Liu Shaoqi and Peng Zhen to take her seriously; and the disadvantages of being a woman. She and most of the Cultural Revolution Small Group were relative upstarts with narrow political bases. On the other hand, she was the Chairman's wife and made up the rest with zeal. Of the three factions, this one was the most idealistic and irresponsible. Jiang Qing and Chen Boda worked to foster revolutionary culture and radical populism. They were the closest to Mao's heart, but they lacked his balance and realism.

Premier Zhou Enlai was a practical administrator, not a zealot. His goals were actually closer to those of Liu Shaoqi. The Cultural Revolution was not his doing, but he went along with Mao from long habit of loyalty and an unerring talent for self-preservation. He took positions that were just radical enough to avoid destruction while he worked to minimize the chaos. His tireless negotiating skills became indispensable when civil strife and anarchy loomed in 1967 and 1968.

Because the three factions strove for different objectives, the directives emanating from Beijing changed as Mao favored one or another. Below there were other layers of power. A middle tier was made up of provincial and lower-level Party committees. Being responsible for the functioning of the system and jealous of their own positions and perquisites, they favored order and the status quo. Also at this level were the regional PLA commands. As these military leaders got dragged into the fray, they had to take up the reins of authority, and their attitudes became much like those of the officials they had displaced.

Down at the basic level in the cities, students of differing backgrounds and persuasions, graduates drifting back from the countryside, factory workers, temporary industrial workers, and suburban peasants created an astonishing array of organizations during the Cultural Revolution. Some were manipulated from above; some were spontaneous. All had a life of their own and were difficult to control. It was they that made the Cultural Revolution so explosive, hopeful, excessive, and ultimately tragic.

Disruption and relaxation followed one another in wavelike oscillations. Viewed broadly, the Cultural Revolution intensified in a long upsurge from May 1966 until September 1967. It then receded irregularly over a period lasting until the spring of 1969. Within this rise and fall, there were briefer pulses of turbulence and calm. The main reason for these waves was that Mao, although a true believer, was prepared to regroup when disaster loomed. Consequently, the Cultural Revolution repeated the familiar pattern (radical upsurge, unforeseen consequences, and adjustment) that had already appeared in 1955, 1957, and 1958.

When Mao attacked Peng Zhen and Luo Ruiqing in late 1955, he did not dream that he was about to decimate the Party. His target was revisionism and the few who tolerated it. But his policies had been repeatedly undercut. Ousting Peng Zhen did not solve the problem because Liu Shaoqi, Deng Xiaoping, and others continued to act in the same way. Finally, an aroused Mao charged personally into the fray and unleashed the student movement to give his colleagues a big lesson in mass politics.

Tidal Wave

Ominous Breakers: May 1966–August 1966

In May, June, and July 1966, Mao emerged from his semiobscurity to resume personal command in a way not seen since the Great Leap Forward. Prior to May he had not appeared publicly for months, and there were rumors of illness and even death. A May 10 newspaper photo showing him with an Albanian delegation dispelled some doubts. On July 16 he found a more spectacular way to dramatize his reentry. Accompanied by hundreds of youths, he swam the Yangzi River at Hankou, covering fifteen kilometers in just over an hour. Nationally reported in red ink headlines a few days later and greeted with drums, firecrackers, and congratulatory festivities, it was the first of many ecstatic communions between leader and masses.

By that time the Chairman had decisively strengthened his hand within the Party and started to push his program of cultural renewal. Most of the major logjams were cleared away in May 1966. *People's Daily* photos published at the time show that Mao was being supported by Lin Biao, Deng Xiaoping, and Zhou Enlai. He had isolated Liu Shaoqi. Actions taken at the enlarged Politburo meeting reflected new power realignments. Former Chief of Staff Luo Ruiqing's ouster was finalized, removing Lin Biao's rival in the PLA. Peng Zhen, together with his Beijing allies in propaganda and culture, was dismissed, which smashed the ''independent kingdom'' and gave Maoists control of the media.

A new conspiracy theory emerged: the anti-Party clique of Peng Zhen, Luo Ruiqing, and others, who were fingered by Lin Biao in his May 18 speech. Here was a ''black line'' that could be ascribed to one's enemies. The Politburo's "May 16 Circular" warned

> Those representatives of the bourgeoisie who have sneaked into the party, the government, the army and various cultural circles are a bunch of counterrevolutionary revisionists. Once conditions are ripe, they will seize power and turn the dictatorship of the proletariat into a dictatorship of the bourgeoisie. Some of them we have already seen through, others we have not. Some are still trusted by us and are being trained as our successors, persons like Khrushchev, for example, who are still nestling beside us . . .[2]

The task was now to carry out the Great Proletarian Cultural Revolution, which Zhou Enlai had proclaimed during the May Day festivities. The press carried criticisms of literature and culture, and the PLA promoted the living study of Mao Zedong Thought. On May 7, 1966, Mao sent a directive to Lin Biao. It came to be regarded as a kind of charter for the movement to unite all civil and military sectors in politics, production, and culture under the banner of Mao Zedong Thought.

The Maoist faction saw promise in high schools and universities. They encouraged radical students and teachers to carry out the Great Proletarian Cultural Revolution by criticizing Party leaders and administrators. The most famous of these early academic rebels was a philosophy instructor at Beijing University named Nie Yuanzi. On May 25 she and six students pasted up a wall poster indicting the president for suppressing student meetings, debates, marches, and posters. School heads throughout the country were thrown on the defensive by these attacks, particularly when Mao himself ordered the press and radio to report Nie's poster on June 1. In subsequent weeks many were dismissed from their posts, no doubt shocked and shaken at being assailed by their students. The following lines from a middle school poster convey the flavor of these assaults.

> Since we want rebellion, the matter has been taken out of your hands! We are going to make the air thick with the pungent smell

of explosives. Toss them over, grenades and stick bombs together, and start a big fight. "Sympathy," "all-sidedness," out
of the way![3]

But the establishment had not entirely lost the capacity to protect itself. Various school administrators implored the Party center to send work teams to direct and contain the students. Liu
Shaoqi responded by dispatching about 400 teams totalling 10,000
cadres to institutions in many cities. These work teams restrained the students' extremism. In this way, although Peng's
anti-Party clique had been purged, the remaining leaders continued to frustrate Mao's mass politics. The structure of authority
leading down from the Party center was still intact as was the
habit of conducting affairs in privileged meetings and of shield-
ing Party cadres from outside attacks.

Nevertheless, pressure from the left was intensifying. In early
June 1966, *People's Daily* and other major publications ran a
series of strident editorials to promote the Cultural Revolution
with such titles as "SWEEP AWAY ALL MONSTERS AND DEMONS"
and "CAPTURE THE POSITIONS IN THE FIELD OF HISTORICAL
STUDIES SEIZED BY THE BOURGEOISIE."[4] At about this same time
it was announced that college admissions were going to be determined by political criteria rather than by entrance exams and
that this year's enrollment would be delayed for six months. A
June 1 editorial proclaimed

> The Great Proletarian Cultural Revolution is advancing with great
> rapidity and intensity. One group of monsters and demons after
> another has been exposed, and one reactionary bastion after an-
> other has been shattered . . .[5]

There is a Chinese saying which Mao now took as his motto:
You must beat a vicious dog even if it has fallen in the water.
Mao, furious at the work teams for suppressing the student
movement, continued to swing his stick. Returning to Beijing
after his swim, he intervened at Qinghua University, where the

work team leader was none other than Liu's wife, Wang Guang-mei. Mao declared in favor of the students, and the work team withdrew. More shock waves pulsed across the country. Mao next summoned a work conference of Party leaders and berated them for opposing the students. He told them to drop their high and mighty posture and go learn from the students. Obediently, they trekked to various universities to talk with students. Liu Shaoqi's daughter later said, "I had never seen my father so upset."[6]

Next, to legitimize his moves, Mao convened the first Central Committee Plenum since the Tenth Plenum of 1962. Even at this point, Party leaders were balky, so he packed the Plenum with people from radical groups and the People's Liberation Army, and he excluded many Central Committee members. While it was in session, he held the Plenum's feet to the fire. On August 1, 1966, he published an open letter of praise to the Beijing middle school activists who made the poster partially quoted earlier. In this letter he used the designation "Red Guards" for the first time, and he praised their slogan, "Rebellion Is Justified!" He also published his May 7, 1966 directive to Lin Biao, mentioned earlier. Perhaps his boldest gesture was on August 5. On the door where the Central Committee met, he put up his own poster entitled "Bombard the Headquarters." In it he attacked the "fifty days" of work team tyranny in the schools and the "leading comrades" who had "enforced a bourgeois dictatorship and struck down the surging movement of the Great Cultural Revolution of the Proletariat . . ."[7]

Under this pressure, the Central Committee took several important actions. It reorganized both the Politburo Standing Committee and the Military Affairs Committee, giving Maoists control of these key bodies. And it issued a directive for the promotion of the Cultural Revolution, called the "Sixteen Points." This document encouraged the creation of mass organizations to criticize the establishment. Its tone recalled the utopianism of the Great Leap Forward, proclaiming the birth of new institutions for mass participation.

> The cultural revolutionary groups, committees, and other organizational forms created by the masses in many schools and units are something new and of great historic importance . . . whereby the masses educate themselves. . . . They are an excellent bridge to keep our Party in close contact with the masses . . .[8]

It continued, evoking one of the sacred chapters in the history of Marxist revolutions.

> [They] should not be temporary organizations but permanent, standing mass organizations. . . . It is necessary to institute a system of general elections, like that of the Paris Commune, for electing members to [them].

Although this document was not published in the public media until a year later, it was sent to all important Party committees, and its contents were widely disseminated. It struck a radical new note by invoking the 1871 Paris Commune. This stimulated a further upsurge of mass political participation and raised hopes for a kind of Party-dominated democracy.

Inundation: From August 1966 to the February 1967 Adverse Current

The August 1966 Plenum sounded the trumpets for the Great Proletarian Cultural Revolution. Beijing authorized students from "Red" families (cadre, military, peasant, worker) to form Red Guard organizations. They were to spearhead a purge of "capitalist roaders" (those taking the road of capitalism) at all levels and of "old" culture in every form. On August 18 a million Red Guards were brought to a rally at Beijing's huge Tian'anmen Square. At dawn Mao appeared to a tumultuous welcome and mingled with the delirious students for six hours. A middle school girl pinned a Red Guard armband on him, reportedly causing the participants to shout, "Chairman Mao is our supreme commander and we are his little soldiers."[9] Lin Biao was hailed as Chairman Mao's "closest comrade-in-arms." Zhou Enlai spoke as did Nie Yuanzi, the radical instructor from Beijing University. Next day, red-ink headlines breathlessly recounted the spectacle to the entire nation. Until cold weather intervened, millions more were brought to the capital to participate in similar events. The last rally in November 1966 reportedly numbered two and a half million.

Never since 1949 had China's youth tasted such excitement. Lauded by their government as "courageous and daring path-breakers," both "vigorous in action and intelligent,"[10] buoyed by adventure and idealism, and delivered from schoolwork and a future of exile in the countryside, they descended on Beijing in a great pilgrimage. Additional hordes, with government permission and free passage, jammed the railways to travel and "exchange experiences" with youths from other regions. Thousands more strode off on foot, bound for famous revolutionary sites in emulation of the Long March. Thus were China's successors being "steeled."

They wore a standard outfit of green PLA fatigues, a wide leather belt, and, most important, a bright red armband emblazoned in yellow with the words Red Guard. They might also wear a prized Mao button from Yanan, Jinggangshan, or other revolutionary shrines. Some changed their given names to more revolutionary ones. They sang "The Great Helmsman" and danced the Loyalty Dance to Chairman Mao. They carried always their *Quotations of Chairman Mao*, and some committed to memory every word of this 270-page catechism. They generated enormous quantities of communications, both from higher authorities and from their own ranks. The many factions published thousands of newssheets at government expense. Red Guard loudspeakers alternately blared propaganda and the strains of the "Internationale" into the small hours of the morning, driving the neighbors to distraction. Enormous energies went into creating and copying the thousands of "big character posters" pasted on walls, proclaiming every conceivable political message, perhaps none repeated more than Chairman Mao's audacious words of 1927:

> A revolution is not a dinner party, or writing an essay, or painting a picture, or doing embroidery; it cannot be so refined, so leisurely and gentle, so temperate, kind, courteous, restrained, and magnanimous. A revolution is an insurrection, an act of violence by which one class overthrows another.[11]

In August and September 1966, the movement became harsh and violent. Assured that "Rebellion Is Justified," and that the "Four Olds" (old thought, old culture, old customs, old habits) must be destroyed, the Red Guards descended on the intelligentsia. Unceremonious bands burst into homes to confiscate books, musical instruments, Western clothes, paintings, and any other possessions considered old or foreign. The frightened intellectuals received verbal and sometimes physical abuse. In many cases, the victims even died from excitation, suicide, or brutal treatment. The young iconoclasts also defaced or destroyed thousands of temples, statues, gravestones, and monuments.

Another target was "power holders taking the capitalist road." From Beijing, Red Guards fanned out to other cities to launch wall poster exposés of cadre corruption and misconduct. But Party officials were better equipped than the intellectuals to withstand the attack. They were practiced at manipulating mass organizations, so nothing was more natural than to establish their own Red Guard units. The children of Party cadres often organized such groups. So long as they proclaimed their loyalty to Chairman Mao, waved their red books, and assailed revisionism, they could claim to be true children of the revolution. These "conservatives" would immediately find themselves in conflict with more radical Red Guards. In the capital the noisy assaults on government included demonstrations against the USSR. For two weeks in late August thousands massed in front of the Russian embassy, plastered the neighborhood with antirevisionist slogans, and blared forth accusations from their loudspeakers.

Mao seems to have been truly surprised by the virulence of the Red Guard attacks.

One big-character poster, the Red Guards, the great exchange of revolutionary experience, and nobody—not even I—expected that all the provinces and cities would be thrown into confusion.[12]

In October and November 1966 Mao and the Cultural Revolution Small Group took a milder tone and tried to steer the Red Guards along a more orderly restrained path. The youth were reminded that not all Party leaders could be capitalist roaders and that most of them could redeem themselves for past mistakes. Mao tried to reassure regional leaders in an October meeting.

> That which you never dreamed of has come to pass. What's come has come. I think that there are advantages in being assailed. For so many years you had not thought about such things, but as soon as they burst upon you, you began to think. Undoubtedly you have made some mistakes, some mistakes of line, but they can be corrected and that will be that! Whoever wants to overthrow you? I don't and I don't think the Red Guards do either.[13]

It is difficult to believe that they went away less nervous about his intentions.

At this same time, workers began to form their own revolutionary associations. In November young industrial workers organized in Shanghai. Beijing industrial contract laborers formed cultural revolution groups. There were organizations of former PLA personnel and of ex-students who had been sent down to the countryside. It was also decreed that students who were not of the "five red" classes could join Red Guard units if they demonstrated revolutionary behavior. These various organizations injected a complex new dimension to the Cultural Revolution. Their positions differed from the Red Guards and from one another. Although some were true Maoists, others attempted to use the upheaval to improve their condition (contract laborers, for example), and still others banded together to protect their interests (such as permanent factory workers).

Power relationships grew increasingly confused. The Cultural

Revolution Small Group, the Military Affairs Committee, and the State Council were supposedly in harmony, but in fact sometimes at odds. Mao supported now one and now another position. The cities pulsated with diverse student, worker, and other Cultural Revolution organizations. They tended to polarize into loose radical and conservative confederations although everyone claimed to represent the true left and swore that their opponents were rightists, ultraleftists, and counterrevolutionaries. Nervously caught in the middle were the central, provincial, and county Party leaders. They were urged "boldly" to take the lead in promoting the new mass politics. But recognizing a threat to their power, they strove to contain the damage and appear revolutionary at the same time. On the sidelines the regional PLA garrisons had orders to facilitate the great debate. It was the PLA, for example, that handled the logistics of the Red Guard rallies in Beijing. During this period Liu Shaoqi and Deng Xiaoping went into complete eclipse. Mao called a conference in October 1966 at which Liu and Deng delivered self-criticisms. By November they were the targets of wall posters and were seen at a rally sitting sullen and quiet. The Cultural Revolution Small Group took over Deng's base of power, the Secretariat.

In December 1966 and January 1967 the Cultural Revolution leaders lost patience with the evasive entrenched cadres. They decided to go after, not just a handful, but the entire Party leadership. This movement climaxed in the "January storm" under the slogan "Seize power!" For a few weeks Shanghai took the center stage. By year's end, two huge worker coalitions, one radical and one conservative, had stolen the limelight from the Red Guards in that city. In January, the radicals defeated their rivals, gained control of the media, withstood counterattacks from the entrenched cadres, and in a climactic meeting of one million workers, forced the Party leadership to resign. Through a complex series of events the "Shanghai Commune" was established in February. It seemed to some that the Shanghai Commune was precisely what the the Central Committees's "Sixteen Points" of early August 1966 meant when it referred to the Paris Commune. Radicals in other places also attempted to follow this model.

Zhou Enlai's State Council was also struck by the tide of power seizures. In January 1967, revolutionary rebels seized power in more than twenty ministries. The State Council soon numbered six active members, down from its much larger normal complement. Particularly ominous was the damage to China's foreign relations. On January 18, the Foreign Ministry was seized. Soon Chen Yi found himself before a struggle meeting of ten thousand reading a self-criticism. Even his wife was repeatedly "struggled."

These events affected relations with the whole world. China's ambassadors, with the single exception of the ambassador to Egypt, were called home. There were numerous international incidents, the most serious being altercations between the Moscow police and Chinese embassy personnel. In Beijing, Red Guards responded by massing outside the Soviet embassy. They belabored and harassed and, in some cases, manhandled Russian diplomats and their families. Moscow began to growl about limits to its patience. From this time Russia began to increase the number of Soviet army divisions stationed at various locations on the Chinese border.

Liu and the other fallen leaders were subjected to humiliating "struggle sessions," standing before Red Guards, a placard hanging from each of their necks, a dunce cap on each of their heads. There were many variations. The struggle session might be scheduled in advance, or the offenders might be jolted suddenly from sleep in the middle of the night. They might be paraded through the streets in a truck. The assembly might be small and relatively restrained, allowing the accused to respond, or there might be tens of thousands shouting accusations. And the victim's strength to cope with the ordeal varied. Crusty Foreign Minister Chen Yi drew laughter from the Red Guards when he asked permission to wear his dunce cap to lunch as he was growing rather attached to it. Others were not so resilient or protected. One of Chen Yi's subordinates cracked from the strain and killed himself.

By late January 1967, violence and chaos were increasing everywhere. Alarmed, Mao once again leaned toward moderation. He turned against the Shanghai Commune as a model. Summoning its leaders, Zhang Chunqiao and Yao Wenyuan, to Beijing, he dashed cold water on their creation just days after it had been celebrated by millions of Shanghailanders.

[The demand heard in Shanghai to do away with all heads] is extreme anarchism, it is most reactionary. . . . In reality there will still always be "heads" . . .[14]

Mao favored developments in the northeast, where a coalition of radicals, "revolutionary" Party cadres, and regional PLA officers seized power. This "three-in-one" combination struck Mao as the pattern for the whole country. He disliked pure populism. "Democratic centralism," not "democracy," was his watchword. The three-in-one formula, with its inclusion of both organization and populism, corresponded more closely to the mass line concept. Immediately the media began promoting power seizures by three-in-one committees, emphasizing that not only the PLA but also cadres were important elements.

PLA commanders began ousting Party committees from power, forming three-in-one revolutionary committees in their place. The leading members were usually military officers. Surviving Party officials were supposed to supply the experience. Revolutionary rebel leaders would represent the masses. But although power seizures could be accomplished with relative ease, formation of revolutionary committees acceptable to all and their certification by Beijing, were processes made tortuous by the raging factionalism.

Resurgent Tidal Wave: Summer 1967

For a brief period in February 1967, beleaguered authorities in Beijing and the provinces were able to take advantage of the new moderate line to shore up their positions. One ministry head staged a "fake" power seizure by revolutionary rebels loyal to himself. Chen Yi repudiated his earlier self-criticism. It was not long before this "February adverse current" was beaten back. Late in the month the Cultural Revolution Group organized rallies to protest the recapture of the government ministries. Simultaneously, the campaign against Liu Shaoqi intensified. Until now Liu's offense had been his Khrushchevite revisionist opposition to Mao. A serious problem, but he was still within the pale. Shorn of power, he lived in the Zhongnanhai compound, discredited but still in the Party.

An augury of worse to come had occurred in mid-January when Liu's son was arrested for allegedly selling state secrets to a foreign power. In late February the theme of treason made its appearance in editorials and wall posters. A "Preparatory Committee for Thoroughly Smashing the Liu Shaoqi Renegade Clique" was formed. It made the astonishing discovery that Liu had headed a secret traitorous conspiracy as far back as 1936. His wife, whose very name, Guangmei, meant "beautiful America" was unmasked as having been a U.S. spy during the civil war in 1947. Liu Shaoqi was now set up for political obliteration. In late March 1967, dozens of people with connections to him were arrested as members of his "renegade clique." Mao summoned a meeting of the Politburo Standing Committee, which divested Liu of all Party and non-Party offices (a legally dubious action). Editorial and wall posters blasted his famous book, *How to Be a Good Communist*. Wang Guangmei was not forgotten. A series of "struggle" meetings culminated in a huge daylong rally during which she received the Red Guards' derision dressed in high heels, a silk dress, and a necklace of ping-pong balls to represent the jewels she had worn as China's first lady.

During this period rebels were once more besieging the state ministries. Chen Yi again became the object of struggle. At the same time a minor diplomat who had been expelled from Indonesia came home to a hero's welcome and became a force in the Foreign Ministry. China's foreign relations deteriorated even more. Starting in May 1967, Hong Kong was wracked with disturbances instigated by mobs possibly acting under the orders of the Cultural Revolution Small Group or possibly under local leadership.

If the campaign against Liu was meant to dampen factionalism in Beijing and the provinces by setting up a common target for all, it failed. Bitter wrangling within and among cliques, groups, and confederations mounted daily. Because the PLA, a source of weapons, had been injected into the scene, the factions were no longer just hurling epithets. There was increasing violence unrelated to any goal other than destroying or not being destroyed. These trends reached a fever pitch in the hot months of July and August in 1967. In Beijing, Peng Dehuai, still paying for his impudence of 1959, was dragged out for a kangaroo trial. Outside the Zhongnanhai milled huge permanent crowds with posters, loudspeakers, and effigies, demanding that Liu Shaoqi, Deng Xiaoping, and others be dragged out for their own trials. This demand received partial satisfaction when a mass condemnation rally of one million was held as the offenders were being "struggled" against by smaller groups in their homes. On one occasion, even Zhou Enlai was beseiged for two days in the State Council offices and managed to fend off the Red Guard demands only by dint of his extraordinary persuasiveness.

Foreign relations hit a nadir. In a move to escalate the crisis over Hong Kong, the Foreign Ministry under its new leadership issued an ultimatum to the British chargé d'affaires concerning the riots there. Failing to get a satisfactory response, a mob broke into the British mission, terrorized the chargé d'affaires and some of his staff, and burned down the chancery.

Meanwhile, serious fighting raged everywhere out in the provinces. Guangzhou (Canton) was in chaos. Weapons destined for Vietnam were stolen and used. The Public Security forces simply gave up attempts to maintain order. There was anarchy and looting. Corpses were seen hanging from trees. Even more serious, if that can be imagined, was the situation at Wuhan in China's heartland. There the local military had supported a conservative worker coalition called "One Million Heroic

Troops," which closed down factories, railways, and bridges and assaulted radical groups. To bring this situation under control, the Cultural Revolution Small Group sent two of its highest members to order the military to support the radicals. In the stifling heat of July 14, 1967, a mutinous division occupied Wuhan, the two emissaries were seized, and one of them received a bad beating. This was serious, for with the Party in shambles the PLA was China's only cohesive organization. If it should fragment, national unity would be at risk.

The Wuhan mutiny was quickly brought under control by the dispatch of central troops. Its disgraced leaders were brought to Beijing for punishment (which was, however, lenient). And when the two emissaries from the Cultural Revolution Small Group returned, they were welcomed by gigantic rallies. This incident set off an even fiercer radicalism. Jiang Qing and others now began to call for the Cultural Revolution to be carried deeper into Zhou Enlai's State Council and into the one heretofore sacred institution, the PLA. "Pull out the handful of capitalist roaders in the army." Clearly the Cultural Revolution was threatening to career totally out of control. Toward the end of August Mao himself came to this conclusion. As he and others following his lead took steps to calm the waters, the great inward tide of the Cultural Revolution peaked and began to recede. But it was not a rapid or steady return to normal.

The Flood Recedes

Turbulent Reflux: September 1967–April 1969

On an inspection tour in September 1967, Mao reportedly exclaimed, "Some people say there is no civil war in China. But I think this is a civil war . . ." [15] He now repented his original faith in the students. His words seem harsh and ironic compared with earlier praise lavished on the "little generals":

the Red Guards . . . would certainly be toppled tomorrow if they
were installed today. This is because they are politically imma-
ture . . . [they] are incompetent; they haven't been tempered. We
can't trust them with things of such major importance. . . . Previously I had the intention to foster successors among the intellectuals but now this plan is far from desirable. . . . [They] embrace the bourgeois world outlook. . . . They don't [rally under
one banner under the Marxist slogan] . . .[16]

With the Chairman's blessing, Zhou, Lin, and others who hoped
to restore order swung into action. On September 1, 1967, Zhou
delivered a major speech demanding discipline among revolutionary groups and respect for the army. New orders went out
to all revolutionary groups, cosigned by Chairman Mao himself,
forbidding seizures of arms, requiring that arms already taken
be turned in, and giving PLA commanders the right to return
fire. To symbolize this return to militarily imposed order, all the
old marshals of the PLA were to be seen with Mao atop the Gate
of Heavenly Peace during the October 1 national celebrations.

As Lin's army and Zhou's organizational talents grew increasingly important, Jiang Qing and her Cultural Revolution
Small Group struggled to protect their position. They toned down
their rhetoric and spoke in support of Lin and Zhou. Jiang Qing
began to assail a conspiratorial group behind the radical excesses and the attacks on Zhou and the army. This heretofore
unknown (and possibly nonexistent) cabal was called the "May
16 Corps." Some second level Cultural Revolution Small Group
people were accused of being members. They were stripped of
their positions in August.

Central to the new emphasis on normalcy was Mao's "Great
Strategic Plan," announced on October 1, 1967. It was a far cry
from "Bombard the Headquarters!" The target was no longer
Party leaders taking the capitalist road but the rank and file of
every unit, and the emphasis was on discipline. Under the slogan "Fight Selfishness and Criticize Revisionism," Mao's great
plan called for factionalism to cease and for self-criticism all

around. "Mao Zedong Thought Study Classes" were instituted with great fanfare. Although it seems astonishing that any Chinese would still require classes to learn Mao's thought, from across the country the new revolutionary committee leaders, many of them military officers, came to the capital to study texts, which they would take back and propagate among their colleagues.

But the genie of chaos was already out of the bottle, and even Beijing's authority, rhetoric, organization, and force could not easily put it back. Mao himself was still hesitant to abandon the radicals. In late January 1968 he allowed—or encouraged— Jiang Qing to renew attacks against various targets, including Zhou's State Council. Mao removed the PLA chief of staff and other high officers, one of whom two weeks earlier had tried to arrest one of Jiang's Cultural Revolution Small Group.

In the provinces, Jiang's call for militancy fanned smoldering fires. Factions and military units had been wrangling for months over representation on the three-in-one revolutionary committees. It was an intense fight because the losers could expect the victors to pay off old scores. By June 1968, partisan warfare reverberated again in the streets of Guangzhou (Canton). Even worse was the neighboring province of Guangxi, where a Red Guard alliance fought a worker-militia alliance, both supported by PLA elements. Weapons destined for Vietnam were again seized and used with bloody effect. Even tanks and artillery saw action. Numerous trussed-up corpses were tossed into the West River and floated past Guangzhou to the sea.

Students in other cities fought vendettas from their campus strongholds. Radicals, sensing repudiation, turned increasingly nasty. They fortified buildings and laid in supplies of bricks, stones, and firearms. Beatings and kidnappings punctuated incidents of gang violence such as the battle at Qinghua University, where fifteen students lost their lives. Among youth not in school, gang activity increased. This is not to say that all young people or workers participated in the ferment. It seems that, in fact, most students had left their schools and gone home, weary of loudspeakers, wall posters, and marches.

JIANG QING

Despite difficulties, order began to return in the summer of 1968. The PLA received tough, new orders to clamp down. They were to round up weapons and punish offenders. As for the students, Mao despaired over their factionalism and began to terminate the Red Guard movement. So-called Worker Mao Zedong Thought Propaganda Teams, usually under military leadership, moved onto high school and college campuses to restore order. Ironically, the student movement, which had begun with Mao's attack on Liu's work teams, was now suppressed by similar teams, dispatched by Mao himself. In late July 1968, Mao summoned the principal Beijing student leaders. Restrained and avuncular, he expressed his disappointment. He taunted a particular brilliant and aggressive student who had complained that a "black hand" was dispatching repressive teams to crush the students.

> Who is the black hand [that has sent the worker teams to the universities to quell the students]? You still haven't captured him. The black hand is nobody else but me." [17]

Meanwhile, Zhou Enlai had been negotiating among contending factions over the formation of revolutionary committees. It was no easy task after two years of bitter division. Working province by province, calling the wrangling parties to Beijing to forge compromises and reconciliation, he was gradually able to fill the administrative map with functioning committees. On September 8, 1968, he announced to a huge gathering in Tiananmen Square that the last provincial committee had been formed. "Now the whole country is red." [18] Few revolutionary committees existed at lower levels, where innumerable grudges persisted. But a glimmering of authority was restored. At this same rally, Jiang Qing, apparently under compulsion, spoke a few words. It was her last occasion to address the Red Guards, whom she had incited to storm the heavens. For her it was a bleak finale.

The new system could now be formally established, and Moscow gave special urgency to the effort. On August 20, 1968, Soviet and Warsaw Pact troops had entered Czechoslovakia to suppress the "springtime of freedom" under Alexander Dubček's liberal regime. By late September the Russians announced the "Brezhnev doctrine" that socialist states had no right to abandon socialism—on pain of military intervention by other bloc countries. The Chinese could not be sure that the Russians would resist the temptation to invade them.

In October the surviving Party leaders, together with Cultural Revolution radicals, provincial revolutionary committee members, and, above all, the PLA officers, met as the Twelfth and last Plenum of the Eighth Central Committee to prepare for a Ninth Party Congress. A draft Party constitution was circulated naming Lin Biao, "Comrade Mao Zedong's close comrade-in-arms *and successor*," and revealing that the "number one person in authority taking the capitalist" road was none other than the "renegade, traitor, and scab," Liu Shaoqi. This plenum also saw a new development, of which the outside world was then unaware. With U.S. deescalation in Vietnam and the growing Soviet threat, Mao and others were beginning to rethink foreign policy. They considered normalizing relations with the United

States as a counterweight to their ominous northern neighbor.

In April 1969, after lower-level Party congresses had studied the relevant documents and selected delegates, the Ninth Congress of the Chinese Communist party convened. In the public eye the joyous official celebrations reflected the resolution of the issues raised by the Cultural Revolution. Maoism was triumphant in a framework of orthodoxy and order. Lin Biao, although looking frail and unhealthy, was Mao's named successor; and the PLA, a central force in administration and Party politics. The new Party constitution signaled continued Party rebuilding although Mao, Mao Zedong Thought, and mass supervision were supposed to make it a different Party from what is was before. But events were to show that the unity was only apparent.

As for the Red Guards, the range and depth of their feelings can scarcely be imagined. Little did it matter that they had trekked to the Gate of Heavenly Peace, Tian'anmen, for instructions from Premier Zhou or Vice-Chairman Lin or Jiang Qing or to touch the hand of Chairman Mao himself. It was of no consequence that they had served as the shock troops of the revolution, writing and reading the posters and struggling against Party leaders opposed to Chairman Mao. Never mind that they had defended their factions, sometimes to the death, against Chairman Mao's enemies. Now soldiers and former cadres controlled the revolutionary committees, occupied their schools, and had little use for student radicals despite all the three-in-one rhetoric. In any case, the entire educational system was in a shambles and would not recover for years.

They were a kind of lost generation, and the only place for them was where they least wanted to go: the countryside. In 1968 and 1969 millions were persuaded and coerced to go down to the villages. It may be doubted that many listened with the old thrill to Mao's encouragement:

All people who have had some education ought to be very happy to work in the countryside if they get the chance. In our vast rural areas there is plenty of room for them to develop their talents to the full.[19]

Starting in October 1968, Party cadres experienced a rather similar fate. "May 7 Cadre Schools" began to be established all over the country. These were special farms set up, manned, and run by cadres of all ranks, assigned in groups for six-months to three years. The rationale was to carry out Mao's May 7, 1966, admonition that cadres, as well as soldiers, workers, peasants, and other groups, should work in other areas. A period of farm work under conditions familiar to peasants would give them a better understanding of the masses. Still, they were better off than the sent-down students because they continued to draw their cadre salaries and, in most cases, expected to return to their old jobs.

Final Assessments

Any political phenomenon as complex and disruptive as the Cultural Revolution is bound to be perceived and evaluated rather differently by different observers. The general opinion in the mid-1980s, both inside and outside China, is that this movement was not a good thing and had very few redeeming motives or outcomes. However, this view has not always prevailed. Although the destructive aspects of the Cultural Revolution have seldom been denied, many have found the chaos justified by the goals aimed for or the results achieved. Here, rather than conclude with an indictment or an apology, the following paragraphs will describe major alternative viewpoints that have been adopted at one time or another. Three positions, not always mutually exclusive, emerge.

The Cultural Revolution was a power struggle between competing factions and groups. This conclusion devalues the announced purposes of Mao and others as merely instruments of political power. Mao Zedong himself, the principal factions in Beijing, Party committees and PLA commands in the provinces, and various social groups at the bottom are seen as locked in a complex struggle to gain or retain power. In this light, Mao appears to be a revolutionary messiah determined to prevent his old comrades-in-arms from usurping his authority. Other versions would have either Jiang Qing or Lin Biao as the prime movers. One such view appears in a biography of Mao's wife.

> No one understood the Cultural Revolution, perhaps because there was nothing to understand; nothing rational beneath [Jiang Qing's] vanity, frustration, and thirst for revenge that triggered it.[20]

Another characterization based on these kinds of assumptions calls the Cultural Revolution

> a rebellion of the dominated against the establishment in most spheres of Chinese society—a rebellion inspired and manipulated by the supreme leader.[21]

Here not only the power appetites of the leaders but also struggles emanating from lower levels are highlighted. Clearly, those who insist on this perspective still have to sort out the different dimensions of the power struggle.

The Cultural Revolution was a much-needed attempt to cope with China's growing political problems: bureaucratism, social inequalities, decline of mass participation, and alienation. This position accepts at least some of Mao's goals. It places social justice at the top of the scale and relegates competing values, such as economic development or individual rights, to a lower standing. Mao's own pronouncement may be cited here. He called the Cultural Revolution

> absolutely necessary and most timely for consolidating the dictatorship of the proletariat, preventing capitalist restoration, and building socialism.[22]

Sympathetic Western observers have argued similarly. One called it

> a nation-wide rejection of the Soviet model of socialism and a daring experiment with a new philosphy of continuous revolution.[23]

The Cultural Revolution was a misguided or quixotic effort that did more damage than it accomplished good. This conclusion may even acknowledge Mao's announced purposes or other legitimate objectives to some extent. It argues either that the means did not justify the ends or that the costs in terms of other values (such as economic development) outweighed the benefits. One version of this negative evaluation is the criticism that Mao's own successors leveled at the Cultural Revolution twenty years later. They characterized it as

> responsible for the most severe setback and the heaviest losses suffered by the Party, the state and the people since the founding of the People's Republic.[24]

Alternately, this point of view may argue that the whole enterprise was simply the fatuous self-indulgence of an aging autocrat. As one of Mao's less charitable critics remarks

> a political egoist is never more evilly employed than when he thinks he is doing others good.[25]

Of course, it is not necessary to subscribe to one of these major viewpoints in its pure form. Many observers recognize all three as offering some insight into a very complex phenomenon. One such more ambiguous evaluation is the following, which calls the Cultural Revolution

> really three things in one: an enigmatic multiple power struggle, wrapped in a crusade, and superimposed on a scattering of more or less spontaneous, more or less politicized student riots, strikes, peasant uprisings, mutinies, and palace coups.[26]

To the extent that we share the Marxist critique of social inequality and dissatisfaction with liberal democracy as an instrument of class domination, we will be sympathetic toward Mao's goals. In a sense, his career was a long search for mass line, that is, for a means other than liberal electoral politics to dis-

203 The Cultural Revolution

cover and give form to the will of the people. During one brief heroic period he seemed to find it in the hills of Yanan, and his subsequent career was an attempt to recover that happy combination of popular mobilization and Party leadership.

On the other hand, the question that rises from the perspective of the Western liberal tradition is, "Why not pluralism?" That cluster of values (individual rights, market freedom, rule of law) poses a challenge to Mao's goals. But it is a complex issue. What right do we have to demand pluralism of a Chinese Leninist whose ideology rejected this as a central value? In China, pluralism has usually been associated with chaos, and Chinese political culture seems to favor authoritarian systems in any case. On the other hand, what right did Mao have to coerce the Chinese people into the views he had chosen for them? In its complexity, the Cultural Revolution forces the examination of such difficult questions.

As for the Chinese citizenry in general, one of the most fascinating aspects of the Cultural Revolution is the emergence of so many spontaneous political groups. All over China young leaders emerged from nowhere to fashion nascent parties and confederations. Their experiences and ultimate destruction demonstrated the importance of organization in politics. Ideals, slogans, and causes abounded, and the participants did not lack commitment. But without a stable structure and resources to translate general ideas into consistent specific policy, their actions amounted to little more than mob violence.

Finally, it is interesting to note the kinship of the Cultural Revolution to the numerous traditionalist or utopian reactions against modernization that have occurred throughout the world. The disruptive effects engendered by the introduction of modern material culture sometimes excite a kind of moral reaction. Those who deplore what they see as the loss of basic human or transcendent values sometimes attempt to reinvigorate the old ways or, alternatively, to bring about some idealized millenium. Modern Chinese history provides dramatic examples of this phenomenon. The massive Taiping Rebellion (1850-1864) was a quasi-

Christian, messianic reaction against social upheavals associated with Western intrusions. The Boxer Uprising (1900) was an attempt by secret societies to drive out Christians and Western influences through traditional magic and symbols.

But such movements are always shot through with ambiguity. The aspects of modern material culture that they wish to destroy are indissolubly connected with other things that they would wish to keep. Because there is no way to separate the desirable from the undesirable, these reactions against change usually prove futile. When they are benign, they end up merely ritualizing a set of symbols and doctrines. When malignant they sow destruction and chaos. Thus, it would seem, ironically, that sometimes those who champion society's deeper values end up, like China's Cultural Revolutionaries, being either irrelevant or dangerous.

Nevertheless, even from this viewpoint, there is a positive side to the Cultural Revolution. The chaos taught an entire generation of Chinese a great historical lesson. In later years the leaders of the People's Republic would be determined not to permit a repeat of these radical spasms.

7

The Cultural Revolution
in Retreat: 1969–76

There is some confusion about the term *Great Proletarian Cultural Revolution*. Its virulent phase began in the spring of 1966 and ended in the spring of 1969 with the move toward stability at the Ninth Party Congress. Strictly speaking, that was the Cultural Revolution. Because the movement was not declared over until after Mao died in 1976, the entire decade starting in 1966 is also commonly called the Cultural Revolution. In those final seven or eight years, triumphant Maoism was replaced by spasmodic radical attempts to stem the moderate tide.

After 1969 many ousted cadres reclaimed their posts in the Party and state bureaucracies. They revived the domestic policies of the early 1960s and initiated a new foreign policy. These "moderates," considered such measures a prescription for healthy modernization and for security in a fast-changing, dangerous world. The radicals, however, were not pleased with what seemed to them like a cancer eating at the soul of the revolution. They, too, held positions of power and did their utmost to resist these changes. Mao Zedong himself energized the resulting struggle as he repeatedly backed and encouraged the radicals. But with each episode the revisionist tide rose a little higher. When Mao died, the radicals lost their patron and were quickly overwhelmed.

Failure to Consolidate Radical Rule, 1969–71

Throughout April 1969 the Ninth Congress of the Chinese Communist party convened in deep secrecy. The carefully selected delegates passed a new Party constitution very different from the one promulgated in 1956. Where the prior document ignored Mao Zedong Thought, the new constitution glorified his person and hailed his ideas as the Party's guiding star, the very perfection of Marxism:

> Mao Zedong thought is Marxism-Leninism of the era in which imperialism is heading for total collapse and socialism is advancing to worldwide victory.

The new charter also enjoined the Party to submit to the "opinions" and the "supervision" of the masses and named Lin Biao as "Chairman Mao Zedong's close comrade-in-arms and successor."[1]

As for the new leadership, it seemed that the Cultural Revolution gains had been secured. Most of the old Central Committee and the Politburo had been hounded out. Liu Shaoqi, being held in Henan Province was soon to die of pneumonia. Deng Xiaoping was under guard in Jiangxi Province, but permitted to labor in a tractor factory. Peng Zhen was also in confinement. The only nonradical member on the Politburo's Standing Committee was Zhou Enlai. In the vacated seats sat mostly Cultural Revolution radicals and military officers. On the Standing Committee were Lin Biao, Chen Boda, and another Maoist. Radicals in the Politburo included Lin Biao's wife, as well as Jiang Qing, and Jiang Qing's two Shanghai associates, Zhang Chunqiao and Yao Wenyuan. Finally, Lin Biao commanded the PLA, which was now the effective governing apparatus throughout the country.

Appearances were deceiving. Lin Biao's frail and sallow look as he addressed the Congress foretold his political future. Within two years he would be sliding toward oblivion on the heels of all who had occupied second place to Mao Zedong. The other radicals were to see power slip from their fingers leaving them able only to block and frustrate their opponents' policies as best they could. Even the PLA gradually drew back from its commanding position.

How could such triumph dissipate so quickly? The answer involves a paradox. The very hand that had beckoned these people to their main chance would not allow them to press their advantage. Mao Zedong lifted them up. But he fancied himself a dialectician. "One divides into two," as he liked to say. The left having prevailed and a new situation having obtained, it was now necessary to tack to the right. Moreover, conditions required a move away from the disorder of the Cultural Revolution. The most important were economic and social disruption, a new constellation of international power, a devastated Party, and the psychological-political threat from Lin Biao.

Economic and Social Policy

First, the disorder in national life had to be addressed. The Cultural Revolution had adversely affected industry and agriculture and had caused foreign trade to decline. Figure 5 in Chapter 5 illustrates that, although the slump in overall national income was not as severe as after the Great Leap Forward, it was nonetheless substantial. The educational system was a shambles, particularly the colleges and universities. With few jobs or educational opportunities for youth, the cities were tinderboxes of unrest and lawlessness. Despite his revolutionary romanticism, Mao could not let this situation deteriorate.

The hope was to fashion a Maoist solution to these problems. This would mean putting politics first and fostering collective spirit, egalitarianism, participation, and self-reliance. In agriculture the epitome of these values was the Shanxi production brigade named Dazhai (pronounced something like "Dodge-eye"). As previously noted, Dazhai was already famous before the Cultural Revolution. It apparently thrived by emphasizing collective agriculture controlled by the production brigade rather than the smaller production team, moral over material incentives, relatively equal distribution of income in preference to payment according to work, grain self-sufficiency over diversified crops, and locally generated investment funds rather than borrowing from the state. In 1970 a big campaign was launched under this slogan: "In Agriculture, Learn from Dazhai." Industry, not to be outdone, had its own Maoist model. It was provided by the newly developed oil fields at Daqing (pronounced "Dah-ching"). Here again a collective spirit, egalitarianism, and a self-sufficient, "can-do" attitude provided an example for other industrial enterprises. So the Dazhai slogan had its industrial counterpart: "In Industry Learn from Daqing."

Education was supposed to embody these same values. Schooling should be proletarianized. Rather than by admissions exams, students in higher education would be selected by their fellow workers and their revolutionary committees. The curriculum should de-emphasize pure academicism to stress practice and production. This would mean regular participation in productive labor, no exams, and no grades. Every school either had its own shop or maintained connections with one or more enterprises where students worked part-time. School life should be political, emphasizing the collective spirit and self-sacrifice. Most middle school graduates were to be mobilized to "go down to the countryside" to make a life as peasants. By the spring of 1976, 12 million had done so.

Although programs after 1969 did embody these values, bits and pieces of pragmatism also began to emerge—always dressed in Maoist rhetoric. Revolutionary committees in industry came under the control of the Party or army secretary, thereby promoting a return to economic discipline. National policy began to favor material incentives, centralized control, less grain self-sufficiency, more economic diversity, and more foreign trade. In December 1971 the Party Center issued a directive against slavishly copying Dazhai.

A New Global Strategy

The importance of economic growth was underlined by new dangers and new opportunities in the world. In the Cultural Revolution, Lin Biao pushed the "Maoist" line that the Third World revolutionaries must oppose both the Tweedledum of Russian "hegemonism" and the Tweedledee of American "imperialism." Now what if Moscow were emerging as a mortal threat, hell-bent on world hegemony while Washington had lost its grip on empire— but remained a useful source of technology? Was it unthinkable to abandon the Maoist doctrine, so fervently promoted in the 1960s, and make peace with bourgeois imperialism?

It has been noted that, during the virulent stages of the Cultural Revolution, Moscow began a large-scale buildup of troops across China's borders. Countervailing forces were placed on the Chinese side. Before long, tensions grew very serious. In 1969 border clashes between Chinese and Soviet troops occurred in the west and in the northeast. Beijing charged that Russia had provoked 429 border incidents in June and July 1969. In August and September the Soviets began to hint at preemptive strikes against Chinese nuclear installations and later allegedly sounded out the American SALT negotiators about joint action against possible Chinese provocation. Both sides strengthened their border armies, and the Chinese began a vast campaign to build urban air raid tunnels.

Fortunately, both countries exercised some restraint. In September 1969, Soviet Premier Aleksei Kosygin stopped off in Beijing. The degree of iciness is reflected in the fact that Mao would not receive him, and Zhou met him only at the airport. Nevertheless, the two came to some sort of understanding about future negotiations and military restraint. Border incidents declined. Still, a hostile tone continued. Moscow denied any plans for a preemptive strike and accused the Chinese of preparing for war. At the same time, Russian frontier forces swelled to formidable proportions.

In April 1970 the Chinese published their most vehement denunciation ever of the Soviet Union, charging their former friend and ally of being even more aggressive than the United States. Although polemics receded somewhat in the second half of 1970, when Chinese and Soviet ambassadors returned to their respective posts, by 1971 the two sides were once again trading recriminations. The brief war between India and Pakistan in December of that year set Russians and Chinese editors into a new round of charges and countercharges.

This extremely serious hostility was one side of the new international equation facing the People's Republic of China. It was counterbalanced by a shift in Sino-American relations. By 1968 and 1969 the Chinese realized that the United States presence in Vietnam would soon end, and concluded that American power in Asia was waning. In June 1969 the first stages of American withdrawal got under way. The following month President Nixon articulated the "Nixon Doctrine" that U.S. allies would henceforth be more responsible for their own defense as Washington reduced its world police officer's role.

Before long, there were increasing hints and signs from both sides that some rapprochement would be welcome. Ambassadorial talks at Warsaw were resumed in January 1970 at about the same time that China hinted it would welcome admission to the United Nations. For the first time ever an American diplomat publicly spoke the words "The People's Republic of China." At the October 1, 1970, National Day celebrations, Mao personally sent a signal. He invited Edgar Snow and his wife to stand beside him on the reviewing stand. Snow was the reporter who had interviewed Mao in 1936 and who had since written sympathetically about China. A photograph of Mao and the Snows appeared on the front page of *People's Daily*, which also carried this statement by Mao: "Peoples of the world, including the American people, are all our friends."[2] President Nixon sent a secret message suggesting that a high American official might like to visit China.

The reconciliation did not proceed entirely smoothly. The United States was still in Vietnam, and Nixon wanted to get out with a minimum loss of face. Consequently, intransigence from Hanoi was answered with U.S. counterattacks and bombings. In May 1970, American forces abruptly invaded Cambodia in the hope of rooting out enemy command centers. Quite aside from the furious public reaction inside the United States, this move prompted a strong personal condemnation from Mao. Again in February 1971, an American-backed South Vietnamese thrust into Laos threatened to expand the conflict, but fortunately for Sino-American relations it failed. In December 1971, American planes flew heavy bombing raids against North Vietnam troop concentrations.

Nevertheless, U.S. disengagement was unmistakable, and the advantages of rapprochement impelled both sides forward. In the course of 1970 and 1971, Washington made a number of gestures. Nixon, too, used the friendly term "People's Republic of China." Travel restrictions for Americans visiting China were eased. The trade embargo was lifted. Washington indicated that it would no longer oppose Chinese admission to the United Nations.

From China came responding signals. In April 1971, the American table tennis team, then visiting Japan, received an invitation to play in China. Thus began the famous "ping-pong" diplomacy, as the journalists accompanying the team reported a warm Chinese welcome. In June 1971, President Nixon's foreign security adviser, Henry Kissinger, secretly flew to Beijing to negotiate a Nixon trip, and a week later the president himself announced that he would soon visit China. When in October the UN took up the question of China's admission, the United States made only a token (and unsuccessful) gesture to preserve Taiwan's General Assembly seat. Thus, both sides—Nixon, the fierce anti-Communist, and Mao, the archfoe of capitalism—had executed a dramatic about-face.

Party Rebuilding

Accompanying these domestic and foreign developments was a shift in political leadership. Many observers, noting the military men on the Ninth Central Committee and Politburo, concluded that the army was "taking over." It was also reasonable to assume an important role for the "three-in-one" revolutionary committees. However, neither expectation proved correct. The revolutionary committees quickly lost out to Party or PLA leaders. The military began to be supplanted by a revived Party structure much sooner than might have been expected.

How could a party, so decimated, ever recover? Leninist "democratic centralism" was deeply ingrained in Chinese communism. Mao dealt the CCP a terrific blow in the Cultural Revolution, but he never intended to annihilate it. In 1967 he had rebuffed Zhang Chunqiao's and Yao Wenyuan's Shanghai Commune precisely because it included no commanding role for the Party. As for Party-army relations, Mao's own famous adage encapsulates the CCP tradition: "Our principle is that the Party commands the gun, and the gun must never be allowed to command the Party."[3]

There are other reasons as well. One is brute numbers. The armed forces, numbering about 4 million, could hardly supplant the 28 million (by 1973) Party members even if every soldier gave up military duties. Moreover in mid-1969 it was urgent to get things back to normal. Revolutionary committees had proved to be fractious and unstable. In turn, they stimulated popular unrest. In the summer of 1969, serious conflicts erupted in Shanxi. Contemporary sources described a serious situation where "a handful of class enemies and bad leaders" who had "wormed their way" into mass organizations and organized armed combat teams assaulted the PLA; sabotaged railroads, highways, and bridges; looted banks, warehouses, and stores; and sabotaged industry and agriculture.[4]

During the two years following the Ninth Party Congress, Party rebuilding proceeded slowly and tortuously. It was necessary to rehabilitate veteran Party cadres and recruit new members. Radicalism had to be diminished. At the top, Jiang Qing's and Chen Boda's Cultural Revolution Group was phased out. In the provinces some leftists were purged. There was an early-1970 witch-hunt of members of the alleged ultraradical May 16 Corps. During this period the PLA continued to assign officers to schools, enterprises, and communes across the country.

It was necessary to reconstitute provincial and lower-level Party committees. The first provincial committee was established in Hunan in December 1970; the last, in August of 1971. Yet rebuilding was still not complete because at the county level only about one-fifth of the Party committees had been rebuilt. Still, the process was well under way. Simultaneously with Party revival, Zhou Enlai was rebuilding the state bureaucracy.

Some new faces emerged during this restoration process. One was a man named Hua Guofeng (pronounced "Hwah Gwo-fung") who headed the new Hunan committee mentioned earlier. Hua was about fifty at this time. Of northern peasant extraction, he had joined the Communist guerrillas as a young man during the anti-Japanese struggle. At the time of liberation, he found himself a cadre in Mao's home province of Hunan. He gradually worked his way up through the Party organization, occasionally coming to Mao's attention for his defense of the High Tide and of the Great Leap Forward. He also had personal responsibility over Mao's native district, which he favored. Hua was a combination Maoist, pragmatist, opportunist with a certain bent for conciliation. He was tall, jowly, and rumpled in appearance, an obscure provincial functionary about to be thrust into the national limelight.

The Fall of Lin Biao

To the radicals, all these changes were unsettling. But they were mere pinpricks compared to the devastating blow of September 1971: Lin Biao's disgrace and death.

How did the Cultural Revolution's greatest beneficiary, the man who shared Mao's sacred niche above all other mortals, suddenly turn traitor? How could the Chairman again choose a successor whom he had to destroy? What caused the falling out? Who turned on whom? These questions elude ready answers, to

say nothing about the plain facts as to what happened. An em-
barrassment of this magnitude brought out the full artistry of the
official obfuscators. Almost all available information was released weeks or years after the event. It is full of improbable
allegations and gaping omissions and cannot be verified—a tan-
talizing puzzle, but an important one in view of Lin Biao's
standing and the consequences of his ruination.

Some facts are reasonably certain. Lin Biao and Chen Boda,
who had become allies, came into conflict with Mao at a Central
Committee Plenum in August 1970. Mao struck back immediately at Chen, the lesser of the two, and abruptly ended his fellow theoretician's career. It is also fairly certain that Mao took
a series of actions in the months that followed to weaken Lin's
position. Several generals and even Lin's wife were forced to
make self-criticisms. Important regional military commanders
were shifted around. In August 1971 Mao toured southern and
central China, getting support. Immediately on the Chairman's
return, Lin Biao met his death, together with his wife, his son,
and several others, including altogether five members of the Politburo. A wave of arrests rounded up scores of Lin supporters
in the PLA.

Almost all the rest of the story must be reconstructed from
alleged facts and inferences. Lin could not rest easy in his high
position. Moderates such as Zhou opposed his economic views.
His revolutionary global strategy was at stake if the United States
should cease to be an enemy. If China abandoned guerrilla warfare for professionalism, his position would also be undercut.
Domestically, his military power base weakened as the Party revived. Lin's fall was also tied in with power struggle. There are
those who argue that Mao was never able to tolerate a near rival
and exhibited a deeply ingrained pattern of turning on his second-
in-command.

Lin's difficulties probably began as early as 1969 over policy
disagreements. Then at the 1970 Plenum Lin and Chen took two
actions that for some reason infuriated Mao. In connection with
a state constitution then being drafted, Lin proposed reviving the

office of head of state. Since Liu Shaoqi's disgrace, the position had, in effect, been abolished. In addition, Lin and Chen Boda proposed that the Party formally endorse the theory of "genius," the theory that Mao Zedong was the kind of genius that appears only once in several centuries.

It would be easier to believe that these two suggestions had been made, rejected, and forgotten than that they had caused the ruin of two such powerful men. But the unbelievable is closer to the truth. It would seem that Mao considered their head-of-state initiative as an attempt to ease him from active power or else as an effort to secure the job for Lin himself. The genius theory was probably Chen Boda's. Although the intention was, no doubt, to honor and flatter Mao, there may have been a fairly transparent ulterior motive, namely, to strengthen the positions of Lin and Chen, who naturally would be the head priests in charge of interpreting Maoist scripture for other mortals.

Was this paranoia in the mind of Mao? Did Lin see, or imagine, that his position was at risk and take desperate action? Was Lin always a cunning schemer, unmasked only at the last minute? The authorities alleged that Lin desperately drew up a plan to assassinate Mao and, when it failed, fled with his closest conspirators. Some have bought this story more or less as offered. Others have refused to believe part or all of it. The plot was too cuckoo to be the work of a great battlefield tactician and experienced politician. It had to be the work of his profligate twenty-seven-year-old son. But would even a twenty-seven-year-old concoct a plan that called for the use of dynamite, bazookas, artillery, exploding oil storage tanks, aerial bombs, and assassins? Surely, Lin Biao fathered a more subtle offspring than this? Still, that is the story.

On finding their plan foiled, the plotters are said to have dashed for the airport, hotly pursued. After a hair-raising takeoff in Lin Biao's personal Trident, they headed for Russia, the inevitable destination of all traitors. But the fuel tanks ran dry, and they had to attempt an emergency landing in Mongolia, where the aircraft burst into flames. There were no survivors. A plane did, in fact, crash in Mongolia. But just who the passengers were, why they were on it, and where they were going remains part of the great puzzle.

The Uneasy Regime of the Moderates: 1972–75

The Radicals Lose Ground

For four years after the fall of Lin Biao, from 1972 through 1975, the rhetorical side of the Cultural Revolution retained great strength whereas actual government policies in most spheres moved increasingly in the direction of the "moderate" thrust of the early 1960s. On the surface, China remained a thoroughly Maoist society, a self-proclaimed model for other peoples hoping to mitigate the social problems of modernization. But underneath, the majority of China's rulers were attempting to modernize in an un-Maoist fashion. Behind them was a broad consensus of veteran cadres at all levels, military commanders, the intelligentsia, sent-down youth in the countryside, permanent industrial workers, and middle peasants.

Trying valiantly to force or cajole that multitude in the direction of equality, justice, and heroic self-dedication was a smaller group strongly attached to the principles of the Great Leap Forward and the Cultural Revolution. Besides radicals like Jiang Qing, they included poorer peasants who benefited from rural egalitarianism, workers without secure employment, and younger cadres who saw their futures limited by entrenched incumbents. Their leaders claimed the revolutionary moral high ground, which they defended in the *People's Daily* and the other propaganda and cultural institutions under their control. Most important, they had Mao's protection—and sometimes his backing.

From 1972 through 1975, these two broadly defined forces engaged in a to-and-fro that had some peculiar qualities. The rhetoric of both sides sounded roughly similar. But behind the words and rituals, the larger side was steadily promoting pragmatic modernization. The other side, with little bureaucratic power, used its ideological weapons and its Mao connection to frustrate this reverse course whenever possible. The result was the familiar seesaw of "moderate" and "radical" policies.

Aftertremors of the Lin Biao affair shuddered through the Party and army for months. In addition to the destruction of Lin's personal faction, well over a hundred central and provincial military commanders were purged. With them fell nearly fifty provincial Party leaders. The Party rank and file must have gaped with amazement as they read top secret directives informing them that Lin was dead after plotting to blow up the Chairman's train and further revealing that Lin had for years opposed Mao and carried on counterrevolutionary conspiracies. Heads must have been shaking as Party committees rounded up Lin's portraits, his calligraphic inscriptions, his books and pamphlets, and even the Party constitution to forward to higher authorities for destruction. "Mao Zedong's close comrade-in-arms and successor" was now that "swindler like Liu Shaoqi," sometimes compared to "dogshit." The *People's Daily* New Year's editorial for 1972 almost pleads, "Practice Marxism, and not revisionism; unite, and don't split; be open and above board, and don't intrigue and conspire."[5]

The October 1, 1971, National Day celebrations had to be canceled. The whole affair was deeply embarrassing not only inside China but also in the world at large at a time when China was being admitted to the United Nations and Henry Kissinger was paying his secret visit. For months, the Chinese leaders could think of no better course than to say nothing. Only in mid-1972 did the official story begin to be released.

Lin's fall and Chen Boda's disgrace undercut the position of the remaining radicals. The stigma on their policies could be partly removed by claiming that Lin and Chen were ultrarightists only feigning to be left. More serious was the fact that the Maoists now had no one of great prestige and institutional power to champion their point of view. Jiang Qing was powerful, principally because of her ties to Mao. Even that relationship eroded in 1972, when Mao learned that, without authorization, she had granted a series of interviews to an American professor, Roxanne Witke. After this the husband and wife stopped living in the same house, and he is known to have rebuked her on several occasions.

Among Jiang Qing's "Shanghai Group," the only person with any credibility as a Party leader was Zhang Chunqiao. However even he was only a figure of provincial stature. Zhang's associate, Yao Wenyuan, was principally a radical propagandist with no claim to broad expertise. The fourth member of the group, Wang Hongwen, had been a security guard at Number Seventeen Cotton Mill when the Cultural Revolution began. In the upheavals, his ability to organize workers was put in the service of Zhang's an Yao's Shanghai Commune. Suddenly in 1969 this handsome young worker was named to the Central Committee, and by the early 1970s, thanks to Jiang Qing's patronage, he had "helicoptered" to the top. Nevertheless, being only in his late thirties and with no great revolutionary prestige or bureaucratic base, he was vulnerable.

Zhou Enlai Takes Charge

In inverse ratio to the radicals' uncertain standing, Zhou Enlai's influence reached a pinnacle. Having spent over a quarter of a century as number three or four in the hierarchy, he now occupied the riskier second spot. The depth and breadth of his political authority were unmatched, in some ways even by Mao. Premier since 1949, Zhou oversaw the State Council and its entire spectrum of administration and planning. He played a particularly prominent role in foreign affairs until 1958 as foreign minister and even thereafter. His legendary capacity for work had been put to the supreme test during the Cultural Revolution, when he kept the central administration together single-handedly. Many Party and military leaders owed their survival to his protection during those trying times.[6]

Lin's sudden disgrace allowed Zhou to push ahead with the

ZHOU ENLAI

modernizing programs already under way. Central to this effort was economic development. The Five-Year Plan and all the activities that took place under its aegis from 1971 through 1975 are a vast and complex subject, not easy to characterize in a few words and not without faults according to more recent assessments. Generally speaking, in all sectors the principles Zhou pushed were pragmatic management, central planning, material incentives, and interdependence, all of which contradicted Lin's (and Mao's) emphasis on decentralization, moral incentives, self-reliance, and politics first.

Zhou got results. Industrial production, which had slumped briefly during the Cultural Revolution, rebounded and moved upward through the 1970s. As for agriculture, already in December 1971, with the wreckage of Lin's presumed escape plane still smoldering in Mongolia, the Central Committee was admonishing cadres against pushing the Dazhai approach. More criticisms followed in succeeding months, even as the slogan "In Agriculture Learn from Dazhai" continued to be plastered all over the country. These signals from the center only strengthened tendencies that were already at work. Not the Dazhai spirit but practicality was the order of the day, and results showed it. Grain harvests, which had slumped during the Cultural Revolution, increased smartly through 1975 with the sole exception of 1972, a year of bad weather. By 1975 the per capita availability of grain finally recovered to levels that had been reached back in the 1950s on the eve of the Great Leap Forward. Figure 5 in Chapter 4 represents the recovery in overall national income during this period.

The massive program of sending down young people to the countryside continued. Radical insistence on "tempering" China's youth converged with the pragmatists' interest in limiting the growth of urban population and attendant unemployment problems. Consequently, this program never flagged until after Mao's death. By the end of 1972, the number of youths who had gone down to the villages since the end of the Cultural Revolution totaled 7 million.

Even education, which the Maoists had adamantly insisted should shake off bourgeois influences, began to be drawn back into more conventional patterns. The radical rhetoric continued, as did the practice of intermixing labor with academic study, selecting college students from candidates recommended by fellow workers or peasants and favoring categories such as workers, peasants, and women. Underneath, a gradual return to academic emphasis and even entrance examinations were creeping in. The government was particularly anxious to rebuild scientific and technical education and research as absolutely essential for economic modernization.

Under Zhou the new thrust in foreign affairs, which Lin had opposed, continued to develop. The most sensational moment came when Richard Nixon, in the *Spirit of '76*, touched down at Beijing airport in February 1972. The famous "Shanghai Communiqué" signed by Nixon and Zhou on February 27 established the basis for improved relations between the two countries by sidestepping the Taiwan issue as a problem that would be solved among the Chinese themselves in due time. Meanwhile, economic, cultural, and other contacts could move ahead. The spring of 1973 saw a high point in the relationship when the two countries established liaison offices in each others' capitals. This was a step toward full diplomatic relations, which, however, did not come about for another six years.

Formal recognition was forthcoming from many other countries. Shortly after Nixon's visit, Sino-Japanese relations changed dramatically. In September 1972, the same Chinese leaders who one year earlier were railing against Japanese militarism and expansion received Prime Minister Tanaka and established diplomatic relations between Beijing and Tokyo. Altogether sixteen more countries granted formal recognition to the PRC in 1972. Fourteen had done so in 1971. In the UN, China took up its role with great seriousness and responsibility and won the general respect of the other delegations. These breakthroughs were part of a broad redefinition of foreign policy. As we noted earlier, Beijing was abandoning the substance, if not always the rhetoric, of encouraging people's liberation movements against both American imperialism and Russian "hegemonism." The new "Three Worlds" thesis divided the world into two superpowers, other developed nations, and undeveloped nations. Of the superpowers, only the USSR was a truly dangerous enemy. Against Russia, China was prepared to join all countries without concern for their revolutionary credentials.

Hostility toward the USSR continued unabated although fears concerning a preemptive Russian strike declined, and border incidents became rare. Large concentrations of troops were still arrayed on either side of the world's longest frontier. By late 1972, perhaps one-third of the Soviet army was there, well supplied with mechanized divisions, air support, and tactical nuclear weapons. But China's own nuclear program had also been making progress. In addition to long-range bombers, medium-range (1,500 miles) and intermediate range (3,000 miles) ballistic missiles were already deployed, and intercontinental ballistic missiles, capable of reaching European Russia, were being rapidly developed. In addition, the tunnels under the cities afforded at least a psychological sense of protection against Russian attack. With these developments, China's sense of security was growing.

The new diplomacy allowed China to tap foreign technology, especially from Japan, Europe, and the United States. Once again, as in the 1950s and the early 1960s, complete "turnkey" plants were imported. From late 1972 to the end of 1974, over 2 billion U.S. dollars' worth were purchased, in large measure thanks to funds available from a reduced military budget after Lin's fall and to export earnings from China's rapidly expanding petroleum exports.

Finally, Zhou's program included further rebuilding of the political and administrative system. Party reorganization continued. The political role of the radicals decreased proportionately. Mass organizations that had been destroyed during the Cultural Revolution (trade unions and the Communist Youth League) reappeared. The Mao cult moderated, and the catechismlike recitations from the Little Red Book ceased with a movement to study complete Marxist classics, including Mao's theoretical essays. Large numbers of former cadres were rehabilitated. In August 1972, at the annual Army Day reception, the two leaders of the 1967 Wuhan mutiny appeared. The hubbub that this caused was small compared with the stir over Deng Xiaoping's reemergence in the spring of 1973. An American visitor observed the electric response of movie audiences when the once familiar face of this former capitalist roader, second only to Liu Shaoqi, reappeared in newsreels.[7]

In August 1973, some 1,200 delegates were gathered for a short and secret Tenth Congress of the Chinese Communist party. This was necessary to formalize the changes since the Ninth Congress of 1969. Lin Biao, now named by name, and Chen Boda were both formally denounced and expelled from the Party, the former as a "bourgeois careerist, conspirator, counterrevolutionary, double-dealer, renegade, and traitor" and the latter as a "principal member of the Lin Biao anti-Party clique, anticommunist Guomindang element, Trotskyite, renegade, enemy agent, and revisionist."[8] A new Party constitution was written, removing Lin as Mao's designated successor.

The new leadership hierarchy emerged. Rehabilitated Party members appeared on the Central Committee, most notably Deng Xiaoping. One of the new faces in the Politburo was the fast-rising Hunan Party chief Hua Guofeng. Military representation was down although by no means insignificant. Only two speeches were delivered at the Congress so far as is known. One of them was Zhou Enlai's. In his section on the economy, after paying lip service to several Maoist slogans, he argued that "planning and coordination must be strengthened, rational rules and regulations improved, and both central and local initiative further brought into full play . . ."[9]

Persisting Radical Influence

Yet Zhou Enlai did not have it all his own way, nor were the radicals ready to be counted out. One new factor was that Zhou had been diagnosed as having stomach cancer in 1972. In May 1973, he entered the hospital, emerging on rare occasions such as the Party Congress. With his days numbered, it was not clear whether he would be able to solidify the modernization programs sufficiently before his death. This was surely one of the main reasons for rehabilitating the able pragmatist Deng Xiaoping.

Secondly, the radicals were not without support for their views. Mao, of course, remained the ultimate fountain of revolutionary values. Presumably, with his backing, the Shanghai Group all had places on the eighteen-member Politburo, and two of them (Zhang Chunqiao and Wang Hongwen) were on its Standing Committee. Wang, in particular, had made a spectacular rise and was now ranked third just after Zhou Enlai. Increasingly, he was talked about as a possible successor to Mao.

The Shanghai Group were not prepared to see moderate programs continue unopposed. They had succeeded in inserting Cultural Revolution principles in the new Party constitution: the need for periodic cultural revolutions, the duty to criticize revisionism, and the revolutionary spirit of "daring to go against the tide." The phrase was emblematic of the leftists as a brave minority against the organization-minded majority.

Immediately after the Tenth Congress, the left began to strike back. As they did not control the administrative machinery at any level or have influence in the PLA, their main instrument was the propaganda and culture apparatus. Consequently, they launched a big campaign to "Criticize Confucius." This would seem innocuous enough, given that Confucius died more than 2,000 years ago. It was political code. "Confucius" meant Zhou Enlai, and the "Criticize Confucius" campaign took aim at his programs.

Actually, there had been a steady tattoo of radical criticism, and it is hard to pinpoint when the campaign began—probably about September 1973. It is also hard to establish just what Mao's connection was. Did he initiate the movement as some claim? At least it would seem that he was in the mood for a dialectical turn away from moderation. At the end of November 1973, when the *People's Daily* quoted him as saying, "Every seven or eight years monsters and demons will jump out," the radicals took this as a signal. The demons and monsters were, of course, revisionists who require to be beaten back periodically with cultural revolutions. Soon a vast amorphous campaign was under way, attacking such diverse evils as *Jonathan Livingston Seagull*, bourgeois music, and material incentives.

The Shanghai Group were not the only ones who knew how to use the media. Early in 1974, Zhou Enlai or his supporters complicated things and deflected the criticism by grafting a "Criticize Lin Biao" campaign onto the existing one. In this complicated way, it became a "Criticize Lin, Criticize Confucius" movement. On one side, the *People's Daily* and other radical-controlled media flailed this improbable pair as rightists while the moderates, in publications such as *Red Flag*, excoriated Lin and Confucius as leftists. Consequently, the campaign lurched forward in a contradictory and ill-defined fashion, it not always being clear to Chinese or to foreigners just who was the target of a given attack. Although no deep inroads were made into the modernization programs, the campaign did have the effect of slowing and, in a few cases, obstructing Zhou's programs.

By July 1974, the campaign to criticize Lin Biao and Confucius had run its course. Possibly because the moderates could point to lagging economic performance and signs of popular resistance since the onset of the campaign and perhaps because the radicals could see they weren't getting very far, the Politburo decided to wind it down. The *People's Daily* editorial for July 1, marking the Party anniversary, proclaimed:

> Of the Party, the government, the army, the mass organizations, and the cultural and educational institutions . . . , it is the Party that exercises leadership in everything. The current movement to criticize Lin Biao and Confucius must be conducted under the centralized leadership of Party committees. Only when Party leadership is strengthened is it possible to organize the various forces and attain UNITY IN THINKING, POLICY, PLAN, COMMAND, AND ACTION . . .[10]

On this same day, the Politburo issued a directive, "The Central Committee Notice Concerning Grasping Revolution and Promoting Production," which ordered work stoppages to cease, production to resume, and wage and management disputes to be deferred. The campaign sputtered on for a few months, but its force was spent.

Late 1974 and early 1975 saw the rehabilitated Deng Xiaoping rise once more to the top, protected by the ailing Zhou Enlai. This caused no little anxiety among Deng's enemies. The radicals launched several ineffectual and slightly desperate initiatives to regain influence. Mao having left Beijing for the south in July 1974, they launched a campaign to build up Jiang Qing's stature as "Expounder of Mao Zedong Thought." But he frowned on her presumption and purportedly scolded her for sticking her nose into everything, lecturing people, and pursuing personal ambition. Also, in October 1974, Wang Hongwen is said to have visited Mao to complain that the radicals had too few high posts and to charge that Zhou, Deng, and others were plotting against the Chairman. Mao took little notice.

The capstone of Zhou's and Deng's efforts, in a formal sense, was the long overdue Fourth National People's Congress in January 1975. Zhou Enlai left his sickbed to preside. Perhaps the most remarkable thing about this Congress is the rebound in the status of Deng Xiaoping that it marked. Languishing in oblivion just two years previously, he now occupied commanding positions in each of the three institutional hierarchies. As ranking vice-premier, he was effectively in charge of the State Council in Premier Zhou's absence. As a vice-chairperson of the Party (an appointment made by a Central Committee Plenum just prior to the Congress), he once again belonged to the Politburo and its Standing Committee. And as chief of staff of the People's Liberation Army, he commanded the military services.

Also noteworthy was the way this Congress formalized the planned program of development. Zhou's keynote address, although hedged with radical rhetoric, was essentially a call to forge ahead with the long-range plan of achieving

> the comprehensive modernization of agriculture, industry, national defense, and science and technology before the end of the century, so that our national economy will be advancing in the front ranks of the world.[11]

This broad objective came to be referred to as the "Four Modernizations." To realize them, Zhou said that the State Council would draw up China's fifth Five-Year Plan (1976 to 1980), together with long-range and annual plans. The new constitution proclaimed

> the planned and proportionate development of the socialist economy, taking agriculture as the foundation and industry as the leading factor . . .[12]

In agriculture, the document reaffirmed the production team as the prime unit of ownership and management and guaranteed peasants their right to have private plots, engage in sideline occupations, and market their products.

However, as was characteristic of this period generally, the Congress was not a unified love feast for pragmatic policies. Despite the importance of this meeting, Mao did not attend, probably signaling his disapproval. It was unlikely that he was ill because he was able, while the Congress was in session, to receive West Germany's Franz Josef Strauss. Aside from Mao, the important radicals were prominently in attendance. Sitting at the rostrum before the 2,800 delegates with Zhou, Deng, and some of their supporters sat the Shanghai Group: Jiang Qing, Zhang Chunqiao, Wang Hongwen, and Yao Wenyuan. Zhang, the most experienced of them, was awarded positions in the State Council, the army, and the Party just subordinate to Deng Xiaoping—perhaps as part of the deal when Deng's promotions were negotiated. Also at the dais was Hua Guofeng, the Hunan leader, who had been named sixth-ranking vice-premier and head of the sensitive Ministry of Public Security.

In the months following the Fourth National Peoples Congress, Deng continued to push the development program. In virtually every sector of the economy, excellent growth was recorded for the year. In addition to current production, the State Council was absorbed with completing the new Five-Year Plan to start in 1976. A number of conferences were organized to determine the needs of agriculture, industry, science and technology, and national defense. Deng called Military Affairs Committee meetings in May and July 1975, where he advocated efficiency, professionalism, better weapons, and Party control. To direct the modernization program, he rehabilitated none other than Luo Ruiqing, the chief of staff in the early 1960s who had opposed Lin Biao, had joined Peng Zhen as the earliest victim of the Cultural Revolution, and had tried twice to commit suicide under radical pressure.

As usual, much of this was anathema to the radicals. The rehabilitation of people like Luo Ruiqing (not to mention Deng!), the downgrading of the human factor in warfare, and the renewed emphasis on technology and expertise all offended against Maoist doctrine. Consequently, it is not surprising that, as had happened after the Tenth Party Congress of 1973, the period following the Fourth National People's Congress saw a surge of radical propaganda and efforts to undercut Deng's program.

Again, it is not clear just how central Mao's role was. A case can be made that, in his dissatisfaction with the Fourth People's Congress, he attempted to sponsor a swing back toward the Left. After returning to the capital in January 1975 (somewhat unusual for a man who preferred to winter in the south), he wrote a new admonition that was featured in the *People's Daily* editorial for February 9. He said:

> Lack of clarity on [exercising proletarian dictatorship over the bourgeoisie] will lead to revisionism. This should be made known to the whole nation.[13]

Here again was Mao's theme of politics in command. In March and April 1975, both Zhang Chunqiao and Yao Wenyuan of the Shanghai Group published attacks on Deng's approach. Zhang warned against the bourgeoisie who assured China's youth that material incentives "like 'stinky' bean curd, smells awful but tastes good."[14] Yao, too, decried material incentives. Zhang urged that, in agriculture, efforts be made to increase the importance of brigades and communes at the expense of the smaller production teams. This propaganda campaign buzzed over the heads of Deng's bureaucrats as they went ahead with their plans.

This radical sniping continued into the summer and fall of 1975, with Mao taking an unpredictable position. In May it seems that he had chastised the Shanghai Group for factionalism and sectarianism. They all wrote letters of self-criticism. But late August found him initiating further attacks on Zhou and Deng through criticism of a popular traditional novel, *Water Margin*. The novel's hero, a stand-in for Deng, was charged with "capitulationism'' (and hence revisionism) to the emperor, that is, to Zhou Enlai presumably. A number of articles echoed this theme, orchestrated no doubt by the Shanghai Group. Yet once again the net effect of the leftist initiatives was marginal. They were unable to reverse Deng's course, but they did force the moderates to dress up modernization with revolutionary rhetoric. In some places, their opposition to material incentives sparked a backlash of industrial unrest. Their patron, however, was growing weaker by the day. Foreigners who visited him during 1975 found a man of sound mind but physically almost as helpless as a baby.

Mao's Final Months and the Arrest of the Gang of Four: 1976

By the end of 1975, the nation had experienced four years of a fluctuating moderate-radical stalemate. The moderates had the advantage in their control over the Party and state systems. Cadres concerned to get on with the job typically had little use for the radicals. In agriculture, even when the Dazhai system was being promoted, thousands of production teams went their own way by underreporting their output, allocating extra private plots, using collective vehicles and facilities for private gain, sending weaker family members to do collective labor while the more vigorous worked on private enterprises, and leaving the village in slack season to work in the cities. A February 1976 report on the situation in Fujian Province complained:

> The restoration of capitalism in the district of Changle has assumed extremely alarming proportions. In reality, the situation there is about the same as during the period of the rule of the Guomindang. The only thing which is missing is the Guomindang flag. . . . There are thirty-five groups of people who produce exclusively for their own benefit. . . . They have distributed the arable land to the individual households and have made the individ-

ual households into a distribution organ. . . . In an entire [county], everybody, cadres as well as the population, [is] busy with speculation. . . . On top of all this, they put on performances of classic Fujian operas."[15]

The radicals' bureaucratic resources were fewer; and their popular support, smaller. Yet there were many cadres who had risen during the Cultural Revolution and other elements, as, for example, students selected under the academically less rigorous criteria, whose interests or idealism aligned them with the Shanghai Group. There were brigades who did, in fact, emulate the Dazhai model. And the radicals' criticism of bureaucratism and elite privilege certainly sounded a responsive chord. But for the most part this camp could do little more than obstruct the moderates through the propaganda media and with Mao's fluctuating support.

At this time, at least a few figures were emerging at the top who might be considered a compromise group between the hardcore radicals and Deng's moderates. Most prominent among them were Hua Guofeng, the Hunan Party chairperson recently promoted to high posts (including the Security Ministry), and Chen Yongguei, the peasant leader from Dazhai. These men had good Maoist credentials, but they were more pragmatic and less confrontational than the Shanghai Group.

Toward the end of 1975, politics heated up. Mao's Parkinson's disease and Zhou's cancer were closing in on their victims. Any day could bring fateful news. Now the succession problem, which had figured in political struggles for years, became acute. The departure of one of these men could leave his protégés fatally exposed. The Shanghai Group reacted to this heightened uncertainty by launching shrill attacks on Deng toward the end of 1975. Already at midyear Jiang Qing had been railing against "friendly gentlemen like Malenkov," by which she presumably meant Hua Guofeng, "but above all people like Khrushchev are still right in our [midst] . . . ," alluding, of course, to Deng.[16] By November the radical media were criticising the "right deviationist wind," which was "reversing correct verdicts," that is, rehabilitating victims of the Cultural Revolution.[17]

At the turn of the year, it got even more intense. Presumably with Mao's support, the radicals launched a campaign against creeping revisionism in education. On New Year's Day the *People's Daily* carried this Mao quote: "Stability and unity do not mean writing off class struggle. Class struggle is the key link and everything else hinges on it."[18] This term, "key link," became a constantly repeated theme.

And then, from Deng's point of view, the worst possible thing happened. Zhou Enlai died on January 8, 1976. Suddenly, the entire nation was in deep and emotional mourning. Zhou's remains were cremated, and a casket containing his ashes was placed in one of the buildings in the Imperial Palace. In subzero temperatures, thousands of mourners stood on line for hours to pay their last respects. For days the airwaves carried nothing but funeral music and tributes to the departed leader. If the people had lost their great folk hero, Deng Xiaoping may have lost his lifeline.

Deng gave the eulogy at the memorial ceremony at the Great Hall of the People, attended by some 5,000 mourners. As it turned out, this was his last public utterance (for the time being). The radical attack now unleashed its full fury against him. A campaign of oblique attacks on the "unrepenting capitalist-roader inside the Party" and on the modernization program now began, with Mao himself adding a barb or two, such as this view of his carried by *People's Daily*: "That man's never been interested in class struggle."[19] Shorn of Zhou's protection, Deng was unable to resist, despite his high positions. He disappeared from view in February or March, 1976. To the complete astonishment of observers inside and outside China, the new acting premier was not Deng, but the virtually unknown Hua Guofeng, whom Mao nominated in January, 1976 as a compromise candidate.

Then a succession of events in early April brought the political struggle to a climax. Several indications point to the conclusion that organized or individual Deng adherents had been working to counteract the radicals. A March 25 Shanghai newspaper article disparaged Zhou, saying that a certain "capitalist-roader in the Party wanted to put back in power a capitalist-roader who had been toppled and is unrepentant to this day."[20] This triggered thousands of protesting telegrams and letters. No doubt convinced that Deng adherents would take advantage of the upcoming Qing Ming Festival to honor Zhou (and thereby Deng), the authorities sent out a directive to all workplaces discouraging participation in any activities, but in vain.

Sunday, April 4, 1976, marked Qing Ming, a traditional holiday for cleaning and repairing family graves. Thousands of Beijing residents came to the massive square at Tian'anmen to express their affection for the departed premier. They came here because his ashes had been scattered, and no grave or monument honored his memory. For some days wreaths had been appearing at the large cenotaph that commemorates heroes of the Revolution. By Qing Ming there was an enormous accumulation of them, reportedly accumulating thirty feet high. People also attached paper slips bearing poems or statements to the nearby hedges. Some of them were barely disguised denunciations of Jiang Qing, the Shanghai Group, or even of Mao himself. Such free expression of dissent was not to be tolerated.

In the early morning hours of April 5, on orders from the highest authority, city officials removed the wreaths. When dawn came and the public discovered this fact, a huge demonstration developed, the famous Tian'anmen Incident. Tens of thousands milled around the square in great agitation. Foreign observers were roughly sent away. Harangues were delivered, slogans chanted, police officers were scolded, scuffles broke out, and some people were beaten. A loudspeaker van was overturned, two or three cars were set on fire, and the police headquarters bordering the square was put to the torch. Finally, in the evening, as the crowds thinned, militia moved in with clubs and cleared the square, with numerous arrests. It was a daylong riot that was answered by demonstrations elsewhere in the country.

Ironically, the Tian'anmen Incident sealed Deng's fate (for the time being). His extraordinary career, just recently revived, ended in a second disgrace. Blaming him for the unrest (on no known evidence), the Politburo stripped him of all offices. He retained only his Party membership. The anti-Deng campaign heated up even more, with extensive wall poster displays detailing his manifold revisionism. At the same time, the radicals began to push again for Dazhai policies in agriculture.

It was not a complete victory for the radicals. Although they ousted Deng, they lacked the power to capture effective leadership for themselves. It was the compromise candidate, Hua Guofeng, who, with Mao's backing, stepped in as a compromise. He succeeded Zhou as premier and became ranking Party vice-chairperson second only to Mao. Moreover, Deng's removal was a solitary demotion, not a sweeping purge. The whole system of cadres and military leaders, many of them Deng supporters, remained in place. Deng himself was taken out of Beijing under the protection of one of the regional military commanders. He is said to have met with several key PLA leaders to work out strategy for the future.

Soon after the Tian'anmen Incident, Mao's health took a turn for worse. Foreign visitors who were received by him in April and May 1976 found a man barely capable of moving and speaking. A May 27 *People's Daily* photo with Pakistani Prime Minister Bhutto showed him scarcely able to sit up. On June 15 the president of Madagascar left China without having had an audience, and shortly thereafter it was announced that the Chairman would no longer receive foreign dignitaries. Mao's deteriorating condition exacerbated the already strong tendency for an inner palace court to form. Increasingly, those who informed the Chairman and transmitted his will to the outside world were in a position to manipulate him. Jiang Qing's influence rose. Mao's nephew, Mao Yuanxin, seemed to function as palace chief of staff. The commander of the Central Guard Division, PLA Unit 8341, which numbered perhaps 40,000 well-armed troops became an increasingly important element in succession politics.

As Mao lay dying, natural disasters revived traditional notions about the fall of dynasties. The old "Mandate of Heaven" belief said that prodigies signaled Heaven's displeasure with the ruler and anticipated the withdrawal of the divine "mandate" to rule. In the spring and summer in 1976, several provinces suffered severe drought. Two major earthquakes struck the southwest in May. In late July a major earthquake hit Tangshan, not far from Beijing, a second quake then striking the capital itself. The Tangshan quake was a disaster of vast dimensions, perhaps the worst in centuries. Internal documents claimed that over 655,000 people died and a million were left homeless. Other sources put the toll at 250,000. In either case, the losses were staggering. "Mandate of Heaven" talk became so common that the Party launched a small campaign to stop it.

Mao died on September 9, 1976. Naturally, the nationwide mourning was deep and prolonged. Visitors testify that the mood was more reserved and formal and less emotional than when Zhou Enlai died. Despite the reverence in which he was held for his early revolutionary leadership, there was a broad, if unspoken, view that his excesses had not served China well. As one writer expresses it, "The very success of Mao's revolution had produced a generation that passed him by . . . [He] was like a speaker addressing an audience that has left for its next engagement."[21] Or as a recently current formula says, "His founding of the Republic was meritorious; his antirightism was mistaken; his Cultural Revolution was criminal."

The day that had been dreaded and anticipated for over fifteen years had finally arrived. Once the giant memorial service was over and the decision made to display Mao's embalmed remains in a memorial hall, the big questions were: Who would inherit Mao's authority, and what direction would the country take? The short-term answers were soon given. Hua Guofeng teamed up with the PLA contingent in the Party and arrested Jiang Qing's faction on October 6, 1976. With their mentor gone, the radicals' position collapsed totally. Now excoriated as the "Gang of Four," Jiang Qing, Wang Hongwen, Zhang Chunqiao, and Yao Wenyuan entered the last phase of their careers as scapegoats for virtually every evil, natural or human, that had afflicted China for the last decade. Incarcerated in Qincheng Prison in the suburbs of Beijing, they would be dragged out for public trial four years later, together with Chen Boda and others.

Now Hua Guofeng seemed to emerge on top. He was appointed to be head of all three major hierarchies: chairperson of the Party, premier of the State Council, and chairperson of the Party's Military Affairs Commission. From October 21 through October 24 in 1976 a series of giant rallies were organized in Beijing and other cities to celebrate the ascent of the new leader.

An End and a Beginning

September and October in 1976 cut a line across modern Chinese history that is equaled only by one other momentous transition. On October 1, 1949, Mao had proclaimed the end of insurgency and the beginning of nation building. Twenty-seven years later, his death terminated an era dominated by Maoism. His preserved flesh and his edited words became holy relics manipulated by others as they addressed problems more complex and daunting than he had been prepared to comprehend.

It has been seen that in 1949 a great challenge faced Mao's talented team of revolutionaries—to organize and develop the world's largest nation. After a phase of copying Soviet formulas verbatim, they had to deal with a Mao-inspired effort to incorporate the spirit of Yanan in the process of modernization. Since 1955 an uneasy tension separated "Maoists" who refused to accept modernization that was not "Red" from a diverse opposition who were prepared to sacrifice some "redness" as the necessary price for modernization. In all that quarter of a century, this issue was never decisively settled. The final episode from 1969 to 1976 saw "radicalism" and "pragmatism" wrestle indecisively back and forth. With Mao's departure and the quick elimination of Jiang Qing's radicals, "Maoism" became, not orthodoxy, but merely one of several positions—and not the strongest one at that.

8

Return to Pragmatism: 1976–84

After Mao: Politics and Problems

The death of the Great Helmsman, although long anticipated, triggered profound changes throughout Chinese society. As for his physical remains, the surviving leaders ignored the long-standing practice of cremating fallen comrades and summoned from Vietnam the experts who had preserved that country's revolutionary patriarch, Ho Chi Minh. Thus, ironically, Mao, who had dominated everyone in the last forty years of his life, became a political pawn. His successors decided to erect a great memorial hall in the center of Tian'anmen Square to house a crystal coffin. Henceforth, as with Lenin in Moscow, thousands would be able to file past his august remains.

Those closest to his way of thinking, the Shanghai Group, now known derisively as the Gang of Four, were eliminated with remarkable speed. Locked up in Qincheng Prison on the outskirts of Beijing, they awaited whatever their victors had in store. In their heyday they had "capped" thousands with humiliating labels. Now they themselves were held up to public scorn as the self-indulgent empress and her claque of fawning courtiers. As they began the months and years of incarceration, their political program declined to the status of a discredited minority viewpoint.

What now became increasingly clear was that the Chinese nation was sick of the zeal and coercion associated with Maoism. Vast numbers had simply wearied of politics, of the endless succession of campaigns, of the ubiquitous loudspeakers. Although individualism has never been the supreme Chinese value, people deeply resented the unreasonable official intrusion into personal life, such as the youth rustication campaigns and work assignments that placed husbands and wives in cities hundreds of miles from one another. People were perhaps even more tired of poverty, which in some rural regions was truly extreme.

Mao's successors also experienced mounting concern over the seriousness and breadth of the country's problems. The economy was riddled with inefficiencies and irrationalities. The environment groaned under massive assaults on forests, cropland, water, and air. The PLA's weaponry was twenty years out of date, and tactical readiness was low. People spoke of a "lost generation," which a crippled education system had either trained poorly or not educated at all. The political system stood in need of radical repair to bring fresh blood into the aging bureaucracies, to reduce the role of cliques and factions, and to restore the Party's legitimacy in the eyes of a cynical nation. The time had come when two overarching and intertwining issues had to be settled. Of prime importance at the outset was a purely political matter: Who would rule? The successors, whoever they might be, would then have to find solutions to the host of problems besetting the country.

Power Struggle: October 1976–December 1978

The Uneasy Prominence of Hua Guofeng

The apparent answer to the first question came during the week of October 21, 1976. A huge rally asembled at Tian'anmen Square to be informed that Jiang Qing and the Gang of Four were counterrevolutionary capitalist roaders and had been arrested. At that,

Beijing and other cities exploded into delirious celebration marked by the "three empties" (empty liquor stores, empty fireworks stores, and empty hospital beds). Three days later another rally saw Hua Guofeng, who was wearing a military uniform for the occasion, declared to be Mao's successor as Chairperson of the Chinese Communist party. It will be remembered that Hua had been an able but obscure provincial leader brought to Beijing in 1971. He worked under Zhou Enlai, eventually becoming head of the security apparatus. He was clearly being groomed as one of the new top leaders. Mao liked him and nominated him as acting premier when Zhou died. This promotion "helicoptered" Hua over the head of Deng Xiaoping (who was just then being attacked by the radicals) and of Zhang Chunqiao (the radical favorite who, however, was unpopular with powerful Party and PLA leaders).

When the April 1976 Tian'anmen Incident triggered Deng's second fall, Hua rose still higher to become full premier. Then when Mao's death set off a power struggle, Hua became the favorite of certain military, security, and Party leaders who were determined to frustrate the ambitions of Jiang Qing. He was respectably Maoist. He claimed that the Chairman had personally given him a note containing these words: "With you in charge I am at ease." This would make him Mao's chosen successor. A competent and sensible bureaucrat, Hua posed no threat to this group, so they supported him in his October *coup* against the "Gang of Four." As mentioned previously, he soon was promoted to head all three major hierarchies: the Party, the government, and the army. Not even Mao himself had worn all three hats.

In China power resides more in persons than in positions. Hua's titles were important, but not decisive. Many of the Party elite remained unenthusiastic about this provincial upstart. Skeptics included victims of the Cultural Revolution and opponents of Maoist policies, with which Hua was too closely associated. Others were reluctant to follow a "helicopter" who lacked an old veteran's aura and connections. Cadres, both inside and outside the Party, wanted a more prestigious leader who could rally the nation. Professional-minded generals, who rejected Maoist guerrilla doctrines, were cool. It would not be easy for Hua to bring those of moderate and pragmatic persuasion into his political camp. Although he had been a center-leftist, the fall of the Gang of Four meant that he himself now occupied the vulnerable left end of the political spectrum.

Hua's supporters set about enhancing his image. A propaganda campaign touted him as the "wise" leader who had saved China from the Gang of Four. Posters and billboards depicted Hua sitting next to a smiling, approving Mao. Hua even let his short hair grow out into a swept-back cut reminiscent of the Chairman's. In an effort to strengthen the force of Mao's approval, Hua's backers began to urge the view that today's successors must faithfully carry out the departed leaders's wishes. In February 1977, one of Hua's faction wrote an editorial in *People's Daily*, urging the following:

> Let us hold still higher Chairman Mao's great banner and implement Chairman Mao's revolutionary line still more consciously. We resolutely defend *whatever* policies Chairman Mao has formulated and unswervingly adhere to *whatever* instructions Chairman Mao has issued . . .[1]

Propaganda could help his cause, but Hua also had to show that he could get results. The economy, in particular, required attention. Twenty years of Maoist economics, relieved by countercurrents of central planning and pragmatism breaking to the surface, had left the economy at a serious impasse. Although agricultural production had kept pace with population growth (no small feat given the huge population increase), a true breakthrough in productivity had not been achieved. The commune system was shot through with irrationalities and inefficiencies. Average peasant incomes were actually lower than they had been in 1957. In 1976, Sichuan Province, with over 10 percent of China's total population, suffered food shortages bordering on famine. This was a disappointing record, to say the least.

Nor was the situation much better in industry. True, China had, with only occasional setbacks, established a record of steady industrial growth that would be the envy of many Third World countries. But this growth had not been accompanied by increases in efficiency and productivity. Rather, it was the product of massive national savings and investment, especially in heavy industry. Less favored sectors, which investment policies had overlooked, were seriously underdeveloped. These included energy and transportation as well as housing and consumer goods. The living standard of workers was lower than in the 1950s, and urban unemployment, which was not even supposed to exist in a socialist society, was becoming serious.

Fortunately, like politicians everywhere, Hua could blame his predecessors, the Gang of Four and Lin Biao, for creating the mess. But to make his leadership credible, he would have to develop policies to treat these ills and bring the economy to a more healthy condition. His approach clarified during 1977 and 1978. It was an awkward mix of shopworn Maoist policies (especially in agriculture), centralized planning, technological solutions (which began to go under the name of "The Four Modernizations"), and time-tested political mobilization. He began to lay out his strategy in the huge December 1976 national agricultural conference on "Learning from Dazhai" and at an industrial conference on "Learning from Daqing," which he called the following April.

Embracing Maoist institutions (such as the communes) while at the same time promoting "modernization" in agriculture, industry, science and technology, and national defense (a formulation that went back to earlier initiatives of Zhou Enlai), he expected that China could launch a new "leap forward." In February 1978, at the Fifth National People's Congress, he announced an extremely ambitious Ten-Year Plan for 1976 to 1985. This plan called for massive investments in industry, technological upgrading of agriculture, a flowering of science and technology, and rapid military modernization. At the same time Hua pushed two Maoist slogans: "Take grain as the key link" and

"Let us go all out, aim high, and achieve greater, faster, better and more economical results in building socialism." [2] In retrospect, this approach seems hopelessly optimistic and hybrid. At the time, however, it was enthusiastically embraced by the general population.

Unfortunately for Hua, neither his political efforts nor his economic policies were enough to save him. The pragmatists were growing stronger. One reason was the return of cadres and intellectuals formerly persecuted by the Gang of Four. Many had already been reinstated by Deng between 1973 and 1976. Now that the radicals had been discredited, it was difficult to resist the rehabilitation of their remaining victims. For Hua this was risky because he and his supporters could not wash away their own association with certain persecutions. Furthermore, his faction had few political connections with these returnees. There was one victim awaiting rehabilitation who cast an especially long shadow. Deng Xiaoping, detested by the Gang of Four, was eagerly awaited by millions as the closest equivalent to Zhou Enlai. He was a formidable leader. He had been Zhou's chosen successor and even had close personal links to Mao from the 1930s. His supporters could be found in all three power hierarchies because he had at one time or another acted as chief executive of the Party, the army, and the state. With the Gang's arrest, the campaign to criticize Deng ceased.

Hua Guofeng could not forget that the April 5, 1976, Tiananmen Incident, which some of his present supporters had crushed and to which he owed his premiership, had also been the event that precipitated Deng's ouster. If the Dengists returned, it was not unlikely that they would seek revenge. But Hua had little choice. Pressures within and outside the Party to redress past injustices were too strong. Deng wrote Hua two letters in which he applauded the Gang's arrest, admitted his own shortcomings, and pledged his support. Hints and rumors about his rehabilitation began to circulate. In January 1977, there was even a popular demonstration in his favor on the anniversary of Zhou's death. At that time much of Tian'anmen Square was fenced off as the construction site of Chairman Mao's Memorial Hall. People came and plastered these fences with posters commemorating Zhou Enlai and in many cases calling for Deng's return. In March 1977, the Party leadership decided to reinstate Deng, and by April he was quietly working in the State Council.

Deng Xiaoping Redivivus: 1977–78

From Deng's return in mid-1977 to late 1978, while Hua Guofeng remained China's apparent leader, Deng rebuild his own political position. He increased his already numerous supporters at all levels and continued to remove Gang of Four loyalists. A key associate in this task was Hu Yaobang, whose career must be sketched here. Hu Yaobang (pronounced something like "Who Yaow-bang") was then in his early sixties. He seemed to be cut from the same cloth as Deng. Neither was much above five feet tall, and both were brilliant, canny, and able administrators. Hu probably never graduated from primary school. Like Deng, he was blunt. During the Cultural Revolution, Red Guards were shocked at his irreverence toward Mao. He said, "If we have to speak [Mao's words] as though we were reciting classical texts, then language and words would eventually become obsolete and dead. That is the way thinking becomes ossified, rigid, and stagnant."[3]

A veteran of the Long March, Hu served under Deng Xiaoping during the anti-Japanese war. From that time forward, his career rose and fell with Deng's. Brought to Beijing by the latter in 1952, he spent fourteen years directing the Communist Youth League, a key organization in the recruitment of new Party members. The Cultural Revolution destroyed the League while both Deng and Hu were purged. When Deng returned in the early 1970s, he rehabilitated Hu, who became Party secretary of the Chinese Academy of Sciences, an important institution in China's modernization. There he worked to liberalize and improve the treatment of intellectuals and scientists. This did not endear him to the Shanghai Group, and, as a result, when Deng fell

again in 1976, Hu was not far behind. With Deng's second res-
urrection, Hu returned to an even more sensitive position at Party
center in charge of personnel. He actively reinstated Cultural
Revolution victims. Because of this, a steady stream of returning cadres marked the last half of 1977 and continued in 1978.
By late 1978 virtually every province experienced dismissals and
new appointments.

Deng Xiaoping quickly became the champion of popular policies, especially in the economy. In contrast to Chairman Hua's
advocacy of collectivism and big-push mobilization, Deng wanted
to revive Chen Yun's policies from the early 1960s and Zhou
Enlai's program of the early 1970s. His supporters turned the
Chinese Academy of Social Sciences into a "think tank." Studies produced there argued that "economic laws" could not be
vitiated by revolutionary rhetoric. They urged planned, systematic growth based on material incentives rather than on spiritual
rewards. In agriculture, this meant private plots, handicrafts, and
markets where peasants could sell their sideline products. They
felt that the state must reduce its massive commitment to heavy
industry while investing more in agriculture and consumer goods
production. To overcome backwardness, China must increase
foreign trade and import technology from the industrialized West
and Japan.

The Dengists also promoted cultural liberalization and openness to the outside world. Tabooed films, foreign and traditional
novels, and traditional art began to make their appearance. In
the spring of 1977, bans on Beethoven and Shakespeare were
lifted. In education, a fall conference called for a return to college entrance examinations, a system of high-quality "key"
schools, high academic standards, and greater status and rewards for teachers and intellectuals. The first entrance examinations were held immediately. Tourism and trade with Western
countries increased rapidly. Relations even improved with Yugoslavia, one of the countries Mao especially detested as revisionist. In September 1977 one might have seen the Chairman
stirring in his crystal coffin as the very first foreign guest en-

tered the newly completed Memorial Hall. It was Yugoslavia's Broz Tito, concluding a friendly state visit.

Party Meetings and the Third Plenum of December 1978

Deng's rise was punctuated by attacks on the Hua camp and by several important Party meetings. In July 1977 the Central Committee met in plenary session. It expelled the Gang of Four from all positions, calling Jiang Qing a renegade, Zhang Chunqiao a Nationalist special agent, Yao Wenyuan an alien class element, Wang Hongwen a new bourgeois element, and all of them "bourgeois careerist, conspirator, counter-revolutionary double-dealers."[4] At the same time, the Plenum formalized Deng's resumption of his old offices.

A month later the Eleventh Party Congress further solidified the new political constellation. The Cultural Revolution was declared over. Deng regained his positions as the Party vice-chairperson, the State Council vice-premier, and the vice-chairperson of the Military Affairs Commission. He delivered the concluding address in his characteristic no-nonsense style.

> We must revive and carry forward the practice of seeking truth from facts. . . . Deed and word must match and theory and practice must be closely integrated. We must reject flashiness without substance and every sort of boasting. There must be less empty talk and more hard work . . .[5]

In June 1978, Deng gave another speech strongly emphasizing the principle that "practice is the sole criterion of truth." He supported his views with Mao Zedong quotations and suggested that even Mao's pronouncements were correct only if they worked. Blind obedience, said Deng, could only stifle progress.

This emphasis on "truth from facts" and "practice as the sole criterion of truth" was the core of Deng's counterattack against the "Whateverist" supporters of Hua Guofeng. By subjecting even Mao's own pronouncements to the test of pragmatism and

DENG XIAOPING

empirical verification, Deng was undercutting the dogmatic reverence on which his rivals depended. In July 1978, to discredit further the "Whateverists," Deng's supporters published for the first time Mao's 1962 talk to a Central Committee conference. Every newspaper ran the item in which Mao admitted that "when it comes to productive forces I still know very little . . . Haven't we done many foolish things during the last few years. . . ?"[6] Surprised readers of this quotation could only ask themselves how anyone could advocate doing *whatever* Mao said if Mao himself admitted to error?

It is impossible to say just when the balance of power altered decisively in favor of Deng Xiaoping's group and away from Hua Guofeng. Certainly, after the lengthy inner-Party meetings in November and December 1978 and the Central Committee's Third Plenum, which followed in late December, Hua and the Maoists were fighting a hopeless rearguard action. Decisive personnel and policy shifts took place. Hua Guofeng, the "Whateverists," and other allies saw their position slip badly. Some were forced to criticize themselves. Some lost posts. From this time forward, the press stopped referring to "our wise leader

Chairman Hua" and simply called him "Comrade Hua Guofeng."

Persons associated with Deng Xiaoping, on the other hand, rose. An important symbolic change was the posthumous rehabilitation of Peng Dehuai, together with others who had suffered at the hands of Mao or the radicals. It was announced that 100,000 people who had been punished as "rightists" after the 1957 Hundred Flowers campaign would be rehabilitated. Chen Yun, Hu Yaobang, and two other Deng supporters were appointed to the Politburo. Hu became secretary general of the Party.

Several formal statements on past events signaled a complete reversal of Maoism. The Tian'anmen riots of April 1976, which had toppled Deng and led to Hua's promotion, were now declared to be "revolutionary," not "counterrevolutionary." The communiqué of the Plenum admitted, albeit in a restrained way, that Mao had made mistakes and that the Cultural Revolution had faults. China's principal intellectual newspaper ran an article strongly criticizing Yao Wenyuan's 1965 attack on the play *Hai Rui Dismissed from Office*. Yao's essay, which had launched the Cultural Revolution, was now decried as "counterrevolutionary" and "Fascist." As was later revealed, Chen Yun encapsulated the views of most, inside and outside the Party, when he told his colleagues:

> Had Chairman Mao died in 1956, there would have been no doubt that he was a great leader of the Chinese people. . . . Had he died in 1966, his meritorious achievements would have been somewhat tarnished, but his overall record still very good. Since he actually died in 1976, there is nothing we can do about it.[7]

Finally, the Third Plenum turned its back on neo-Maoist economic policies. The directions that had been established under Deng in 1975 were vindicated. What was most important, the pragmatic agricultural policies of the early 1960s reemerged while the collectivist Dazhai approach went into complete eclipse.

By the end of 1978, the Deng alternative had overshadowed

Hua Guofeng. The first phase of the post-Mao era was over. The question had been settled, at least for the short run and probably for the longer run, as to what kind of leadership and policies China would have. Under Deng, China would abandon revolutionary radicalism. It was yet to be seen whether the existing Party, state, and military structures could successfully be remolded into a modified socialist system capable of coping with the complex problems facing China in the late twentieth century.

Deng Takes Charge: 1979–81

Liberalization and Democracy Wall

To a degree that surpassed anything yet seen under the People's Republic, the Party meetings of November and December 1978 took place against a background of unrestrained ventilation of public opinion. Mobilization of mass opinion was, of course, a favorite technique of the Chinese Communists. But except for brief spasms in the "Hundred Flowers" campaign and the Cultural Revolution, such public outbursts had always been orchestrated from above. Now, like a mild rain after long drought, appeared the famous Democracy Wall in Beijing and similar spots in other cities. By late November 1978, it was clear that the Party was not going to crack down on the numerous expressions of opinion that had been appearing in posters at the wall in front of Beijing's municipal bus station. Even the following charge against Mao, which in earlier times would have earned immediate punishment for its author, went unmolested by the security personnel who monitored the wall:

> Try and ask yourself the question: How could Lin Biao rise to such power without Chairman Mao's support? . . . Did Chairman Mao realize the true nature of Jiang Qing? . . . How could the Gang of Four start an anti-Rightist campaign to topple Vice-Premier Deng from power without Chairman Mao's knowledge?

. . . How could the Tiananmen Incident get labeled a counter-revolutionary act without Chairman Mao nodding his head?[8]

The public response at this place and at other walls around the country was electric, especially when it became known that Deng Xiaoping approved. A steady throng of citizens visited, read, and copied down the texts of the hundreds of posters, which expressed a broad spectrum of views. Scores of unofficial magazines were published and hawked openly on the street. Although this "democracy" was but a fragile blossom, for only official toleration allowed it to exist, still the depth and intensity of feeling manifested there gave the leaders a clear reading of the public mood. For Deng's purposes it was very useful.

The liberalization strengthened Deng's hand against the radicals at the Third Plenum and then persisted even after that Plenum adjourned. The pragmatists had not yet consolidated their control and found Democracy Wall a useful source of continuing pressure on the radicals. Another positive feature of this movement had to do with Sino-American relations. On December 15, 1978, just on the eve of the Third Plenum, both countries announced that full diplomatic relations would be established on the first day of 1979. By late December negotiations were under way for a visit to America by Deng Xiaoping. An impression of increasing civil rights in China would help neutralize the conservative opposition in America. Moreover, the leaders recognized that successful modernization hinged on the enthusiasm of the intelligentsia, who had suffered grievously in the Cultural Revolution. For these reasons, through the early months of 1979, the Democracy Wall movement was given a latitude far greater than either the 1957 Hundred Flowers campaign or the liberalization of 1961 and 1962.

In a variety of ways, the Party signaled its support for the warmer breeze. Spontaneous expressions of dissent went unchecked, as in the case of the tens of thousands of wretched peasants who descended on Beijing and other cities to press for relief for the political injustices they had suffered. Little was done to discourage wall posters, which were being pasted up not only in approved places but virtually all over the capital as well.

The official press joined the criticisms of the Left. In January 1979, *Liberation Army Daily* published an account by nieces and nephews of Peng Dehuai that described their uncle's pathetic death in 1974. According to them, he was held in solitary confinement as his health failed, deprived of reading material, writing instruments, or even such a tiny luxury as natural light. Meanwhile, Radio Beijing and the New China News Agency criticized the Antirightist Movement of 1957, the Great Leap Forward, and the 1976 cashiering of Deng Xiaoping. The Gang of Four, until now labeled ultra*rightists*, were redesignated ultra*leftists*—a signal that radicalism could now be criticized.

In February 1979, an editor of *People's Daily* made a speech likening Mao to Stalin. He voiced the widely held view that Mao should take responsibility for the Gang's excesses and for Lin Biao. He even charged that Mao had been trying to destroy Zhou Enlai during his last years. Although this speech circulated only as a classified document within Party circles, its sensational charges were widely disseminated through the political grapevine. Veiled criticisms of Hua Guofeng appeared in the press. Attention was called to his share of responsibility for mislabeling the Gang of Four as rightists and for Deng Xiaoping's dismissal in 1976. Other steps were also taken to demonstrate the Party's seriousness. In January 1979, class labels were removed from former landlords and their families, who had been persecuted for years. Then in February three Guangzhou (Canton) men who had been jailed in 1974 for posting a famous manifesto called "Socialist Democracy and a Legal System" were released and exonerated.

The unprecedented openness to the outside world, which had accelerated since 1977, continued to grow. Suddenly there were hundreds of thousands of foreign tourists and overseas Chinese in the major cities. Although these visitors were subtly insulated from too much unsupervised contact with the ordinary Chinese, foreign journalists were now able to interview people and meet

Chinese citizens. Never in the history of the PRC had people enjoyed such free contact with foreigners and so much information about the outside world. Shortly after Chinese and American ambassadors assumed their posts, Deng Xiaoping visited the United States. Television and the press gave extensive coverage to his trip. Viewers saw exotica like Disneyland and views of the typical American household, a cornucopia of consumer goods. These programs had a sensational impact, especially coming on the heels of a widely viewed travelogue on life in Japan.

In Beijing and other cities, large numbers of people responded to these signals. Most striking were the wall posters and some of their authors. Although posters had frequently been, and continued to be, produced by Party factions, in the winter and spring of 1978–79, unofficial posters of every description vastly outnumbered the others. Among the most notorious was the "Nineteen Point Declaration" of a gentle, daring human rights activist named Ren Wending, one of the first individuals to sign his own name instead of a pseudonym. Appearing in early January, this poster called for reforms that would have transformed the People's Republic into a liberal democracy: free elections, an independent judiciary, a multiparty system, an end to special perquisites for Party members, and more freedom of information.

Even more remarkable was a younger, even bolder man named Wei Jingsheng. He was the son of an important Party cadre with ties to Chen Yun. Wei ranks as the most brilliant of the dissidents. His alienation was especially remarkable because his family was thoroughly Communist and he enjoyed the benefits of being a cadre's son. He had been a Red Guard and an officer in the PLA. But apparently the Cultural Revolution had shattered his faith. In wall posters and in a magazine called *Explorations*, Wei marshaled devastating arguments against oppression. His first famous poster, entitled "The Fifth Modernization," proclaimed that "democracy is a prerequisite for rapid economic modernization. Without this precondition modernization of production and livelihood is impossible, all pledges by any Great Man to the contrary notwithstanding.''[9] With unblinking directness he challenged his readers:

> according to the definition of the Marxist ancestors, socialism means that the people, or the proletariat, are their own masters. Let me ask the Chinese workers and peasants: With the meager wages you get every month, whose master and what kind of master can you be?[10]

Another figure who gained some attention at this time was a young woman municipal worker named Fu Yuehua. A few years before, her superior cadre had raped her, but when she brought charges against him, it was she who suffered ostracism while he went completely free. Her deep sense of injustice impelled her to take up the cause of the thousands of peasants demanding redress. She organized these inarticulate people into marches and chants, hoping to goad the system into taking up their cases.

The Clampdown Against Democracy Wall

In late January 1979, after leading a large procession, however, Fu Yuehua was quietly arrested. This was one sign that what had happened during three or four months of loosened restraints had pushed the leaders beyond the limits they would tolerate. Cadres at all levels of the Party had been complaining about the posters and protests, arguing that they were creating chaos.

At about this same time, a crisis developed regarding urban youth who had been sent down to the villages. Shanghai and some other large metropolises assigned young people permanently to distant regions. (In most other cities they went to nearby villages.) These distant exiles were permitted to visit home for Chinese New Year. There were many others who, in one way or another, filtered back to the cities from their rural assignments. During the first half of 1979, around five million of them returned, leaving an equal number still in the villages. Since 1977 rumors circulated that the rustication program would be terminated. But there was no indication that those already sent down would be allowed back permanently. Outright defiance exploded in February as several hundred thousand desperate Shanghai youth bluntly refused to return to a peasant existence. Demonstrations erupted. The railroad station was seized. Similar events occurred elsewhere, answered with arrests.

Later in the month, as the public was being told about China's great success in punishing Vietnam (see further on), Wei Jingsheng passed on to foreign correspondents a Defense Ministry document that revealed heavy casualties and listed the names of the commanding officers. Although this document was of no real strategic importance, Wei's action could be construed as a breach of national security. This and the increasing extent to which Canadian, American, and other Western journalists were building friendships and contacts with ordinary Chinese people alarmed the government.

The reaction was a crackdown. In March 1979, shortly after Fu Yuehua's arrest, the security police took Wei Jingsheng into custody. In early April, Ren Wending, who ironically disliked Wei and disagreed with his radical ideas, nevertheless pasted up a poster against the jailing of Wei. This only precipitated his own arrest. Other activists in several cities were seized. That the government was concerned with foreign reaction is evidenced by the fact that the entire Western press corps was lured out of Beijing on a trip to the southwest just prior to the clampdown on Democracy Wall.

On the eve of his arrest, Wei Jingsheng expressed his chagrin. Lashing out at Deng Xiaoping's apparent betrayal, Wei said, "He now want[s] to strip off his mask of protector of democracy and suppress the democratic movement. He is prepared to . . . resolutely safeguard dictatorial politics"[11] But perhaps Wei should not have been surprised. Certainly, there were those whose longer memories made them suspicious of the liberalization. One old man had warned:

The so-called freedom is limited to the Democracy Wall. Never use this freedom in your own unit or any other place where you are well-known. Remember the historical lesson of "luring the snake out of the hole" in 1957, and don't forget the label of "counter-revolutionary." Otherwise, what you say now is like money deposited in the bank. As soon as a movement comes, it will come back to you, capital and interest.[12]

However, the repression was neither widespread nor decisive because the pragmatists were ambivalent, desiring to ease cultural and political restrictions while maintaining the Party's unquestioned dominance. Subject to pressures from both sides, they were alternatively permissive and restrictive through the rest of 1979 and 1980. Unofficial magazines that had emerged in 1978 continued to be tolerated. Peasant protesters were still to be seen in Beijing in the fall of 1980. Beijing students demonstrated against the continued military occupation of university buildings, a legacy of the 1968 suppression of the Red Guards. In Changsha, students also demonstrated over Party interference against a non-Communist candidate for election to the local people's congress. In the National People's Congress in September 1980, there were even a few negative votes cast, an unprecedented occurrence in this rubber-stamp legislature. All the while, dissent of a different sort was under way as thousands, mostly from Guangdong Province, fled to Hong Kong. (These migrations had continued steadily since 1949, sometimes at a trickle and sometimes in a flood.)

On the other hand, the government sporadically moved against the liberalizing trends. The wall posters were controlled by various means. In March 1979, Deng enunciated "four basic principles" that poster writers were not permitted to criticize, namely, socialism, the dictatorship of the proletariat, the leadership of the Communist party, and Marxism-Leninism and Mao Zedong Thought. These constraints were reminiscent of the boundaries to free expression with which Mao had signaled the end of the Hundred Flowers campaign in 1957. Restrictions were imposed

on places where posters could be displayed. The security police
sometimes harassed their authors. Wei Jingsheng and Fu Yuehua went on trial and, although they defended themselves valiantly, were declared guilty and sent to prison as examples to
others. Democracy Wall itself was declared closed in December
1979, replaced by an inaccessible wall on the outskirts of the
city, which dissidents dubbed "Bureaucracy Wall." Unofficial
magazines were suppressed in 1980. Finally, in August 1980,
the formal right to free expression through wall posters and other
media was blithely eliminated from the constitution by the National People's Congress. Contacts between Chinese and foreigners trickled off to almost nothing under the pressure of renewed restrictions and retaliations. Yet this did not amount to
complete repression. Although the government would not tolerate all views, it also stopped far short of the violent overreaction
of 1957, in which hundreds of thousands were persecuted.

Vietnam

In 1978 and 1979, China's worsening relations with Vietnam
exploded into open warfare. Although it was not a full-scale or
prolonged war, the repercussions were widely felt, especially in
the economy. The heart of the conflict was China's dispute with
the Soviet Union. Although both countries had supported North
Vietnam against the United States, they had done so with much
disagreement and bickering. China's proximity and cultural af-
finity may have been advantages in dealings with Vietnam. But
these were offset by Russia's greater resources and by China's
new friendliness toward the United States. The fiercely independent North Vietnamese were less than enthusiastic when Zhou
Enlai and Richard Nixon signed the Shanghai Communiqué in
1972.

The Chinese made the situation worse through their obsessive
anti-Sovietism. By 1975, as American power waned, they worried about growing Russian influence in Southeast Asia, and they
badgered Hanoi to line up against Moscow as the price for Chinese
support. This made it difficult for the Vietnamese to remain

equidistant from both powers. When it came to a choice, Moscow had more to offer and demanded less in return. Consequently, by late 1978, the Vietnamese were ready to sign a friendship and mutual defense treaty with the Soviet Union. In Beijing's eyes this seemed like unforgivable ingratitude in view of China's contribution of manpower (over 300,000 people) and money (billions of Chinese dollars) to Hanoi's war against the United States.

The issue that brought China and Vietnam to blows was Cambodia. That unfortunate country had been dragged into the Vietnamese conflict in 1970 with a coup by Lon Nol, an openly anti-Communist general. His regime, in turn, succumbed to a Communist insurgency in April 1975, the same month in which the South Vietnamese government surrendered to North Vietnam. This seemed to bode well for China, for the People's Republic had influence with the Khmer Rouge, the Cambodian guerrilla organization. If Cambodia became a client state, China would have a counterweight to Russia's growing influence in Vietnam. To be sure, Cambodia was far smaller and weaker than Vietnam, but it was better than nothing at all. Immediately, Beijing moved to support the new regime, which called itself "the State of Democratic Kampuchea" as of January 1976. Economic and military aid in the reported amount of nearly one billion U.S. dollars was promised over the next five or six years. Chinese arms and advisers began to flow into the country.

Unfortunately, China and her new ally overplayed their hands, with disastrous results. The new government under Pol Pot showed itself to be one of the most radical and callous regimes in the world. The policy of brutally removing the entire urban population to the countryside,, shocked world opinion. Thousands upon thousands of people perished while still other thousands became refugees, either into Thailand to the west or into southern Vietnam to the east. Kampuchea also quickly alienated the Vietnamese communists. Like many of the general population, ethnic Vietnamese in Kampuchea were badly treated, and Pol Pot soon became belligerent toward Hanoi.

By the spring of 1977, Kampuchea and Vietnam were beginning to engage in armed clashes, a dangerous prospect for the smaller and greener Kampuchean forces. Later in the year, Hanoi became furious on discovering Chinese complicity in Phnom Penh's aggression. In January 1978, Vietnamese forces thrust into Kampuchea, then withdrew. Subsequent attacks led up to a full-scale military intervention the following December by 100,000 Vietnamese troops and 20,000 friendly Kampucheans. They took the capital, Phnom Penh, on January 7, 1979.

Sino-Vietnamese relations were further poisoned by Hanoi's policies toward its large Chinese minority. Hostility toward these people stemmed partly from China's involvement in Kampuchea. Anti-Chinese resentment deepened when Beijing withdrew all aid and technical assistance from Vietnam in the summer of 1978 (reminiscent of, although less abrupt than, Khrushchev's withdrawal from China in 1960). Another source of hostility was Hanoi's program of expropriating the capitalists in the south, many of whom were Chinese. By 1978 thousands of refugees were streaming into China from north Vietnam while still more thousands were fleeing the south, bound for non-Communist countries despite high seas, rickety vessels, and pirates. These were the famous "boat people," two-thirds of them ethnic Chinese.

Thus as Deng Xiaoping and his followers were gaining control of the government in 1977 and 1978, they had to confront these serious developments in Southeast Asia. Incensed over the treatment of ethnic Chinese, embarrassed by the horrid reputation of their ally Pol Pot, dismayed by Vietnam's invasion of Kampuchea, and alarmed by the loss of influence in the region, the Chinese resorted to military pressure. Even while Deng was visiting the United States in January 1979, plans were being finalized for the invasion. On February 17, soon after Deng's return, 75,000 to 85,000 PLA troops "counterattacked" at twenty points along the northern Vietnamese border. They hoped for a quick success like the 1962 surgical strike into India, where the enemy had been quickly subdued and Chinese forces could withdraw without costly delays or casualties. In the course of sixteen days, the Chinese attained several of their military objectives (strategic positions along the frontier and the capture of four provincial towns), but without the ease of the 1962 war. Their casualties were high, and it became apparent that the PLA was not an effective instrument of modern warfare. They failed to force Vietnam to withdraw significant troops from Kampuchea. By mid-March all Chinese forces had been withdrawn, proclaiming that they had taught Hanoi a lesson.

Soviet military forces on China's border increased during this period, and Moscow made ominous rumblings over the Vietnam invasion. But Moscow, in effect, declined to intervene against China, probably because of the danger of starting a worldwide conflict. Although Soviet inaction may have demonstrated that in Moscow détente came first and Hanoi second, still the Chinese failed to lessen Vietnamese dependence on the USSR. Moreover, Laotian support for Vietnam and the expulsion of Chinese advisers from Laos accomplished a total eclipse of Chinese influence in Indochina. Since that time a state of armed hostility has existed along the Sino-Vietnamese frontier, with Beijing very unhappy over what it considers Soviet encirclement of the People's Republic.

Economic Reforms

The Third Plenum at the end of 1978 marked the start of a fundamental change in economic policy. It was increasingly apparent that Hua's continued allegiance to elements of Maoism and his overly ambitious Ten-Year Plan had not even begun to clear away the economic difficulties. Many problems enumerated earlier in this chapter continued to fester. Among other things, one-fourth of all state enterprises were operating in the red, placing a heavy burden on the government's budget. Hua's Ten-Year Plan had triggered a binge of industrial investments far in excess the state's ability to pay for them, and some were so ill-planned that they simply represented gigantic waste. For example, new steel plants threatened to consume half of the available electricity in a province, and many projects would soon be sitting half-finished for want of basic building materials. Scientific and technical personnel as well as middle-level managers were in desperately short supply. Agriculture was still barely keeping pace with population growth, and rural-urban income differences remained scandalously wide. To compound the problem, the heavy costs of the Vietnam hostilities put further pressures on the government's budget.

Consequently, at the Third Plenum, decisions were taken to abandon the ten-year program and to initiate a cooling-down period. More modest investment, especially in heavy industry, would allow agriculture and consumer goods production to begin catching up. By the middle of 1979, Hua Guofeng himself was forced to admit that his ten-year program had been unrealistic and that the years 1979–81 would be three years of "adjustment, reconstruction, consolidation, and improvement." There would be less investment and increased consumption. Funds for the expansion of industries such as steel, machinery, and chemicals would be curbed. This led in 1979 to halting hundreds of large projects and thousands of small ones. Concurrently, investment in agriculture and consumer goods industries increased (although total investment in these sectors still remained considerably below the level of industry). Chen Yun, the perennial exponent of economic pragmatism, reemerged to head economic policy in the State Council. In August 1980, Deng spoke at a Politburo meeting, saying that the defects of the system must be corrected; otherwise "people will say: 'Why is the socialist system incapable of solving problems that the capitalist system has already solved?'" [13]

Socialism received a new bare-bones definition: public ownership plus remuneration according to labor. So long as these two requirements were met, any arrangement could be called "socialist." Maoist "moral" incentives gave way to material rewards. Thus, a fundamental tenet of the economic system was replaced by its opposite: Productivity would henceforth be promoted through individual rewards rather than collective political

Table 3. China's Foreign Trade

	1950–60	1961–70	1971–76	1977–83
Average annual trade with all countries (billions of $ U.S.)	2.8	3.6	12.4	37.6
Trade with Communist countries (% total Chinese imports and exports)	65%	31%	17%	8%
Trade with non-Communist countries (% total Chinese imports and exports)	36%	69%	83%	91%

Sources: A. Doak Barnett, *China's Economy in Global Perspective* (Washington, D.C.: Brookings Institution, 1981), 152–53; Nai-Ruenn Chen, *China's Economy and Foreign Trade, 1981–1985* (Washington, D.C.: U.S. Department of Commerce, International Trade Administration, 1984), 41–42.

exhortation. At the same time, efforts were made to improve the problem-ridden management practices in the industrial sector because the huge hierarchy of economic ministries and enterprises desperately needed a thorough, long-term revamping. Another Maoist shibboleth, "self-reliance," disappeared. Rather than recoiling from the idea of contact with the outside world, new policymakers showed a fresh openness to foreign loans, foreign technical consultants, and even foreign investment. In 1980 four "special economic zones" were established in south coastal China, where foreign businesses could establish joint ventures to manufacture export products with cheap Chinese labor, an arrangement that Mao would have abhorred as capitalistic exploitation. Table 3 illustrates not only the increase in China's foreign trade, especially since Mao's death, but also the dramatic way in which China's exports and imports, once exchanged predominantly with Communist countries, have come to be traded overwhelmingly with non-Communist countries.

In agriculture the Dazhai model was repudiated as was the Maoist policy of requiring grain production everywhere. And the beginnings were laid for the most dramatically successful reform of all, the so-called "responsibility system." These rural production arrangements were first tried out in selected provinces, most notably starting in 1977 in troubled Sichuan under the leadership of Zhao Ziyang (see further on). In 1979 the new arrangements were promoted nationally and by the early 1980s overtook virtually the entire rural sector. There were many variants, but the essence of the system was a long-term contractual relationship between production teams (villages) and households. These contracts specified which parcels of land would be assigned to each household and established a fixed amount of grain to be sold to the state. Above-quota production belonged to the household and could be sold for profit. Agricultural sideline occupations and specialized households (such as in forestry, fishing, and transportation) also expanded rapidly under official encouragement. It would be incorrect to label these new changes "capitalism" as has often been done because ownership of the land remained with the production team, and the state retained the right to intrude in a variety of ways. Still, the commune, the jewel of the Maoist system, became a pale shadow of its former self. With management devolving on teams and households, communes and brigades were increasingly left with only small-scale rural industries to manage.

Consumerism flourished. Per capita GNP for 1980 was nearly 12 percent higher than in 1977 and output of food and specific products such as cloth and bicycles increased dramatically. The hundreds of thousands of overseas Chinese who were now permitted to visit relatives entered the country bringing large quantities of televisions, appliances, and other desired goods. Books and entertainment became more diverse and more available, even including many foreign and traditional works. Product advertising even began to appear in some cities.

These bold new policies were, of course, unable immediately to cure the accumulated ills stemming from a basically underdeveloped economy and a problem-ridden bureaucratic structure. For example, although agriculture and light industry immediately began to rebound, it proved difficult to reduce overall levels of investment because many ministries, localities, and enterprises were determined to expand no matter what. The government began to incur large budget deficits. China's steady price level, long held up as a model for capitalists to envy, began to rise. There was still the huge population, basically poor and rather starkly divided between the worse off and the better off. Illiteracy and lack of skills slowed modernization. Nevertheless, in the two or three years after Deng Xiaoping became China's preeminent leader in 1978, shifts in economic policy showed promise of effectively addressing the country's massive problems. Figure 5 in Chapter 4 shows that overall national income, adjusted for price changes, took a slight downturn in 1976 and then began a long-term resumption of growth under the emerging new policies.

Deng's Triumph and Political Reforms

Although the Third Plenum of late 1978 signaled the emergence of Deng Xiaoping's power, the transition was not yet complete. Hua Guofeng remained the formal head of Party, army, and government, and Deng continued to defer ceremonially. But Deng was as determined to make fundamental changes in the political system as he was to reform the economy. He was also determined to replace the remaining Maoists with moderates and to begin the transfer of power to a new generation of leaders.

In fact, the Party and state apparatus was badly in need of overhaul. Ten years of Cultural Revolution and radicalism—the tumult, purges, and agitation for mass participation—had corroded the inner working of the organization. In the absence of clear, accepted procedures, the role of factions had increased to the point where the system was a vast congeries of political machines. "Connections" meant everything. Not rational and legal procedures, but bribes, favors, and the arbitrary exercise of authority determined what got accomplished. In the eyes of the public, both these characteristics and the remembrances of the Cultural Revolution undercut the legitimacy of the regime. As one student of the subject describes it:

> The leadership's capacity to acquire good information, to base decisions on the substantive merits of issues, to have those deci-

sions implemented in a prudent and conscientious way, and to elicit support from the population for this entire process had all seriously eroded between 1966 and 1976.[14]

In late 1978 and early 1979, several prominent victims of the Cultural Revolution were rehabilitated. Notable was Peng Zhen, who had been an early casualty of the Red Guards. He now took on the important task of overseeing the creation of legal codes and of orchestrating the trial of the Gang of Four. Liu Shaoqi's widow, Wang Guangmei, was released from Qincheng Prison. The deceased Peng Dehuai was honored with a memorial meeting, thus ending nearly twenty years of public disgrace. Lesser figures were remembered as well, as, for example, the sadistically murdered Zhang Zhixin. (Back in 1975 her executioners had first cut her larynx so that she would be unable to shout, "Long live Chairman Mao!") Most stunning of all, admitting that he had been grievously maligned, the Party announced in September the posthumous rehabilitation of Liu Shaoqi, "China's Khrushchev."

As these rehabilitations took place, two new men were rising, Hu Yaobang and Zhao Ziyang. Hu, long associated with Deng Xiaoping, reemerged with his old boss in 1977, as noted earlier, and helped engineer the return of moderates to power. His role within the Party became increasingly important. By early 1980 he had been named general secretary of the Party (Deng's former post) and made a member of the Politburo. Zhao Ziyang entered the picture slightly later and via a different route. Because he quickly became a central figure, it is necessary to pause and describe his background.

Zhao was born into a landlord family in 1919. His education stopped with graduation from senior middle school, probably because of the anti-Japanese war. At thirteen he joined the Communist Youth League in his home province of Henan. In 1938 shortly after the war broke out, he was admitted as a full member to the Party. He was not yet twenty. Zhao spent the years of the anti-Japanese war serving the Party in various capacities in and around his home region. Then shortly after liberation he was sent south to Guangdong Province as part of a general dispatch of outside personnel to spur on land reform. He arrived there in 1951 and over the next fifteen years built his career in Guangdong, where he became the second-ranking Party leader. His duties ranged across the spectrum, but his special expertise was agriculture. He emerged during this period as an exponent of pragmatic measures to increase farm output.

The Cultural Revolution temporarily ended Zhao's career. After the January "power seizure" of 1967, he seems to have been assigned to a May Seventh Cadre School in Inner Mongolia. This exile may have been a blessing, for it kept him away from the more populous areas where the Red Guards ran rampant. Surfacing in 1971 in Inner Mongolia, he was soon transferred back to Guangdong, perhaps as part of Zhou Enlai's national shake-up after the Lin Biao affair. Gradually, he reemerged as a provincial leader. He also became a Central Committee member in 1973, indicative of his growing national prominence. He supported the pragmatic policies of Zhou Enlai and Deng Xiaoping although he knew how to spout leftist rhetoric when necessary.

His big opportunity came in late 1975, when he was transferred to Sichuan Province as Party first secretary. This huge province, China's most populous, was suffering acute economic hardship and political disarray after a decade of radical turmoil and shifting policies. Zhao Enlai's efforts to ameliorate these problems halted with Zhou's death and the second fall of Deng. Finally in mid-1977, with Mao gone and Deng returning to power, Zhao Ziyang introduced pragmatic agrarian and industrial reforms in Sichuan. These policies included using material incentives, allowing planned and market economy to coexist, promoting rational management techniques and expertise, looking abroad for expertise, promoting academic reforms, and encouraging birth control. During 1977, 1978, and 1979, these measures produced dramatic improvements in all sectors of Sichuan's economy, making the province a model for others. They also vastly enhanced the national reputation of the pleasant, gregarious Zhao, with his Mao-style haircut and horn-rimmed glasses. Finally, in early 1980, Deng brought him to Beijing to oversee the day-to-day operations of the State Council. In September the National People's Congress confirmed him as premier in place of Hua Guofeng.

Deng and Hu Yaobang worked steadily to rehabilitate and promote their own people and to chip away at Hua Guofeng's support. One important step was to reduce Mao Zedong's myth down to human dimensions. In 1977 and 1978 the anniversary of the Chairman's death was barely noted. By early 1979 the media carried criticisms of Mao's policies, his excessive personality cult, and his support for the Gang of Four. Even "Mao Zedong Thought" began to be redefined, not as the ideas of one man, but as the collective wisdom of China's Communist leaders. Meanwhile, figures living and dead who were associated with Hua Guofeng came under attack. Most important were the "Whateverists," those who had advocated following whatever Mao had said. Other targets included Kang Sheng, the deceased head of public security and Hua's mentor when he came to Beijing in the early 1970s. Kang's ashes were removed from Babaoshan Cemetery, and he was reviled and posthumously expelled from the Party for his part in police excesses.

No radical institution was safe, not even Dazhai, the production brigade so long held up as a model for collective agriculture. Hua's 1976 rural policies had featured a program to promote the transformation of entire counties to predominantly Dazhai-type systems. During 1979 and 1980, however, this brigade and its famous leader, Chen Yongguei, came under attack. Allegations emerged that the brigade was not actually the solid success it claimed to be. It had received state subsidies, and its production figures had been falsified. Moreover, far from being a model society, Dazhai had seen many excesses during the Cultural Revolution, led by Chen Yongguei himself. Chen's own son allegedly took advantage of his father's high position and special privileges. By late 1980 the slogan "In Agriculture Learn from Dazhai," had been totally repudiated.

As Hua's supporters and pet programs drew fire, his own decline was only a matter of time. Already in the spring of 1979
he was criticized in high Party circles both for his role in Deng's
purge and associated leftist errors and for his unsuccessful economic policies. By late in the year it was an open secret that
Hua held his position only at the sufferance of Deng Xiaoping.
The end came in the fall and winter of 1980. Hua first resigned
as premier in August, dutifully recommending Zhao Ziyang as
his replacement. Then in June 1981 he formally resigned as Party
chairperson. Into this post stepped Hu Yaobang. The Party head's
ex officio post as head of the Military Affairs Committee (MAC)
was taken over by Deng Xiaoping (a constitutionally irregular
move, because the Party chairman should automatically head up
the MAC).

Aside from removing Hua Guofeng and his faction, Deng's
group labored throughout 1979 and 1980 to reform the system.
Their objective was to create a more effective and responsive
Party and government. There were millions of Party members
recruited since the 1969 Ninth Party Congress, many of whom
still cherished radical ideas. Aging Party members constituted
another problematic category. The majority of both of these groups
lacked higher education and special expertise, and yet they were
often in charge of government offices and enterprises by virtue
of wearing more than one official hat (for example, provincial
party first secretary and head of the provincial government).
Corruption and abuse of office were rife, as noted previously.

An important move in addressing these problems was the creation of a Central Commission for Inspecting Discipline, headed
by Chen Yun, to restore rules and regulations for inner-Party
discipline and to remove undesirable cadres. In addition to in-
vestigating cases such as Liu Shaoqi's, this large commission
drafted "Guiding Principles for Inner-Party Political Life." There
were analogous committees at lower levels of the Party. The
media began to attack corruption and abuse of office. One tactic
was to associate major radical figures with misconduct. Jiang Qing
was widely known to have enjoyed Greta Garbo films and nu-

merous other bourgeois pleasures while prescribing drab revolutionary entertainments for the masses. The son of Dazhai's leader, Chen Yongguei, was exposed as a corrupt wastrel. One of the "Whateverists" was publicly charged with lavishing public money on his private residence.

In the fall of 1979, publicity was given to the extraordinary case of a young peasant who had posed as the son of a high military official in order to get a ticket to a Shanghai play. One thing led to another, and during the course of two months he was feted and favored by the city's elite, even to the point of becoming engaged to a former capitalist's daughter. When finally found out, he protested that, if he really had been the son of a high cadre, his privilege-seeking would not be considered wrong. *What If I Really Were?*, a play based on this incident, enjoyed great popularity. In the final scene, the young man defends himself, saying:

> I was wrong to be a fake. [But] if I really were the son of Zhang Senior or another leader, then everything I've done would be completely legal.[15]

Other cases of abuse were publicized, and new regulations on official perquisites were issued. Striking and also illustrative of the difficulties of reform was the experience of Shanghai's newspaper *Liberation Daily*. In October 1980, it offered to look into any charges of official misconduct that readers would bring to its attention. The paper was flooded with thousands of letters, and people even came in person to lodge their complaints. But a month later, in a long report, the editors gave up, publicly acknowledging that their efforts had been ineffective in the face of official defensiveness and uncooperativeness.

There were institutional changes as well. Revolutionary committees, Mao's great innovation of the Cultural Revolution for leading institutions at all levels, ceased to exist. Multiple candidate elections for lower-level Party committees were implemented, a principle later extended to the National Party Congress. As for the state government, in July 1979 a new election law provided for multicandidate elections to local people's congresses. The center took pains (although not with complete success) to restrain local Party officials from interfering in the nominating and electing process. Lifetime tenure in office was formally ended although implementing this policy would not be easy. The Party also took measures to remove the police and security apparatus from politics, where it had exercised great influence since the Cultural Revolution.

Steps were taken to begin reorganizing the state administrative structure. This included simplification and restructuring of the ministries under the State Council, restoring the statistical bureau, and strengthening mass organizations such as labor unions and the Federation of Women. Finally, legal reforms were necessary for reducing the arbitrary exercise of power. The rehabilitated Peng Zhen, who earlier in his career had been active in this area, took charge of drafting a new criminal code, criminal procedures, and civil and commercial codes. Although the trials of Wei Jingsheng, Fu Yuehua, and the Gang of Four showed that law remained subordinate to politics, some procedural regularity and predictability did return.

The Trial of the Gang of Four and the Sixth Plenum

The capstone of this whole process of moderate victory and Maoist decline came in the trial of the Gang of Four and in the Central Committee Plenum that followed not long thereafter. The proceedings were delayed because of disagreements over whether a revised verdict on Mao should first be reached and over how much Mao and even Hua would be implicated in the testimony. Finally on November 20, 1980, the trial got under way. Thirty-five special judges in black Mao suits, a corps of prosecutors in similar gray suits, a handpicked audience excluding foreign correspondents, and a handful of defense counsel assembled. Completing the cast of characters were Jiang Qing, her three confederates (Zhang Chunqiao, Wang Hongwen and Yao Wenyuan),

Chen Boda, and five generals associated with Lin Biao. It was announced that, were they not already dead, Lin, his wife, and his son would also be in the dock.

All defendants were charged with plotting against the Party leadership and persecuting hundreds of thousands during the Cultural Revolution, resulting in nearly 35,000 unjust deaths. The Gang of Four was additionally indicted for plotting a military coup after Mao's death, and the generals for allegedly conspiring to assassinate Mao in 1971. The proceedings were half trial, half stage play. The goundwork and most of the participants had been carefully prepared, the parts having been rehearsed beforehand. Only edited excerpts were aired on television. Not all defendants had counsel; the defense lawyers present made no objections, cross-examined no witnesses, and presented no defense.

The excitement was provided by the sensational testimony, Jiang Qing's behavior, and the unspoken presence of Mao. Witness after witness accused the defendants of horrible excesses. Jiang Qing was said to have a private torture chamber. Tape recordings of groaning victims were played. For her part, Jiang Qing matched the official theatrics with her own star performance. She projected confusion and innocence, then scorn and defiance. Her basic defense was that all her actions had been at Mao's behest and in accordance with his directives. She contrasted her own fidelity to Mao with her judges' questionable motives.

> Don't forget, for thirty-eight years [I] was Mao's wife. . . . In the war years, I was the only woman with Chairman Mao at the front. Where were you hiding then? . . .
>
> [Your] purpose is to make me stink, and through me to make Chairman Mao stink, so as to revise the development of Marxism-Leninism and the immense contributions Chairman Mao made. . . .[16]

In counterpoint to her dazzling display, Zhang Chunqiao refused adamantly to recognize the tribunal and sat totally unresponsive and unspeaking from beginning to end. The other defendants, however, had adopted the safer posture of confession, cooperation, and begging for the court's mercy. Chen Boda, a badly deteriorated old man who had been presumed dead for a decade, owned that shooting was too good for him and that decapitation was probably more fitting.

The verdicts came after two months of trial and additional weeks of delay. Jiang Qing and Zhang Chunqiao received the death penalty, which was, however, postponed for two years to allow for repentance. Wang Hongwen was sentenced to life imprisonment, and all the others got from sixteen to twenty years. (Later the two death sentences were commuted indefinitely, and Chen Boda and the generals were released because of failing health.)

The unspoken results were more important. Deng Xiaoping had delivered an additional massive blow to Maoism. In condemning the radicals, the court had pronounced on the culpability of Mao himself. In its summary statement, the prosecution even explicitly admitted that Mao must be held responsible for the Cultural Revolution and for tolerating the machinations of Lin Biao and Jiang Qing—although it added that the people would never forget his great contributions to the Revolution. The trial also proclaimed, by the very fact that it was held, that the days of arbitrary seizure and punishment were over.

Yet it had serious negative repercussions, too. Although an improvement over the hysterical vigilantism of the Cultural Revolution, it, too, was patently predetermined, a political rather than a judicial event. The accused were assumed guilty in advance and had no opportunity to present a defense. Deng's own outburst to the interviewer Oriana Fallaci shortly before the trial, although never published in China, exemplified the position taken by China's leaders on Jiang Qing:

> She is a very, very evil woman. She is so evil that any evil thing you say about her isn't evil enough, and if you ask me to judge her with the grades as we do in China, I answer that this is im-

possible, there are no grades for Chiang Ching, that Chiang Ching is a thousand times a thousand below zero . . .[17]

The contrived nature of the trial was obvious to all, and after the initial sensation wore off, the public apparently became rather indifferent. The fact that Jiang Qing and Zhang Chunqiao remained uncooperative was also injurious to the overall result. Although widely despised, Mao's widow elicited a grudging respect for her absolute refusal to be cowed. At the very end, while being dragged from the courtroom in handcuffs, she was shouting the slogan that ushered in the Cultural Revolution, "To rebel is justified!"

There were certain groups that particularly may have taken offense. Elements in the military resented the humiliation of the old and terribly feeble generals. Also the many cadres who had entered public life after 1966 and who may still have believed in Maoism to some degree were bound to be upset by Deng's triumph of revenge. The trial could not have satisfied either those who longed for totalitarian dictatorship or the advocates of rule by law. It was one more example of the difficulty of straddling the line between Maoism and reform.

The final denouement in the political transition to the Deng Xiaoping era occurred in June 1981. The Party's Central Committee met in its sixth plenary session. This Sixth Plenum put the finishing touches on the transfer of power that the Third Plenum of December 1978 had anticipated. Hua Guofeng, who for some months had obviously been in a very weak political position, resigned as chairperson of the Party and of the Central Committee's Military Affairs Committee. As noted earlier, the former post then went to Hu Yaobang; and the latter, to Deng Xiaoping. (This was not a bloody purge, however, as Hua was merely demoted, not purged. Subsequently, he sank gradually from public view.)

It may be asked here why, if Deng Xiaoping had now emerged as the undisputed leader of China, he did not make himself chairperson of the Party? Probably this was not a deliberate stratagem worked out in advance, but an arrangement that simply evolved. Considerations that must have played a role in Deng's restraint include the following. A central political task at that moment was to downgrade the "personality cult" tendencies exhibited by Mao Zedong. For Deng to grab at the supreme position would have deprived this movement of much of its force. Contrariwise, his restraint would serve as a lesson for others. Secondly, Deng desired to groom a younger group of leaders to take over, for he and the handful of surviving Yanan generation chiefs were in their late seventies or older. If the succession was to stick, the formal changes would have to be made at the earliest moment. Finally, not to occupy the highest Party post had virtually no impact on Deng's real power. His prestige was extremely high, and in view of their still tenuous positions, respectively, as Party chairperson and premier, Hu Yaobang and Zhao Ziyang could be expected to defer to him. Also as chairperson of the Military Affairs Committee, Deng did, in fact, occupy an extremely powerful and sensitive post.

The Sixth Plenum accomplished a second important piece of business relating to the political transition: a summing up of the Party's history and the role of Mao Zedong. It was vital to express a consensus on matters that would affect the regime's legitimacy. What were the Party's and Mao's major achievements? How were shortcomings and mistakes like the Great Leap Forward and the Cultural Revolution to be assessed? Who should bear responsibility? What was the relationship between Mao and Mao Zedong Thought on the one hand and the Party on the other? To address these issues, the Central Committee adopted a "Resolution on Certain Questions in the History of Our Party Since the Founding of the People's Republic of China." [18]

The resolution praised Mao as a great revolutionary leader who had made matchless contributions. But it also accused him of grave shortcomings. From the mid-1950s he allegedly indulged an excessively leftist view of class struggle while also yielding to the temptations of arbitrary rule and the personality cult. These defects violated the principle of collective leadership that he himself had established. Things got even worse during the Cultural Revolution when he allowed "careerists" like Lin Biao and Jiang Qing to exploit his weaknesses. But the "chief responsibility" for this grave leftist error must rest with Mao Zedong himself. Finally, in 1975 he "triggered" the attack on Deng Xiaoping, who was laboring to repair the damage of the Cultural Revolution. As for "Mao Zedong Thought," the resolution considered it a collective Chinese adaptation of Marxism-Leninism and not the personal property of Mao. By these formulations, the Central Committee sought realistically to assign praise and blame in a way that corresponded to widely shared views about Mao's excesses. At the same time, it rescued Mao Zedong Thought as the Party's sacred doctrine, not affected by the Charman's personal failings.

9

Socialist Modernization and Its Discontents

The post-Mao reforms were remarkable in the degree to which they were sustained and extended. In 1985, more than six years after the changes began, they were still going strong, and additional innovations were appearing regularly. Through the sheer accumulation of such changes, it is possible that the diminutive Deng Xiaoping, who labored for so many years in the shadow of Mao and Zhou, will have had a more lasting impact on China's modernization than any other member of the Yanan generation, the Chairman himself not excepted.

Achievements and Dilemmas of Socialist Modernization: 1981–85

The Economy

Revolutionary is a word that could legitimately be applied to China's economic policies in the 1980s. The People's Republic began down the path that socialist bloc countries have entered in an attempt to invigorate their problem-ridden and innefficient socialist systems while preserving the principles of public own-

273

ership and central planning. Yugoslavia and Hungary are the countries most often cited for such efforts. But the Soviet Union itself and even Vietnam have at various times instituted significant modifications of their economic systems.

In China undoubtedly the most successful turnaround occurred in agriculture. The High Tide, under Mao, had collectivized the entire rural sector in the brief space of two and a half years (1955–57). In a dramatic and equally rapid tide of reversal, cooperative agriculture was essentially dismantled (1980–83). Various types of contractual arrangements for family or small-group farming, the so-called responsibility system, took over. By the spring of 1983, the responsibility system was virtually universal. Economic activity was organized by families or by private, collective, or state-run companies, all operating through contracts instead of the old cadre command structure. As a result, communes were virtually defunct; even their strictly governmental functions returned gradually to the reconstituted "townships," which the communes themselves had displaced during the Great Leap Forward. Diversification also increased, with millions of peasant families becoming "key" households specializing in transportation, distribution, services, handicrafts, or the growing of cash crops.

The outstanding overall results suddenly made agriculture, in effect, the economy's leading sector. Between 1979 and 1982 the annual agricultural growth rate averaged 7.5 percent. The 1983 and 1984 grain harvests were excellent, 1984's 400 million tons representing a whopping 25 percent jump over 1980. Not surprisingly, peasant incomes rose dramatically. From 1979 to 1982 the average net annual income of rural individuals doubled to approximately 135 U.S. dollars, the number of prosperous households jumped sharply, and the number of extremely poor ones declined. To encourage peasant entrepreneurs and assure them that it was all right to make money, the government promoted the slogan "Let some localities and peasants get rich first" and publicized economic success stories. Exceptional families began to have incomes equivalent to thousands of U.S. dollars per year, for example, by raising ducks for export to Hong Kong. Others prospered in the transportation business with privately or collectively purchased buses. The variations were endless. Living standards jumped. There was a veritable house-building boom. Consumption of consumer goods (such as watches, radios, televisions, and sewing machines) rose sharply.

In the cities changes were also significant. Possibly the most radical innovation was the appearance of individual and collective small enterprises. This policy emerged in 1979, when it became clear that millions of young people would no longer go down to the countryside and yet could not be provided with state jobs. In response, over the following years millions of people got permission to set up small restaurants, repair shops, services, and manufactures. In 1980, "market socialism" experiments began in state-owned enterprises as well. Although all this has frequently been called "capitalist," the label is inapt for several reason. Most of the people in individual enterprises were reluctant entrepreneurs who would have preferred secure state jobs with higher pay and benefits. They were restricted in the number of employees and apprentices they could hire. And although these small-scale undertakings received attention in the Western press, they still constituted only a tiny proportion of the urban work force. State enterprises, where the great majority of urban workers were employed, experienced more limited change. Still, these reforms made an important contribution in dealing with massive unemployment.

Numerous other innovations invaded the industrial sector. The "open door" to Western trade, technology transfer, investment, and tourism rapidly ended the relatively self-contained system that Mao had tried to preserve. Although the four "special economic zones" mentioned earlier encountered some difficulties, one of them, Shenzhen near Guangzhou (Canton), grew rapidly with hundreds of millions of U.S. dollars worth of capital pouring in from Hong Kong and other foreign sources. In the spring of 1984, it was announced that fourteen ports, from Dalian in the north on the Liaodong Peninsula to Beihai in the south near the Vietnam border, would be opened to foreign investment, with special inducements to attract outside capital.

The 400,000 state and collective enterprises were scheduled for significant changes in their operations. Rather than turn over all profits to the state, they began to pay taxes and retain profits. They were to begin shouldering more responsibility for profits and losses, thus preparing for the day when the government would stop subsidizing thousands of money-losing operations. Changes in management practices began putting greater decision-making authority in the hands of those in charge. Competitive elements were introduced as were incentive-based pay schemes for workers.

In October 1984, the Central Committee approved a sweeping decision to reform the urban economy. The central premise running through these measures was that industry could be revitalized only if enterprises were run by technically competent managers, operating under the loose guidelines of central or regional planners, and responding to prices and markets. To implement this principle, the authorities would have to overhaul the price system to reflect actual costs. Government subsidies for inefficient enterprises and supports to keep down urban food prices would be prudently eliminated. (This last item had become a huge drain on the state budget.) Enterprise managers would have to have more decision-making authority, and large numbers of young managers would have to be trained. Government officials would be expected to stay out of economic management, playing instead a guiding and supporting role. Diversity would have to be promoted along with openness to foreign aid and technology. As the government, in typical bureaucratic prose, explained the rationale for all this:

> proceeding from the overall need to build socialism with Chinese characteristics by integrating the basic tenets of Marxism with actual conditions in China, we must go a step further with the policy of invigorating the domestic economy and opening to the outside world and accelerate the restructuring of the national economy as a whole,

with the focus on the urban economy, so as to create a new, better situation for our socialist modernization.[1]

In the mid-1980s the economic system was producing results far superior to those achieved under earlier policies. Agriculture, industry, foreign trade, and technological development were all steadily on the upswing. Without adjusting for inflation, gross industrial output rose by nearly 8 percent annually over this period. Foreign trade increased at 9.5 percent per annum. Not all industries participated equally, steel and petroleum being important examples, but the overall results were most impressive, especially when compared with the spotty performances in preceding periods. Emblematic of the country's enthusiastic appetite for the latest know-how was the emergence of Haidian, a Beijing suburb that became China's little "silicon valley."

Yet the country still faced formidable obstacles and dilemmas in its goal of fully modernizing the economy by the turn of the century and quadrupling overall prodution between 1980 and the year 2000. On the most general level, there was a real question as to whether a mixed socialist-market system could emerge. Authoritarian political structures and bureaucratic red tape in government industries (state operations employed around three-fourths of the nearly 100 million industrial workers) inevitably worked against the surrender of government control that a true market system would require. In fact, dogging the reform effort was a continuing but hard-to-measure undercurrent of resistance, comprised in part of cadres who saw their power undercut by the new system. City dwellers who enjoyed subsidized food prices could be expected to oppose reform in this area. When and if the supports were removed, urban living costs could rise substantially. Yet continued subsidies would constitute a debilitating drain on the government budget. Another big question centered on industrial productivity. Up into the mid-1980s, reforms had failed to result in a more efficient manufacturing sector. Management was all too often lacking in the spirit of innovation and unwilling to make decisions. Workers resisted hiring systems that would end their "iron rice bowl" (lifetime job security irrespective of performance). It had yet to be demonstrated that state enterprises generally could become truly competitive.

Even though agriculture represented the single most successful part of the reform efforts, there were also questions about whether the gains would continue there. Perhaps the rapid growth of the early 1980s was a onetime development resulting from pent-up potential that had been blocked by the collective system. Formerly, teams and brigades undertook capital formation projects such as irrigation systems, as well as welfare, education, health, and other communal responsibilities. Under the new individualized arrangements, it was not clear that such functions would continue to be adequately performed. Also, under the old system, incomes within given teams and brigades were more or less evened out because the team divided up its net receipts according to work points earned by its members. Under the responsibility system, certain families and certain regions were able to do a great deal better than others. This created potential discontent that could surface if the reform impetus slowed. Technically, there was a question as to whether the common practice of assigning several small plots to a given family would block the introduction of larger, more efficient cultivators and other improvements. Finally, it remained to be seen whether sufficient employment would be created outside strictly agricultural pursuits to absorb the nearly 200 million peasants who would probably have to leave farming by the year 2000.

Economic inequalities created by the new, more open system raised issues across society, not just in villages. They could conceivably nourish a backlash of opposition. Even under Mao, despite the egalitarian rhetoric, great disparities existed between cadres and people, between rural and urban sectors, and between one region and another. Under Deng's regime, the situation became more complex. On the one hand, as the general level of wealth increased, there was more to go around for everyone. Also, in many cases, the power and perquisites of local cadres were reduced. On the other hand, city workers, who had few opportunities to earn extra incomes, began to resent the prosperity of peasant entrepreneurs. And, within agriculture, families with little labor power and regions with poor endowments made out much worse than the well-publicized success stories.

Political Reforms

In politics and government, which in their own way were as problem-ridden as the economy, Deng Xiaoping's quest for change could not be satisfied merely by eliminating the Hua Guofeng faction in the winter of 1980. Institutional transformation was still necessary to address lingering problems. Millions of Party members, recruited during and after the Cultural Revolution, still lacked education and expertise and remained confirmed Maoists. They had to be culled out. Even many of the nearly 3 million rehabilitated Party victims of the Cultural Revolution had to be removed for reasons of age or incompetence. The ministries under the State Council were too numerous and heavily bureaucratized; they required pruning. Party heads at intermediate and lower levels typically wore several hats, doubling as heads of government or economic entities, positions for which they frequently lacked the expertise. Since the Cultural Revolution, the People's Liberation Army and the Public Security apparatus had continued to involve themselves in politics, a practice that Deng wished to curtail.

Progress occurred in all these areas. For example, when the Party convened in its Twelfth Congress in September 1982, many members of the old Central Committee were dropped in favor of newcomers. There were fewer from the military. The new Party constitution stiffened membership rules, and a three-year campaign to weed out unqualified or uncooperative Communists was scheduled for 1983 through 1985. Central ministries, provincial administrations, and other entities experienced reorganization and the infusion of new leadership.

Ensuring an orderly transfer of power received high priority.

Deng, who turned eighty in 1984, began to play a less public role in order to allow Zhao Ziyang, Hu Yaobang, and other new leaders to establish their standing. Thus, a critical transition that Mao began to prepare for in 1959 but then abandoned was now being negotiated with apparent success by Deng. Zhao's stature as premier continued to grow, especially as a result of China's continued economic progress but also through activities in other areas. For example, he began to play an increasingly important role in foreign affairs, visiting the United States in early 1984. Hu, for his part, spoke with increasinly authority as first secretary of the Party (the office of chairperson was abolished in 1982 Party constitution).

A less tangible but no less important problem was the crisis of legitimacy. Beginning about 1979, there were signs of serious erosion of belief in China's principles and institutions. Disillusionment ranged from the belief that Maoism had been betrayed to the conclusion that Marxism was a hollow sham or that official promises would not be kept or that the entire system was corrupt. Opinion polls in late 1980 and early 1981 revealed that the majority of students had little faith in socialism and feared that radical leftism could return. Some demobilized soldiers, unable to cope with a non-Maoist society where they no longer occupied a charmed status, engaged in criminality and protests. In 1981, for example, the so-called Heartbreak Army of unemployed and demobilized soldiers formed into guerrilla groups and raided grain depots and other installations. In increasing numbers, young people from Guangdong Province attempted to make it over the border to the uncertain capitalist world of Hong Kong.

Inside the Party itself, if the complaints of the leaders were to be believed, widespread doubts about Marxism festered. Even the Party's highest cultural commissar admitted that "alienation" (presumably a capitalist disorder) could occur in socialist societies as well. Creative intellectuals, always among the dissatisfied, also complained. The *People's Daily* published several articles criticizing political censorship, the most dramatic being the deathbed testament of a famous actor. Consumed by cancer and having "nothing more to lose in speaking openly," he cried out against political controls on writers and artists. To censor literature and the arts, he charged, was to kill them.[2]

This crisis of faith was not a problem that could be solved by more brainwashing or by coercion. If China were going to advance rapidly, the legitimacy of the system would have to be restored in ways that would elicit people's willing participation. There were a great many policy changes, small and large, to achieve this. The new leaders began to transform their heretofore "totalitarian" regime, in which almost everything that anyone did was viewed as political, into a merely "authoritarian" rule that (through retaining a strict monopoly over political power) limited its intrusions into personal life and tolerated a wider spectrum of expression. Millions of cases of injustice dating back to the antirightist movement of 1957 and the Cultural Revolution were reversed, thereby restoring some faith in justice. At the local level, multiple candidate elections took place. The Chinese began to appear in brighter, more individualized clothing. Intellectual and cultural life grew freer. As a sign of the latter, the China Writers Association concluded a conference in January 1985 that featured new promises of creative freedom. Hu Qili, permanent secretary of the Party's Secretariat and one of the rising new generation, addressed the gathering to this effect. Although they were still expected to respect Marxism-Leninism and the Communist party, the organization's charter encouraged writers to

> develop a great variety of new themes, styles, forms and genres and start a free competition so as to raise the ideological and artistic levels of literary creation.[3]

Another response was the old standby, the campaign (itself something of a paradox because the new leaders publicly renounced mass campaigns as an instrument of policy). There was a campaign to emulate Lei Feng. There was a "Four Beauties and Five Stresses" campaign to restore good manners, presumably lost since the Cultural Revolution. In the winter of 1983–84 a major commotion erupted over a campaign against "spiritual pollution." This movement grew out of some remarks in a speech by Deng Xiaoping. The targets were undesirable foreign ideas and habits worming their way into the country along with Western trade and technology. None of these campaigns was able to sustain itself. In the case of the campaign against spiritual pollution, unreconstructed Maoists and enemies of Hu Yaobang seized the opportunity to implement it with excessive vigor, sparking the widespread fear of a new Cultural Revolution. There were reports, for example, that entry to some Beijing municipal offices was blocked to women wearing long hair or makeup. Hu Yaobang and Zhao Ziyang, backed by Deng himself, quickly moved to restrict and limit the campaign, and within a few weeks it was dead.

Another aspect of reviving the system was the recasting of Communist ideology to fit changed conditions. This "socialism with Chinese characteristics" downplayed prominent features of Maoism. The extreme personality cult disappeared. Some of the rooms in Chairman Mao's Memorial Hall on Tian'anmen Square were dedicated to other great leaders: Zhou Enlai, Liu Shaoqi, and Zhu De. The media freely discussed Mao's errors. "Mao Zedong Thought" was redefined as the collective wisdom of the Party leaders and the Chinese masses. "Practice," not dogma, became the "sole criterion for truth." Class struggle ceased to be emphasized, and talk of exporting revolution to the Third World stopped. Most striking of all (or outrageous from a Maoist perspective) was the open admission that some capitalist practices might be applicable to current conditions in the name of achieving rapid economic growth. Ideological flexibility even went to the point where the *People's Daily* reported this comment by Hu Yaobang: "One cannot expect the works of Marx and Lenin written in their time to solve today's problems." This stark statement, which could be misconstrued as a repudiation of Marxism, was quickly corrected to read that the works of Marx and Lenin could not "solve *all of* today's problems." [4]

The sum total of these political changes constituted a remarkable and vigorous effort to put new life into the system. But the changes were by no means completely effective, as, for example, against incompetence, corruption, and other ills of bureaucracy. Even to the extent that they were successful, they confronted problems and contradictions. The new ideological formulations may have been more pragmatic than Maoism, but they packed far less emotional power. China was left with a hodgepodge of Marxism-Leninism, Maoism, modernizing pragmatism, and traditional beliefs. Ambiguity and confusion resulted. Socialists who frowned on individualism encouraged peasants to "get rich first." Party members, who had always considered themselves the soul of the Revolution, were being ordered to get out of the experts' way. Although clearly defined laws and procedures were essential for modernization, any guarantees of civil rights diminished the Party's power to intervene in the name of the Revolution. Increased material well-being and openness to the world economy were widely welcomed, but not the influx of pop culture and pornography.

Foreign Relations

In the 1980s in foreign affairs, the People's Republic moved in directions that had begun to be explored in the early 1970s. Much had changed since the days of the First Five-Year Plan when, as a member of the socialist block, China blasted American imperialism, and also since the 1960s, when Mao attempted to make China the radical pied piper of the Third World. From the early 1970s onward, the country's principal foreign policy goals had less and less to do with promoting revolution either at home or abroad. Nor did they include the socialist bloc, which China now regarded as defunct. Rather, it was the threat from the USSR that came to dominate foreign policy. That fear persuaded Mao himself to agree to a rapprochement with so unlikely a friend as Richard Nixon in 1972. An added stimulus was the need for a stable world environment in which Zhou Enlai's revived economic modernization policies could proceed without hindrance.

Under Deng Xiaoping this new orientation developed further, the four modernizations becoming an even weightier factor than the Russian threat. To be sure, pressure from that quarter continued to be regarded as serious: half a million Soviet troops along the borders, subversion of ethnic minorities in China's far west, Russia's Pacific fleet and dominant influence in Indochina, and the invasion of Afghanistan. But the probability of actual attack or invasion had diminished greatly since 1969, and in this same period the need for an all-out assault on economic backwardness seemed to require new initiatives, not all of which would have been approved by Mao. Increasingly, the developed countries (Japan, the United States, and the nations of Europe) became important elements in the modernization program. They were the suppliers of badly needed goods and technologies. They were also markets for exports and tourism. And they were sources of capital necessary for industrial development. Driven by these considerations, foreign policy in the Deng era came to be characterized by the "open door" to the West while at the same time China maintained a cold posture toward the Soviet Union.

Although the basis of China's relationship with the United States continued to undergo a fundamental shift in the early 1980s, the road was not a smooth one. The issue of Taiwan, combined with numerous trade-related problems, put repeated strains on relations. Already in 1980 the United States Congress had passed the Taiwan Relations Act, which called for de facto, if unofficial, relations with Taiwan and for continued arms sales to the island. This extremely irritating gesture was compounded by the position of Ronald Reagan during his campaign and in the first two years of his first term. His administration continued to explore expanded arms sales to Taiwan. It seemed otherwise interested in China mainly as a strategic ally against the Soviet Union, a position that made Beijing nervous in view of Reagan's chest-thumping toward Moscow. Under these new circumstances, China attempted to strike a somewhat more equidistant posture toward the two superpowers at the Twelfth Party Congress in September 1982.

Sino-American relations improved considerably beginning in 1983 as the Reagan administration moderated its position on Taiwan and as economic ties became increasingly central. Although Japan remained the leading trading partner of the People's Republic, U.S. trade grew, and American investors became the most important source of foreign capital. Thousands of Chinese students, experts, and scholars were in the United States. A sequence of important visitors marked this newly improved situation. In 1983 and 1984 American secretaries of state, defense, and commerce visited Beijing, and the Chinese foreign minister and defense minister came to Washington. These exchanges culminated in Zhao Ziyang's January 1984 trip to the United States, followed by President Reagan's return visit in April of that year.

However, problems persisted. Whereas the American desire for markets and investment opportunities coincided in general with China's need for Western products, know-how, services, and investment, there were important irritants and economic conflicts between the two countries. Chinese textiles flowed into the U.S. market in rapidly increasing quantities. This exacerbated a more general American fear of a deluge of foreign manufactures displacing domestic goods and U.S. jobs. Washington then imposed import restrictions, which angered the Chinese.

On another front, during 1983 and 1984, Beijing failed to honor its purchase commitments under a five-year grain sale agreement covering the years 1980–84. A number of factors contributed to this, notably Chinese irritation over the textile question, the high prices caused by a strong dollar, and excellent Chinese harvests. Strategic restrictions inhibited or slowed down technology transfer, in which the Chinese were extremely interested. Only in 1983 was the way finally cleared for reasonably unrestricted sale of many high-tech American products to China. Even so, trade in this area continued to run into delays and red tape. It was also apparent that although Chinese and American interests coincided in important respects, there were matters over which Beijing continued to disagree strongly with Washington. American policy elsewhere in the world was one such area. China strongly criticized the Reagan administration's initiatives in such diverse spots as Grenada, Central America, and the Middle East.

China's relations with the Soviet Union remained prickly during the early 1980s although some public easing was visible by mid-decade. The fundamentally threatening and expansionist posture of Moscow had created what to Beijing's eyes was an encirclement far more threatening than the American containment policy of earlier decades. That and Beijing's fierce need for autonomy created a lasting standoff between the two former friends. Beijing repeatedly proclaimed that until the Russians reduced their military presence along the borders, in Afghanistan, and in Indochina, little progress in bilateral relations would be possible. Nevertheless, trade and cultural exchanges began to increase significantly in mid-decade.

In general, China's earlier tilt toward Washington was replaced by greater flexibility and a somewhat more equidistant posture between the United States and the Soviet Union. Beijing continued to try, without results, to lure Taiwan into some form of association with the mainland. On the other hand, negotiations with Great Britain over the future status of Hong Kong resulted in an agreement to reassert Chinese sovereignty over the colony while preserving its economic and social system for half a century. It remained to be seen whether such an agreement could be sustained, especially in view of the absence of any tribunal to oversee the new arrangement. In international bodies such as the United Nations, the People's Republic continued to present itself as a steady, dependable participant. China's strong showing in the 1984 Summer Olympics clearly demonstrated an intention to claim a respected place among nations.

Education

Education was another area where China faced difficulties of mammoth proportions. Ideally, the government should have been able to mobilize massive resources to universalize primary and secondary schooling, and it should have built up higher education in order to graduate the hundreds of thousands of experts and managers vital for economic development. Simultaneously, it should have provided a fair educational opportunity to all citizens, whether urban or rural, male or female, cadre or ordinary citizen, Han Chinese or ethnic minority.

Unfortunately, there were not nearly enough resources to realize this ideal. Difficult choices had to be made between uplifting the general educational level and producing experts, between promoting fairness and rapid results. Under Deng, China's approach radically reversed earlier directions. Maoist educational policies emphasized socialist equity and ideology whereas the Dengists placed economic development unambiguously in the highest priority. Where the earlier system stressed primary and secondary education, the new policies allocated much greater resources to higher education. Where access to education was formerly based on political and social criteria and skewed in favor of disadvantaged groups, the new system admitted students on the basis of competitive examinations.

The new policies achieved positive results. Building up from the devastation left by the Cultural Revolution, staffs and facilities were rebuilt, and a growing and increasingly able student body was selected. Curriculum revisions followed patterns used in Japan and the United States. Over 700 institutions of higher education emerged, about 100 of which were "keypoint" schools, that is, institutions specially favored and assigned the task of providing the highest quality of training for the brightest students. Numbers of college graduates dramatically increased.

However, these positive achievements could not totally obscure the continuing difficulties, inadequacies, and potential problems. Even the higher education system, which received the most budgetary support, was hard pressed to produce the personnel needed for rapid economic development. Lower down on the ladder, primary and secondary education have actually experienced reduced enrollments. The proportion of school-age children entering primary schools went down, and the dropout rate went up. Junior middle schools and especially senior middle schools experienced sharply reduced enrollments. The government made a clear decision to reduce the number of regular secondary schools and partially offset this by developing vocational tracks. But the latter did not come close to offsetting the declines in secondary enrolment. The 1982 census revealed an illiteracy rate of 25 percent among the twelve-to-forty-five age group. This was unlikely to decline under continued policies of reduced emphasis on primary and secondary education.

The issue of appropriateness and fairness was also not well addressed. Under Mao, children of the intelligentsia and other "bad" social groups were discriminated against. Under the new system that policy was reversed, but new sources of inequity took its place. Peasants and women began to confront heavier discrimination. Peasants had almost no chance of getting into the primary and secondary tracks leading to higher education. Urban workers were not much better off. As for women, biases in the lower levels produced a female population unable to compete in the rigorous secondary and higher-level entrance exams. The female proportion of higher education students declined from around one-third under Mao to about one-fifth under Deng. By a wide margin, the persons most favored in the stiff battle for the most sought-after programs were bright sons of urban intellectuals and urban cadres.

There was also much justifiable criticism of the heavy focus on cramming for the college entrance examination, which became the overwhelming focus of urban middle schools. Authorities widely deplored the apparent drop in dedication and idealism as students focused on the best strategies for their individual careers. One observer concluded:

One can only wonder, therefore, how long the Chinese Communists—with decades of rhetoric behind them and a political constituency based on an ideological appeal to workers and peasants—will be able to maintain the undiluted elitism inherent in the present education policies.[5]

Population Control

Maoists had never considered overpopulation a problem. Indeed, Marxism generally has a fundamental bias against any doctrine smacking of Malthus, the early English economist who argued that people could increase faster than food. Consequently the three previous efforts to control population (prior to the Great Leap Forward, just after the Great Leap Forward, and in the early 1970s) had been neither strongly grounded in ideology nor thoroughly carried out.

With Deng's return in ever greater influence in 1978, birth control efforts reemerged with more emphasis. Important Party leaders were put in charge of the effort. Various means were used, including a new oral contraceptive and extensive recourse to abortions, as well as efforts to promote late marriages and set a maximum of two children per family. The year 1978 appears to have shown results of these efforts: The population growth rate, which had varied between 2.22 percent and 1.62 percent during the 1970s, dropped to 1.2 percent.

In the early 1980s, the government began to take the population problem still more seriously. By 1979 zero population growth by the turn of the century had become the government's announced goal. There was an increasing realization that forests and agricultural land had contracted ominously during the preceding three decades (see later) and a sense that any further reduction in the ratio of resources to population could have tragic consequences for the future. Signs of what might happen were not hard to find. Drought in Hebei Province and floods in Hunan in 1980 and 1981 resulted in near famine conditions for as many as 20 million people, causing Beijing for the first time to request foreign relief assistance.

In the wake of these difficulties, population policies received even higher priority in the early 1980s. The first complete census in over thirty years was planned with United Nations assistance. Carried out in the summer of 1982, it revealed a total population of slightly over one billion people. The State Family

Planning Commission, a powerful new body set up under the State Council in 1981, began calling for one child per urban family as the only way to keep growth lower than maximum allowable levels. Later that policy was extended to the rural sector and even to ethnic minorities, who had heretofore been exempt from childbearing limits. The government marshaled an array of negative and positive inducements: propaganda and education, economic incentives and sanctions, and coercion where all else failed. Even the constitution, revised in December 1982, stated that "both husband and wife have the duty to implement fertility planning."[6]

Although China was widely hailed for these bold efforts in a world where many Asian, African, and Latin American states seemed quite unable or unwilling to control their populations, Beijing's program was fraught with difficulties and dangers. Birth control in China suffered from a dearth of reliable theoretical and empirical studies. Two decades of recurrent Maoism, starting with the Great Leap Forward, virtually destroyed statistics gathering and did away with academic studies in demographics, sociology, and law. Consequently, the goals that were set, the means that were employed to reach them, and the side effects all received only hastily consideration.

The one-child family was one of the most radical social policies imaginable. In a society celebrated for its family centeredness, roughly half of all couples were being asked, not only to bear just one child, but also to accept the extinction of the family line should that offspring be female. From a culture possessing a large lexicon of terms to distinguish minute gradations of kinship, China promised to become a land where few people even had a cousin. Other implications were numerous. It would be small wonder then if the one-child program did not prove difficult to implement and conducive to unanticipated problems. This was especially so in the countryside. There not only did traditional attitudes retain more force, but also people's welfare, especially in their old age, was directly affected by the number and sex of their children. In the absence of urban-type retirement benefits, which the government could not begin to afford for hundreds of millions of elderly peasants, rural couples could be expected to embrace the one-child family with limited enthusiasm.

One especially troubling result of the new policy was female infanticide. Many couples, whose preferences were to have at least two children and at minimum one boy, were tempted to do away with a baby rather than have only a single, female child. A report from one province indicated that 12 percent of female babies had been killed.

Even with its draconian qualities, which also included a eugenics component, the birth control policy appeared to be failing to keep natural increase low enough to meet the desired target. In 1982 and 1983 the population growth rates were around 1.4 percent and 1.3 percent respectively whereas they should have been around 1 percent. There were indications of peasant resistance and dissatisfaction among ethnic minorities in the strategically sensitive western provinces. In short, the whole problem proved both insistent and intractable.

Environmental Damage

In the 1980s, China began to address herself to both the cessation and the repair of massive damage to the country's land, water, and air. A population of around 550 million people was already placing a heavy burden on the environment when the Communists came to power in 1949. Since that time, a combination of massive additions to the population, industrial development, and environmentally shortsighted policies had wreaked havoc.

Since 1949 almost one-fourth of the forests had been destroyed. China's per capita production of wood was minuscule. This is to say nothing of the erosion caused by the loss of trees, a problem so serious that in the north, for example, silting rendered an expensive irrigation project on the Yellow River all but useless. Huge amounts of agricultural land were also lost, mostly because of encroachment by suburbs and villages. As a recent comprehensive survey of environmental deterioration expresses it:

> farmland, capable of sustaining some 200 million people (the equivalent of both Germanies, the United Kingdom, and France put together!) is gone—while China's population grew during [1957–77] by about 300 million people.[7]

Figure 7 illustrates the relationship between a relentlessly increasing population and a static and even declining supply of arable land.[8] Adding to these problems were the growth of deserts in the north and west and the widespread shrinking of freshwa-

FIG. 7 China's population and arable land.

ter lakes in the center and south through the encroachment of cropland.

China's water resources were in serious jeopardy, not only from the silting of rivers mentioned earlier, but also from urban and industrial pollution and from the overuse of aquifers. The air also deteriorated because of headlong industrialization. Inefficient combustion of low-grade coal, both for domestic and industrial uses, released enormous volumes of smoke. Increasingly, these pollutants were being supplemented by the emissions of refineries and other large-scale industrial operations. In north China this was compounded by wind-borne dust, which obscured the sky many days each year. One result of all this was a sharp increase in the incidence of lung and other cancers among city dwellers. Acid rain and photochemical smog were two other plagues that promised to grow increasingly serious with time.

Even for a prosperous country with an abundance of scientific and technical expertise, these problems would be formidable. For a developing country without a modern tradition of environmental conservation and whose people understandably often attempted to mitigate their poverty by actions destructive of the long-term environment, they seemed especially daunting. In the 1980s, China's leaders finally become aware of the staggering task ahead. Whether or not they would be up to it, time alone would tell.

Looking Backward

On October 1, 1984, China celebrated the thirty-fifth anniversary of the founding of the People's Republic. Celebrations throughout the country were led by the great parade in Beijing, presided over by Deng Xiaoping, the last major Yanan generation leader. Next to him stood Zhao Ziyang and Hu Yaobang, his chosen successors. The occasion amounted to a celebration of Deng's achievements and optimism about a future under his like-minded protégés. China's national power was on display.

In striking contrast to the motley assortment of confiscated American and Japanese weapons that marked the 1949 parades, the 1984 military displayed improved tanks, self-propelled howitzers, submarine-based medium-range missiles, and intercontinental missiles capable of delivering fifty megaton warheads to targets 8,000 miles away. All these weapons were of Chinese manufacture. Although still no superpower, the People's Republic was announcing that it was not an enemy to be taken lightly.

The festivities also continued the process of laying Mao's ghost. Rather than singling out the Great Helmsman for exclusive veneration, the parade featured a small pantheon of leaders. Some marchers carried huge busts of Mao, Zhou Enlai, Liu Shaoqi, and Zhu De, and others bore representations of the writings of these four plus those of the still living Deng Xiaoping and Chen Yun. Other floats celebrated economic progress and well-being. There were a huge papier-mâché chicken and a great refrigerator stuffed with food. Another float presented in living montage an idealized Beijing street with citizens amusing themselves and helping one another. Still other floats carried Chinese Olympic gold medalists waving to the crowds.

Such was the picture of national power and socialist abundance that China's leaders wished to project into the future. But did the parade leave anything out? What more can be said? What does an overview of the first thirty-five years of the Revolution prepare one to encounter in the next thirty-five? As one thinks about such questions, perhaps the first requirement is to expect the unexpected. It is striking how the history of the People's Republic has been full of surprises. In 1947, Stalin did not contemplate a rapid Communist victory in the civil war. MacArthur was caught unprepared by China's entry into the Korean fighting. When Khrushchev withdrew his experts in 1960, he did not imagine that Beijing would remain completely intransigent. Outside observers did not foresee the deep Sino-Soviet split. No one, not even in China, could have predicted the Cultural Revolution; its chaos caught Mao himself by surprise. Lin Biao's fall rocked the entire nation. Richard Nixon's visit was doubly stunning both in its unexpectedness and in its marvelous historical irony. The list is a long one.

Yet there may be reasons for presuming that violent fluctuations will not happen with such frequency in the future. In broad outlines the Chinese Revolution has followed the trajectory seen in other great revolutions. After initial victory, a period of increasing radicalism, marked by terror, gradually gives way to a more stable and predictable situation. For better or worse, the Revolution has settled down just like its precursors in France, Russia, and elsewhere. Mass mobilization will probably give way to more regularized and institutionalized ways of doing things.

Some of the themes mentioned in the introduction to this volume might provide further guidance in contemplating the next thirty-five years. One theme is poverty. Throughout the PRC era, China has struggled with this condition. Despite many setbacks, a gradual march toward improved living conditions has taken place. Perhaps the best indication of that is the finding in the 1982 census that the life expectancy for the average person had risen to sixty-nine years. Yet, as has been indicated, formidable barriers to rapid development remain. On balance, one should expect progress to continue but not attain the ambitious goals such as quadrupling national income by the year 2000. Poverty will continue to limit China's capacity to deal with problems. Every issue discussed in this book, from education to national defense, is made more difficult because of an acute shortage of resources to deal with it.

A second theme was the tension between Maoist orientations and more regularized and bureaucratized approaches to nation building. This tension manifests itself both in the choice between more rapid economic development and more social justice and in the choice between institutionalized means and mobilization to achieve national goals. Clearly, the "pragmatists," those who prefer economic development and institutional approaches, have come out on top in the mid-1980s. Yet these tensions are unlikely to disappear completely in the future. Maoism has been discredited because it failed to achieve economic improvements and because the political cost of pursuing its social programs was too high. But the Maoist ideal has not disappeared. There are significant groups who do not share equally in the current progress. Should the present policy directions at some time bog down, should Dengism come to be perceived as a failure, it would not be surprising to see the old dialogue between social justice and economic development revived in new form.

A third set of themes relates to the nature and evolution of the political system. Here the experience of thirty-five years provides very mixed and ambiguous signposts to the future. It has seemed as though the regime cannot decide what it wants to be. Leninist democratic centralism is a cardinal principle of all Soviet-inspired governments, and one should not expect the 40-million-member CCP to disband or welcome other parties into the political arena. Yet there is a question about how effectively a one-party dictatorship can cope with the complexities of modernization. Monopoly of power carries heavy costs, of which the Party leaders are well aware. Efforts to root out abuses and corruption and to upgrade the technical competence of Party cadres have become an ongoing agenda. In addition, Zhao Ziyang, as head of the State Council, has worked to separate the state and the Party functions in an effort to upgrade the efficiency of the economic system. These developments require clear procedures and a predictable, dispassionate judiciary. But deferring to experts and honoring rules imply relinquishing power, which the Party may ultimately not be prepared to do. This is compounded by the fact that in the provinces Party power has become entrenched in old-boy networks, which seem impervious to central discipline. In the economic sphere, the more efficient market sector may find itself unable to compete for state investment funds against the socialized bureaus and enterprises.

Other political questions center around leadership. What sort of succession is to be expected with the demise of Deng Xiaoping? Positioned to succeed him are two able men, one with a base in the Party, the other being premier of the State Council.

Assuming an orderly succession, will this duality of authority resolve itself, as in the Brezhnev-Kosygin case, in favor of the Party head? That would produce Hu Yaobang as the new chief. Yet he himself will be in his seventies, and so the next succession would already become an important question. Other outcomes are conceivable, not all of them orderly. Finally, the great issue of popular support and cooperation looms as always over this system. Wei Jingsheng, the hero of Democracy Wall, may be in prison, but the issue he raised is not dead: is it possible to achieve fully the "four modernizations" without a fifth—namely, democracy? To the extent that this proposition is true—and it is not just an odd notion held by one or two dissidents—how much democracy is enough to support modernization without at the same time threatening the dictatorship of the proletariat?

China's place in the world is also a subject of some interest. There is scarcely another country during the past generation whose diplomatic posture has gone through so many dramatically different transformations. Chinese rulers seem to have both hugged and shaken their fists at just about everyone. Does this suggest similar instability for the future? As indicated earlier, the People's Republic appears to have left its volatile revolutionary phase and entered a more stable period of nation building. Given the apparent long-term stasis in world power relationships, one could expect China to negotiate a steady course of restrained opposition to the Soviet Union, conditioned cooperation and intercourse with the industrial West, and warm but mostly verbal support for the Third World.

Until recent years it was common to hear about the Chinese "model" of modernization. Many believed that Mao and his colleagues had found a formula that could satisfy the desire for a fair and humane society while also creating economic well-being. Such discussion has lost popularity in the post-Mao era. Under pragmatic leadership the country's central vision has gotten rather blurred. China's position in the world and her policies are too ambiguous to constitute a model. The People's Republic has been busy borrowing technology and methods from abroad and has been acting much like any other stable major power. Moreover, as continuing massive problems have come to light, it is not certain that China will ultimately overcome her own difficulties, let alone light the way for others.

But, finally, a certain humility is called for in evaluating this great Revolution. It has exhibited excesses and imperfections in abundance. But excesses and imperfections are not unique to China, as any review of Western history will show. Moreover, China's difficulties have been very serious. Even as legitimate complaints abound over one or another aspect of the system, one cannot but be impressed by what has been accomplished and hope that Mao's dictum of 1959 is rather more appropriate now than it was then:

The achievements are tremendous, the problems are numerous, the experience is rich, and the future is bright.[9]

Notes

Introduction

1. Author's translation. For the Chinese text and another translation, see Mao Tse-tung, *The Poems of Mao Tse-tung*, trans. Willis Barstone (New York: Bantam Books, 1972), 92–93.

Chapter 1

1. G. William Skinner, "Regional Urbanization in Nineteenth-Century China," in *The City in Late Imperial China*, ed. G. William Skinner (Stanford, Calif.: Stanford University Press, 1977), 211–49; Central Intelligence Agency, *People's Republic of China Atlas* (Washington, D.C.: U.S. Government Printing Office, 1971), 39, 59.

2. Skinner, "Regional Urbanization," 223.

3. R. H. Tawney, *Land and Labor in China* (Boston: Beacon Press, 1966), 42. Compare Lucian W. Pye, *China, an Introduction* (Boston: Little, Brown, 1978), 89–90.

4. Ramon H. Myers, *The Chinese Economy Past and Present* (Belmont, Calif.: Wadsworth, 1980), 16. Compare similar figures for the middle of the twentieth century in John G. Gurley, *China's Economy and the Maoist Strategy* (New York: Monthly Review Press, 1976), 239; and Isabel and David Crook, *Ten Mile Inn: Mass Movement in a Chinese Village* (New York: Pantheon, 1979), 8.

5. Edgar Snow, *Red Star Over China* (New York: Grove Press, 1961), 16.

6. For Mao's classic statement on mass line, see Mao Tse-tung, *Selected Works of Mao Tse-tung* (Peking: Foreign Languages Press, 1965), vol. 3: 226.

7. Helen Foster Snow, who visited Yanan, used this term. See Helen Foster Snow, *The Chinese Communists: Sketches and Autobiographies of the Old Guard* (Westport, Conn.: Greenwood, 1972), xiv.

8. James Pinkney Harrison, *The Long March to Power: A History of the*

Chinese Communist Party, 1921–1972 (New York: Praeger, 1972), 454. Later figures are from *Beijing Review* (September 6, 1982): 20–24.

9. Ibid., 294, 396.

10. Congressional Quarterly, *China: U.S. Policy Since 1945* (Washington, D.C.: Congressional Quarterly, 1980), 84.

11. Tang Tsou, *America's Failure in China* (Chicago: University of Chicago Press, 1963), 495.

12. Donald W. Klein and Anne B. Clark, *Biographic Dictionary of Chinese Communism, 1921–1965*, 2 vols. (New York: Columbia University Press, 1981), 626.

13. Mao Tse-tung, *Selected Works of Mao Tse-tung*, vol. 2 (Peking: Foreign Languages Press, 1953), 272.

14. Raymond F. Wylie, *The Emergence of Maoism: Mao Tse-tung, Ch'en Po-ta and the Search for Chinese Theory, 1935–1945* (Stanford, Calif.: Stanford University, 1980), 13.

15. Helen Snow, *The Chinese Communists*, 164.

16. Klein and Clark, *Biographic Dictionary of Chinese Communism*, 109.

17. Ibid., 821.

18. Edgar Snow, *Red Star over China*, 294.

19. Chung Hua-min and Arthur C. Miller, *Madame Mao: A Profile of Chiang Ch'ing* (Hong Kong: Union Research Institute, 1968), 53–54, cited in Parris Chang, *Radicals and Radical Ideology in China's Cultural Revolution* (New York: Research Institute on Communist Affairs, 1973), 72.

20. Quoted in Robert C. Tucker, *The Marxian Revolutionary Idea* (New York: Norton, 1969), 16.

21. Ramon H. Myers, *The Chinese Economy*, 36.

22. Ibid., 180–82.

Chapter 2

1. Mao Tse-tung, *Selected Works of Mao Tse-tung* (Peking: Foreign Languages Press, 1977), vol. 5: 17.

2. Yu-ming Shaw, "John Leighton Stuart and U.S.-Chinese Communist Rapprochements: Was There Another 'Lost Chance in China'?" *China Quarterly*, 89 (March 1982): 82. See also John Gittings, *The World and China, 1922–1972* (New York: Harper & Row, 1974), 170.

3. Herbert Feis, *The China Tangle* (Princeton: Princeton University, 1953), 140–41.

4. Stuart R. Schram (ed.), *Chairman Mao Talks to the People: Talks and Letters, 1956–1971* (New York: Pantheon, 1974), 102–3.

5. Ibid., 191.

6. Gittings, *The World and China*, 170.

7. James Pinkney Harrison, *Long March to Power: A History of the Chinese Communist Party, 1921–1972* (New York: Praeger, 1972), 446.

8. A. Doak Barnett, *Cadres, Bureaucracy and Political Power in Communist China* (New York: Columbia University Press, 1967), 18.

9. MAO, *Selected Works,* vol. 5: 143.

10. Ibid.

11. Ibid., vol. 5: 26–31.

12. Melvin Gurtov and Byong-Moo Hwang, *China Under Threat: The Politics of strategy and Diplomacy* (Baltimore: Johns Hopkins University Press, 1980), 52.

13. *The New York Times,* November 16, 1950.

14. Mao, *Selected Works,* vol. 5: 43.

15. Dean Acheson, *The Korean War* (New York: Norton, 1971), 66.

16. John Gardner, "The *Wu-fan* Campaign in Shanghai: A Study in the Consolidation of Urban Control," in *Chinese Communist Politics in Action,* ed. A. Doak Barnett (Seattle: University of Washington Press, 1969), 477.

17. Mao, *Selected Works*, vol. 4: 419.

18. Mao, *Selected Works*, vol. 5: 115.

19. Gurtov and Hwang, *China Under Threat,* 31.

20. Mao, *Selected Works,* vol 5: 53; 45–56 passim.

21. Merle Goldman, *Literary Dissent in Communist China* (New York: Atheneum, 1971), 92.

22. Stuart R. Schram, *Mao Tse-tung* (New York: Simon & Schuster, 1967), 73*n*. A few years later, Mao was expressing himself in similar fashion concerning Russian flatus (see Mao, *Selected Works*, vol. 5: 317). The fact that the CCP's own dogma was a Western import only adds to the paradox.

23. Mark Selden, "The Yenan Legacy: The Mass Line," in *Chinese Communist Politics in Action,* ed. Barnett, 105.

24. Schram, *Mao Tse-tung,* 269–70.

25. Mao, *Selected Works,* vol. 5: 122.

26. Ezra Vogel, *Canton Under Communism: Programs and Politics in a Provincial Capital, 1949–1968* (New York: Harper & Row, 1971), 85.

27. Goldman, *Literary Dissent in Communist China,* 35.

28. Vogel, *Canton Under Communism,* 87.

29. Gardner, "The *Wu-fan* Campaign in Shanghai," 524.

30. Mao, *Selected Works*, vol. 4: 438.

31. Derk Bodde, *Peking Diary: 1948–1949, A Year of Revolution* (Greenwich, Conn.: Fawcett, 1967), 117.

Chapter 3

1. John G. Gurley, *China's Economy and the Maoist Strategy* (New York: Monthly Review Press, 1976), 238–40.

2. Mao Tse-tung, *Selected Works of Mao Tse-tung* (Peking: Foreign Languages Press, 1977), vol. 5: 192.

3. Christopher Howe, *China's Economy: A Basic Guide* (New York: Basic Books, 1978), xxvii. See also Alexander Eckstein, *China's Economic Development: The Interplay of Scarcity and Ideology* (Ann Arbor, Mich.: University of Michigan Press, 1975), 308–10.

4. Parris Chang, *Policy and Power in China* (University Park, Pa.: Pennsylvania State University Press, 1975), 10.

5. Mao, *Selected Works*, vol. 5: 201.

6. Ibid., vol. 5: 172.

7. Ibid., vol. 5: 185.

8. Ibid., vol. 5: 196.

9. Donald J. Munro, "Egalitarian Ideal and Educational Fact in Communist China," in *China: Management of a Revolutionary Society*, ed. John M. Lindbeck (Seattle: University of Washington Press, 1971), 296.

10. Stuart R. Schram (ed.), *Chairman Mao Talks to the People: Talks and Letters, 1956–1971* (New York: Pantheon, 1974), 138.

11. Dick Wilson, *The People's Emperor, Mao: A Biography of Mao Tse-tung* (New York: Lee Publishers Group, 1979), 312.

12. Chang, *Policy and Power in China*, 225.

13. Mark Selden, *The People's Republic of China: A Documentary History of Revolutionary Change* (New York: Monthly Review Press, 1979), 351.

14. Marle Goldman, *Literary Dissent in Communist China* (New York: Atheneum, 1971), 150–51.

15. Schram (ed.), *Chairman Mao Talks to the People*, 70.

16. Wilson, *The People's Emperor, Mao*, 317.

17. Mao, *Selected Works*, vol. 5: 244.

18. Schram (ed.), *Chairman Mao Talks to the People*, 72.

19. Ibid., 75.

20. Mao, *Selected Works*, vol. 5: 443–44.

21. Roderick MacFarquhar, *The Origins of the Cultural Revolution, 1: Contradictions Among the People, 1956–1957* (New York: Columbia University Press, 1974), 87–88; also Chang, *Policy and Power in China*, 26–27.

22. Quoted in Wilson, *The People's Emperor, Mao*, 327.

23. Mao, *Selected Works*, vol. 5: 243-44.

24. Chang, *Policy and Power in China*, 226.

25. Wilson, *The People's Emperor, Mao*, 345.

26. Ibid., 347.

27. Ibid.

Chapter 4

1. Chinese Statistical Bureau, *Chinese Economic Yearbook: 1984* (in Chinese) (Hong Kong: Xianggang Jingji Daobao Chuban She, 1984), 29, 454.

2. Harvard University Center for International Affairs and the East Asian

Research Center, *Communist China, 1955–1959: Policy Documents with Analysis* (Cambridge, Mass.: Harvard University Press, 1965), 329.

3. Dick Wilson, *The People's Emperor, Mao: A Biography of Mao Tse-tung* (New York: Lee Publishers Group, 1979), 348. See also Roderick MacFarquhar, *The Origins of the Cultural Revolution, 1: Contradictions Among the People, 1956–1957* (New York: Columbia University Press, 1974), 289ff.

4. Harvard Center, *Communist China, 1955–1959*, 179.

5. MacFarquhar, *Origins of the Cultural Revolution: 1*, 287.

6. Mao, *Selected Works*, vol. 5: 482.

7. Harold C. Hinton (ed.), *The People's Republic of China, 1949–1979: A Documentary Survey* (Wilmington, Del.: Scholarly Resources, 1980), vol. 2: 605.

8. James Pinkney Harrison, *The Long March to Power: A History of the Chinese Communist Party, 1921–1972* (New York: Praeger, 1972), 474. See also Frederick C. Teiwes, *Politics and Purges in China* (White Plains, N.Y.: M. E. Sharpe, 1979), 349.

9. Harvard Center, *Communist China, 1955–1959*, 16.

10. The following discussion and quotations are taken from Stuart R. Schram, ed., *Chairman Mao Talks to the People: Talks and Letters: 1956–1971* (New York: Pantheon, 1974), 91–124.

11. Hinton (ed.), *The People's Republic of China, 1949–1979*, vol. 2: 639–40.

12. Harvard Center, *Communist China, 1955–1959*, 167.

13. Ibid., 424; also Hinton (ed.), *The People's Republic of China, 1949–1979*, vol. 2: 638.

14. Hinton (ed.), *The People's Republic of China, 1949-1979*, vol. 2: 638.

15. Parris Chang, *Policy and Power in China* (University Park, Pa.: Pennsylvania State University Press, 1975), 83.

16. Richard H. Solomon, *Mao's Revolution and the Chinese Political Culture* (Berkeley: University of California, 1971), 344. Translation altered.

17. Mark Selden, *The People's Republic of China: A Documentary History of Revolutionary Change* (New York: Monthly Review Press, 1979), 413.

18. Chang, *Policy and Power in China*, 114.

19. Han Suyin, *Wind in the Tower* (Boston: Little-Brown, 1976), 128–29.

20. Hinton, *The People's Republic of China*, vol. 2: 685.

21. Kenneth Lieberthal, *A Research Guide to Central Party and Government Meetings in China, 1949–1975* (White Plains, N.Y.: International Arts and Sciences Press, 1976), 133–34.

22. Schram (ed.), *Chairman Mao Talks to the People*, 129.

23. Ellis Joffe, *Between Two Plenums: China's Interleadership Conflict* (Ann Arbor, Mich.: University of Michigan, 1975), 17.

24. Seldon, *The People's Republic of China*, 480.

25. Chang, *Politics and Power in China*, 120.

26. David A. Charles, "The Dismissal of Marshal Peng Te-huai," *China Quarterly*, 8 (1961): 32.

Chapter 5

1. Shigeru Ishikawa, "China Economic Growth Since 1949—An Assessment," *China Quarterly* 94 (June 1983): 247.

2. Harold C. Hinton (ed.), *The People's Republic of China, 1949–1979: A Documentary Survey* (Wilmington, Del.: Scholarly Resources, 1980), vol. 2: 862–69 (translation slightly altered).

3. Ibid., vol. 2: 881. The earlier editorial may be found on pp. 874-76 of vol. 2.

4. Sven Lindqvist, *China in Crisis* (New York: Crowell, 1965), 77.

5. Hinton, *The People's Republic of China*, vol. 2: 909f.

6. Stuart R. Schram (ed.), *Chairman Mao Talks to the People: Talks and Letters: 1956–1971* (New York: Pantheon, 1974), 187.

7. Ibid., 167.

8. Nicholas R. Lardy and Kenneth Lieberthal, *Chen Yun's Strategy for China's Development: A Non-Maoist Alternative* (White Plains, N.Y.: M. E. Sharpe, 1983), 194.

9. Richard Baum, *Prelude to Revolution: Mao, the Party, and the Peasant Question, 1962–1966* (New York: Columbia University Press, 1975), 17.

10. Schram, *Chairman Mao Talks to the People*, 190.

11. Frederick C. Teiwes, *Politics and Purges in China* (White Plains, N.Y.: M. E. Sharpe, 1979), 511.

12. Stuart R. Schram, "Introduction: the Cultural Revolution in Historical Perspective," in *Authority, Participation, and Cultural Change in China* (Cambridge: Cambridge University Press, 1973), 84.

13. Ellis Joffe, *Between Two Plenums: China's Intraleadership Conflict, 1959–1962* (Ann Arbor: University of Michigan Center For Chinese Studies, 1975), 54.

14. Hinton (ed.), *The People's Republic of China*, 912.

15. Thomas P. Bernstein, *Up to the Mountains and Down to the Villages: The Transfer of Youth from Urban to Rural China* (New Haven: Yale University Press, 1977), 56.

16. Ibid., 96–98.

17. Merle Goldman, *China's Intellectuals: Advise and Dissent* (Cambridge, Mass.: Harvard University Press, 1981), 108.

18. Ibid., 77.

19. Teiwes, *Politics and Purges in China*, 579.

20. K. H. Fan (ed.), *Mao Tse-tung and Lin Piao: Post Revolutionary Writings*, (Garden City, N.Y.: Anchor-Doubleday, 1972), xv.

21. Goldman, *China's Intellectuals,* 93.

22. A. Doak Barnett, *China After Mao* (Princeton: Princeton University Press, 1967), 128–29, 149.

23. Roxanne Witke, *Comrade Chiang Ch'ing* (Boston: Little Brown, 1977), 310.

24. Ellis Joffe, "The Chinese Army Under Lin Piao: Prelude to Political Intervention," in *China: Management of a Revolutionary Society,* ed. John M. Lindbeck (Seattle: University of Washington Press, 1971), 359–60.

25. Barnett, *China After Mao,* 123.

26. Byung-joon Ahn, *Chinese Politics and the Cultural Revolution: Dynamics of Policy Processes* (Seattle: University of Washington Press, 1976), 184.

27. Martin Ebon, *Lin Biao: The Life and Writings of China's New Ruler* (New York: Stein & Day, 1970), 224–25.

28. Quoted in Frank E. Rogers, "Sino-American Relations and the Vietnam War, 1964-66," *China Quarterly,* 66 (June 1976): 303.

29. Baum, *Prelude to Revolution,* 143.

30. Ahn, *Chinese Politics and the Cultural Revolution,* 196–97.

Chapter 6

1. Richard Baum, "China: Year of the Mangoes," in *China in Ferment: Perspectives on the Cultural Revolution,* ed. Richard Baum (Englewood Cliffs, N.J.: Prentice-Hall, 1971), 156n.

2. K. H. Fan, *The Chinese Cultural Revolution: Selected Documents* (New York: Grove Press, 1968), 132.

3. David Milton, Nancy Milton and Franz Schurmann (eds.), *People's China: Social Experimentation, Politics, Entry onto the World Scene, 1966 Through 1972* (New York: Vintage Press, 1974), 284.

4. Harold C. Hinton (ed.), *The People's Republic of China, 1949–1979: A Documentary Survey* (Wilmington, Del.: Scholarly Resources, 1980), vol. 3: 1318–19.

5. Ibid., vol. 3: 1521.

6. Byung-Joon Ahn, *Chinese Politics and the Cultural Revolution: Dynamics of Policy Processes* (Seattle: University of Washington Press, 1976), 223.

7. Hinton (ed.), *The People's Republic of China,* vol. 3: 1553.

8. Fan, *The Chinese Cultural Revolution,* 169.

9. Hinton (ed.), *The People's Republic of China,* vol. 3: 1577.

10. Fan, *The Chinese Cultural Revolution,* 163.

11. Mao Tse-tung, *Selected Works of Mao Tse-tung* (Peking: Foreign Languages Press, 1965), vol. 1: 28.

12. Stuart R. Schram, *Chairman Mao Talks to the People: Talks and Letters: 1956–1971* (New York: Pantheon, 1974), 265.

13. Ibid., 273.

14. Ibid., 277.

15. David Milton and Nancy Dall Milton, *The Wind Will Not Subside: Years in Revolutionary China—1964–1969* (New York: Random House, 1976), 291.

16. Edward E. Rice, *Mao's Way* (Berkeley: University of California Press, 1972), 424 (translation altered).

17. Milton and Milton, *The Wind Will Not Subside*, 321.

18. Ibid., 335.

19. Rice, *Mao's Way*, 454–55.

20. Ross Terrill, *The White-Boned Demon: A Biography of Madame Mao Zedong* (New York: Morrow, 1984), 298.

21. Tang Tsou, "The Cultural Revolution and the Chinese Political System," in Baum (ed.), *China in Ferment*, 192.

22. Hinton, *The People's Republic of China*, vol. 4: 2224.

23. Milton et al., *People's China*, 218.

24. *Beijing Review*, 27 (July 6, 1981): 20.

25. Dennis Bloodworth, *The Messiah and the Mandarins: Mao Tsetung and the Ironies of Power* (New York: Atheneum, 1982), 249.

26. Richard M. Pfeffer, "The Pursuit of Purity: Mao's Cultural Revolution," in Baum (ed.), *China in Ferment*, 205.

Chapter 7

1. Harold C. Hinton (ed.), *The People's Republic of China, 1949–1979: A Documentary Survey* (Wilmington, Del.: Scholarly Resources, 1980), vol. 4: 2239 (romanization changed).

2. Ross Terrill, *Mao: A Biography* (New York: Harper & Row, 1980), 342.

3. Mao Tse-tung, *Selected Works of Mao Tse-tung* (Peking: Foreign Languages Press, 1965), vol. 2: 224.

4. Quoted in Philip Bridgham, "Mao's Cultural Revolution: The Struggle to Consolidate Power," *China Quarterly*, 41 (January–March 1970): 22.

5. Thomas Fingar, "Introduction: The Quest for Independence," in *China's Quest for Independence: Policy Evolution in the 1970s*, ed. Thomas Fingar (Boulder, Colo.: Westview Press, 1980), 43.

6. However, Zhou's writ did not reach everywhere. In 1968 he was unable to prevent the torture and death of his own adopted daughter. And in 1972 all he could do for the relatives of Peng Dehuai, who had long been held incommunicado in solitary confinement, was to express his concern and report on Peng's health. See Fox Butterfield, *China: Alive in the Bitter Sea* (New York: New York Times Books, 1982), 355; and Foreign Broadcast Information Ser-

vice, *Daily Report—People's Republic of China* (U.S. Department of Commerce, National Technical Information Service), January 24, 1979, E5–E8.

7. Ross Terrill, *Flowers on an Iron Tree: Five Cities of China* (Boston: Little Brown, 1975), 201.

8. Hinton (ed.), *The People's Republic of China*, vol. 4: 2477.

9. Ibid., vol. 4: 2468.

10. Ibid., vol. 4: 2484.

11. Ibid., vol. 4: 2497.

12. Ibid., vol. 4: 2504.

13. Ibid., vol. 4: 2529.

14. Ibid., vol. 4: 2534 (translation altered).

15. Jurgen Domes, *Socialism in the Chinese Countryside: Rural Societal Policies in the People's Republic of China, 1949–1979* (Montreal: McGill-Queen's University Press, 1980), 90 (romanizations have been changed).

16. Ibid., 93.

17. Tang Tsou, Marc Blecher, and Mitch Meisner, "National Agricultural Policy: the Dazhai Model and Local Change in the Post-Mao Era," in Mark Selden and Victor Lippit, *The Transition to Socialism in China* (Armonk, N.Y.: M. E. Sharpe, 1982), 274.

18. Terrill, *Mao*, 406.

19. Ibid., 413.

20. Philip Short, *The Dragon and the Bear: China and Russia in the Eighties* (New York: William Morrow, 1982), 201.

21. Terrill, *Mao*, 409.

Chapter 8

1. Harold C. Hinton (ed.), *The People's Republic of China, 1949–1979: A Documentary Survey* (Wilmington, Del.: Scholarly Resources, 1980), vol. 4: 2655–56. Emphasis added.

2. Ibid., vol. 4: 2826–27.

3. Quoted in Roger Garside, *Coming Alive: China After Mao* (New York: McGraw-Hill, 1981), 210.

4. "Quarterly Chronicle and Documentation," *The China Quarterly*, 72 (December 1977): 858.

5. Hinton (ed.), *The People's Republic of China*, vol. 4: 2719.

6. Quoted in Philip Short, *The Dragon and the Bear: China and Russia in the Eighties* (New York: William Morrow, 1982), 243.

7. Garside, *Coming Alive*, 206.

8. John Fraser, *The Chinese: Portrait of a People* (New York: Summit Books, 1980), 209.

9. James D. Seymour, *China: The Fifth Modernization: China's Human*

Rights Movement, 1978–1979 (Stanfordville, N.Y.: Human Rights Publishing Group, 1980), 63.

10. Ibid., 50.

11. Ibid., 198.

12. Short, *The Dragon and the Bear*, 291.

13. Ibid., 386.

14. Kenneth Lieberthal, "China's Political Reforms: A Net Assessment," *Annals of the American Academy of Political and Social Sciences*, 476 (November 1984): 20.

15. Perry Link (ed.), *Stubborn Weeds: Popular and Controversial Chinese Literature After the Cultural Revolution* (Bloomington: Indiana University Press, 1983), 248.

16. Ibid., 434.

17. *The New York Times*, August 31, 1980.

18. See *Beijing Review*, 27 (July 6, 1981); also David S. Goodman, "The Sixth Plenum of the 11th Central Committee of the CCP: Look Back in Anger?" *China Quarterly*, 87 (September 1981): 518–27.

Chapter 9

1. *Beijing Review*, 27: 44 (October 29, 1984): 111.

2. *Foreign Broadcast Information Service, Daily Report: People's Republic of China*, October 9, 1980, L9.

3. *The New York Times*, January 6, 1985.

4. Ibid., December 17, 1984.

5. Suzanne Pepper, *China's Universities: Post-Mao Enrollment Policies and Their Impact on the Structure of Secondary Education* (Ann Arbor: University of Michigan Center for Chinese Studies, 1984), 116.

6. Quoted in Wong Siu-lun, "Consequences of China's New Population Policy," *China Quaterly*, 98 (June 1984): 221.

7. Vaclav Smil, *The Bad Earth: Environmental Degradation in China* (Armonk, N.Y.: M. E. Sharpe, 1984), 70. This section draws extensively from Professor Smil's distressing study.

8. Nicholas R. Lardy, *Agriculture in China's Modern Economic Development* (Cambridge: Cambridge University Press, 1983), 5.

9. Mark Seldon, *The People's Republic of China: A Documentary History of Revolutionary Change* (New York: Monthly Review Press, 1979), 480.

Suggested Readings

The enormous literature on China cannot be adequately represented by a brief list. The student who wishes to get a sense of the breadth of scholarship in this field is invited to examine the book review sections of publications such as *China Quarterly* or *Journal of Asian Studies*. What follows here is a sampling of some of the more important and interesting writing accessible to the serious general reader.

General History

Guillermaz, Jacques. *The Chinese Communist Party in Power, 1949–1976.*
    Translated by Anne Destenay. Boulder: Westview Press, 1976. A
    well-documented general history of the People's Republic up to the
    death of Mao.

Hinton, Harold C. (ed.). *The People's Republic of China, 1949–1979: A Doc-
    umentary Survey.* 5 vols. Wilmington, Del.: Scholarly Resources,
    1980. A comprehensive collection of previously translated materials
    covering every aspect of domestic and foreign policy.

Mao Tse-tung. *Chairman Mao Talks to the People: Talks and Letters: 1956–
    1971.* Edited by Stuart Schram. New York: Pantheon Books, 1974.
    A collection of Mao's utterances revealing the the colorful and con-
    tradictory character of the revolutionary leader.

———. *Selected Works.* 5 vols. Peking: Foreign Languages Press, 1961–77.
    Edited speeches and writings from 1927 to 1957.

Meisner, Maurice. *Mao's China and After: A History of the People's Repub-
    lic.* New York: The Free Press, 1985. A revision of the author's *Mao's*

China and a general history of the People's Republic with a pronounced political science orientation.

Rice, Edward E. *Mao's Way*. Berkeley: University of California Press, 1972. A detailed discussion of politics and power struggles, with strong emphasis on the Cultural Revolution.

Selden, Mark (ed.). *The People's Republic of China: A Documentary History of Revolutionary Change*. New York: Monthly Review Press, 1979. Documents and commentary from the civil war years to Mao's death.

Short, Philip. *The Dragon and the Bear: China and Russia in the Eighties*. New York: William Morrow, 1982. An attempt to uncover comparable political patterns in the Soviet and the Chinese Communist systems by a journalist familiar with both nations.

History of Specific Periods

Bao, Ruo-wang. *Prisoner of Mao*. London: Andre Deutsch, 1975. A rare account of China's prisons in the early 1960s by a French-Chinese.

Barnett, A. Doak. *Communist China: The Early Years, 1949–1955*. New York: Praeger, 1964. An account of the consolidation period by one of the most eminent American experts.

Baum, Richard. *Prelude to Revolution: Mao, the Party, and the Peasant Question, 1962–1966*. New York: Columbia University Press, 1975. A study of the Socialist Education movement (1962–66) providing insights into the nature of mobilization campaigns.

Bernstein, Richard. *From the Center of the Earth: A Search for the Truth About China*. Boston: Little Brown, 1982. A wide-ranging, reportorial account of China during the early 1980s.

Bonavia, David. *The Chinese*. New York: Lippincott and Crowell, 1980. A description of rural and urban social life in the post-Mao era with comparisons drawn to the Soviet Union.

Brandt, Conrad, Benjamin Schwartz, and John K. Fairbank. *A Documentary Survey of Chinese Communism*. Cambridge, Mass.: Harvard University Press, 1959. Important documents from the early days of the CCP until liberation.

Butterfield, Fox. *China: Alive in the Bitter Sea*. New York: New York Times Books, 1982. A description of post-Mao China by a *New York Times* correspondent, treating topics ranging from bureaucratic structure to love and sex. The Chinese government loudly objected to this critical book.

Center for International Affairs and the East Asian Research Center. *Communist China 1955–1959: Policy Documents with Analysis*. Cambridge, Mass.: Harvard University Press, 1965. Documents relating to the First Five-Year Plan and the Great Leap Forward.

Cheng, J. Chester, ed. *The Politics of the Chinese Red Army: The Translation of the Bulletin of Activities of the People's Liberation Army*. Stanford, Calif.: Hoover Institution, 1966. Translations of classified documents that reflect conditions in China in the aftermath of the Great Leap Forward.

Fan, K. H. *The Cultural Revolution: Selected Documents*. New York: Grove Press, 1968. Translations of important pronouncements and other documents.

Fraser, John. *The Chinese: Portrait of a People*. New York: Summit Books, 1980. A rather personal account of a Canadian journalist's experiences in Beijing during the time of the Democracy Wall movement (1979).

Goldman, Merle. *China's Intellectuals: Advice and Dissent*. Cambridge, Mass.: Harvard University Press, 1981. A study of establishment and dissenting intellectuals and how they played a role in the political events before and during the Cultural Revolution.

Heng, Liang, and Judith Shapiro. *Son of the Revolution*. New York: Knopf, 1983. Autobiography of a man who grew up during the Cultural Revolution and after many vicissitudes met and married an American. The book is critical of the system.

Hinton, William. *Fanshen: A Documentary of Revolution in a Chinese Village*. New York: Random House, 1966. A famous firsthand account of revolutionary transformation in north China during the years leading up to and immediately after liberation.

Hunter, Neal. *Shanghai Journal: An Eyewitness Account of the Cultural Revolution*. Boston: Beacon Press, 1971. Describes the early years of the Cultural Revolution as experienced by a firsthand observer in Shanghai.

Joffe, Ellis. *Between Two Plenums: China's Intraleadership Conflict, 1959–1962*. Ann Arbor: University of Michigan Center for Chinese Studies, 1975. A good brief summary of politics during the immediate crisis period following the Great Leap Forward.

Lee, Hong Yung. *The Politics of the Chinese Cultural Revolution: A Case Study*. Berkeley: University of California Press, 1978. A many-faceted survey and analysis, which emphasizes cleavages and factionalism within the Party, the Red Guards, and the worker rebels and between the Party and the people.

Lindqvist, Sven. *China in Crisis*. New York: Crowell, 1965. Observations of a Swedish student in China during the post-Great Leap Forward crisis of the early 1960s.

MacFarquhar, Roderick. *The Origins of the Cultural Revolution, 1: Contradictions Among the People 1956–1957*. New York: Columbia University Press, 1974. A detailed study of pre-Great Leap Forward period politics, particularly the Hundred Flowers movement.

———. *The Origins of the Cultural Revolution, 2: The Great Leap Forward*. New York: Columbia University Press, 1983. The continuation of MacFarquhar's multivolume study. Rich in detail.

Milton, David, and Nancy Dall Milton. *The Wind Will Not Subside*. New York: Pantheon, 1976. A sympathetic account of the Cultural Revolution by American language teachers who lived in Beijing at the time.

Mosher, Steven W. *Broken Earth: The Rural Chinese*. New York: The Free Press, 1983. A critical and controversial account of rural China in the early 1980s by an anthropologist who lived in and studied a southern village.

Pepper, Suzanne. *Civil War in China: The Political Struggle, 1945–1949*. Berkeley: University of California Press, 1978. A study of the civil war years that brings out the weaknesses of the Nationalist regime.

Robinson, Thomas W. *The Cultural Revolution in China*. Berkeley: University of California Press, 1971. Analyses of the Cultural Revolution by several specialists.

Seymour, James D. (ed.). *China: The Fifth Modernization: China's Human Rights Movement, 1978–1979*. Stanfordville, N.Y.: Human Rights Publishing Group, 1980. This collection contains materials written by dissidents, some of whom were subsequently imprisoned.

Snow, Edgar. *Red Star Over China*. Revised and enlarged ed. New York: Grove Press, 1968. Influential reportage of the Chinese Communists on the eve of the anti-Japanese war; first published in 1938. Contains unique autobiographical material on Mao.

Wolfgang, Marvin E. (ed.). *China in Transition, Annals of the American Academy of Political and Social Sciences*, 476 (November 1974). A collection of essays by specialists in various aspects of China, discussing recent and probable future developments.

Fiction and Poetry

Ansley, Clive. *The Heresy of Wu Han: His Play "Hai Jui's Dismissal" and Its Role in China's Cultural Revolution*. Toronto: University of Toronto Press, 1971. This is the famous historical play that triggered the Cultural Revolution.

Ch'en Jo-hsi. *The Execution of Mayor Yin, and Other Stories from the Great Proletarian Cultural Revolution*. Bloomington: University of Indiana Press, 1978. A collection of powerful short stories about the waning years of the Cultural Revolution, written by an overseas Chinese who returned to the motherland and then left in disillusionment.

Chen, Yuan-tsung. *The Dragon's Village*. New York: Penguin Books, 1980. A novel about the land reform period, portraying the experiences of idealistic young Party workers who come from Shanghai and must cope with the complexity and violence of a miserable northern village.

Goodman, David S. G. *Beijing Street Voices: The Poetry and Politics of China's Democracy Movement*. London: Marion Boyars, 1981. Translations and analyses of poems written during the Democracy Wall period.

Link, Perry (ed.). *Stubborn Weeds: Popular and Controversial Chinese Literature after the Cultural Revolution*. Bloomington: Indiana University Press, 1983. Poems, stories, humor, and drama, including the controversial play *What If I Really Were?*

—— (ed.). *"People or Monsters" and other Stories and Reportage from China After Mao*. Bloomington: University of Indiana Press, 1983. A collection featuring Liu Binyan's famous exposé of a notoriously corrupt Party cadre.

Shen, Rong. *At Middle Age*. Beijing: Panda Books, 1982. A novel about a woman doctor who almost kills herself with unselfish overwork. The book explores the frustrations and the practical and financial problems faced by middle-level intellectuals in the years since the Cultural Revolution.

Yang, Jiang. *Six Chapters from My Life "Downunder"*. Hong Kong: The Chinese University Press, 1984. An intellectual woman's sensitive and understated account of her rustication during the Cultural Revolution.

Biographies

Dittmer, Lowell. *Liu Shao-ch'i and the Chinese Cultural Revolution*. Berkeley: University of California Press, 1975. A political biography of Mao's second-in-command and a study of the Mao-Liu rupture from perspectives of personalities, styles, and policies.

Ebon, Martin. *Lin Piao: The Life and Writings of China's New Ruler*. New York: Stein & Day, 1970. Biographical information and documents on Lin and other radicals, compiled just prior to Lin's fall.

Klein, Donald W., and Anne B. Clark. *Biographic Dictionary of Chinese Communism, 1921–1965*. Cambridge, Mass.: Harvard University Press, 1971. A two-volume biographical dictionary of all major figures during the early years and up to the Cultural Revolution.

Pye, Lucian. *Mao Tse-tung: The Man in the Leader*. New York: Basic Books, 1976. A stimulating and exploratory psychobiography of Mao that attempts to explain his personality primarily by his relationship to his mother.

Robinson, Thomas W. "Chou En-lai and the Cultural Revolution in China." In *The Cultural Revolution in China*, edited by Thomas W. Robinson. Berkeley: University of California Press, 1971. An illuminating comparison of the political styles of Zhou Enlai, Mao Zedong, and Lin Biao.

Schram, Stuart R. *Mao Tse-tung*. New York: Simon & Schuster, 1967. An authoritative account of Mao's life not including the last decade.

———. *Mao Zedong: A Preliminary Reassessment*. New York: St. Martin's Press, 1984. An examination of Mao's development as a political thinker, starting with his early contributions and ending with the Cultural Revolution years when Maoism itself became a major problem.

Spence, Jonathan D. *The Gate of Heavenly Peace: The Chinese and Their Revolution, 1895–1980*. New York: Viking Press, 1981. An absorbing account of the lives of major leftist intellectuals from the turn of the century through the 1970s. The author is one of the more stimulating and wide-ranging students of China writing today.

Terrill, Ross. *The White-boned Demon: A Biography of Madame Mao Zedong*. New York: Morrow, 1984. A popular biography of Jiang Qing that uses many unorthodox sources.

Wilson, Dick. *Zhou Enlai: A Biography*. New York: Viking Press, 1984. A carefully crafted and much-needed survey of the public life of China's most-admired revolutionary leader.

Witke, Roxane. *Comrade Chiang Ch'ing*. Boston: Little Brown, 1977. A biography of Mao's wife built around interviews granted to Professor Witke in 1972. Publication of this book helped poison the relationship between Mao and Jiang Qing.

Politics and Foreign Policy

Camilleri, Joseph. *Chinese Foreign Policy: The Maoist Era and Its Aftermath*. Seattle: University of Washington Press, 1980. An excellent broad survey of China's foreign policy.

Chang, Parris. *Policy and Power in China*. University Park: Pennsylvania State University Press, 1975. A study of the policy-making process prior to the Cultural Revolution, examining whether the earlier monolithic structure had been replaced by a "struggle between two lines."

315 Suggested Readings

Gittings, John. *The World and China, 1922–1972*. New York: Harper & Row, 1974. An overview of China's foreign affairs that explores connections between the pre-Communist and PRC policies. Based on careful analysis of Chinese sources.

Gurtov, Melvin, and Byong-Moo Hwang. *China Under Threat: The Politics of Strategy and Diplomacy*. Baltimore: Johns Hopkins University Press, 1980. An excellent examination of five case studies in foreign policy-making (from 1950 to 1965), arguing that domestic issues have been the primary determinants.

Harding, Harry (ed.). *China's Foreign Relations in the 1980s*. New Haven: Yale University Press, 1984. A collection of essays examining the relationship between domestic reforms and the new "open door" toward the industrialized west.

———. *Organizing China: The Problem of Bureaucracy, 1949–1976*. Stanford, Calif.: Stanford University Press, 1981. Excellent study of the development of organizational policy affecting the Party and the state administration.

Kim, Samuel S. (ed.). *Chinese Foreign Policy in the Ninteen Eighties*. Boulder, Colo.: Westview Press, 1984. Another collection of essays on post-Mao foreign policy.

Kraus, Richard Curt. *Class Conflict in Chinese Socialism*. New York: Columbia University Press, 1981. A study of the policies toward class designations after 1949 showing how the bases for class attribution changed from economic background to political behavior to entrenched interests.

Nee, Victor, and David Mozingo (eds.). *State and Society in Contemporary China*. Ithica, N.Y.: Cornell University Press, 1983. Essays by prominent American political scientists on the nature and exercise of state power before and after Mao.

Pye, Lucian. *The Dynamics of Chinese Politics*. Cambridge: Oelgeschlager, Gunn, and Hain, 1981. A psychocultural analysis of factional behavior in Chinese politics.

Solomon, Richard H. *Mao's Revolution and the Chinese Political Culture*. Berkeley: University of California Press, 1971. A provocative analysis of Chinese politics from the perspective of political culture, socialization, and Mao's personality.

Teiwes, Frederick C. *Politics and Purges in China*. White Plains, N.Y.: M. E. Sharpe, 1979. An analysis of organizational norms governing political behavior within the Party elite and the degree to which Mao respected them.

Whyte, Martin King. *Small Groups and Political Rituals in China*. Berkeley: University of California Press, 1974. Systematic study of the "small group," a key institution for organizing criticism and self-criticism. The study is based on interviews with Hong Kong refugees.

Yahuda, Michael. *Towards the End of Isolationism.* New York: St. Martin's Press, 1984. A broad study of the geopolitical basis for the continuity in foreign policy since the death of Mao.

Economic Development

Barnett, A. Doak. *China's Economy in Global Perspective.* Washington, D.C.: Brookings Institution, 1981. An encyclopedic survey of all facets of the Chinese economic system.

Ho, Samuel P. S., and Ralph W. Huenemann (eds.). *China's Open Door Policy: The Quest for Foreign Technology and Capital.* Vancouver: University of British Columbia Press, 1984. A collection of essays concerning the possibilities and effects of the new policy of opening up to Western economies.

Howe, Christopher. *China's Economy: A Basic Guide.* New York: Basic Books, 1978. A good introduction to the economic system prior to the recent reforms.

Lardy, Nicholas R. *Agriculture in China's Modern Economic Development.* Cambridge: Cambridge University Press, 1983. An important analysis of the spotty performance and difficult prospects of China's agricultural sector.

Smil, Vaclav. *The Bad Earth: Environmental Degradation in China.* Armonk, N.Y.: M. E. Sharpe, 1984. An important survey of revelations made in the late 1970s concerning China's deteriorating environment.

Social Conditions

Bennett, Gordon A. *Huadong: The Story of a Chinese People's Commune.* Boulder, Colo.: Westview Press, 1978. A description of the agricultural commune system through study of a model commune in Guangdong Province.

Chan, Anita, Richard Madsen, and Jonathan Unger. *Chen Village: The Recent History of a Peasant Community in Mao's China.* Berkeley: University of California Press, 1984. A study of the effects of changing policies on the people of a single south China village, based on systematic interviews of exiles in Hong Kong.

Chu, Godwin C., and Francis L. K. Hsu. *Moving a Mountain: Cultural Change in China.* Honolulu: University Press of Hawaii, 1979. A collection of studies on how different segments of Chinese society have reacted and adapted to the government's efforts at political and social transformation.

Cohen, Jerome A. *The Criminal Process in the People's Republic of China, 1949–63: An Introduction.* Cambridge, Mass.: Harvard University Press, 1968. A pioneering study of the judicial system as it existed prior to the Cultural Revolution.

Croll, Elisabeth. *The Politics of Marriage in Contemporary China.* Cambridge: Cambridge University Press, 1981. An attempt to identify and analyze patterns of mate selection and marriage.

———. *Chinese Women Since Mao.* Armonk, N.Y.: M. E. Sharpe, 1983. A brief assessment of the achievements and shortcomings of gender-related policies, especially since 1976, showing how other objectives, such as general economic development, frequently conflicted with full equality for women.

Davin, Delia. *Woman-Work: Women and the Party in Revolutionary China.* Oxford: Clarendon Press, 1976. A study of official policies toward women from the time of the Soviets in the 1930s, with particular emphasis on the 1950s. A painstakingly researched work.

Davis-Friedman, Deborah. *Long Lives: Chinese Elderly and the Communist Revolution.* Cambridge, Mass.: Harvard University Press, 1983. A study of policies toward China's growing population of elderly.

Dixon, John. *The Chinese Welfare System.* New York: Praeger, 1981. A broad examination of social welfare policies and their effects.

Frolic, B. Michael. *Mao's People: Sixteen Portraits of Life in Revolutionary China.* Cambridge, Mass.: Harvard University Press, 1980. Revealing individual and composite depictions of individuals and their adaptation to the revolution.

Li, Victor. *Law Without Lawyers: A Comparative View of Law in the United States and China.* Boulder, Colo.: Westview Press, 1978. An examination of values, institutions, and practices in the Chinese and American legal systems, especially criminal law. The author argues that China's less procedural and more political approach has been functional for a society undergoing revolutionary transformation.

Parish, William L., and Martin King White. *Village and Family in Contemporary China.* Chicago: University of Chicago Press, 1978. A comprehensive and highly respected study of rural life in Guangdong Province.

Shirk, Susan, L. *Competitive Comrades: Career Incentives and Student Strategies in China.* Berkeley: University of California Press, 1982. A revealing study, based partly on interviews with individuals, of the effect that revolutionary educational policies had on the behavior of urban students in the period prior to the Cultural Revolution.

Unger, Jonathan. *Education Under Mao: Class and Competition in Canton Schools, 1960–1980*. New York: Columbia University Press, 1982. Examines the effect of changing class policies on the educational opportunities facing various social groups.

Wolf, Margery, and Roxanne Witke (eds.). *Women in Chinese Society*. Stanford, Calif.: Stanford University Press, 1975. A collection of ten essays on the status of women in Chinese society both before and after liberation and also in Taiwan. Authored mostly by women, from a variety of perspectives: historical, anthropological, sociological, and literary.

Young, Marilyn B. *Women in China*. Ann Arbor: University of Michigan Center for Chinese Studies, 1973. A collection of articles by American feminist sinologists, exploring the struggle for women's rights in twentieth-century China.

Index

Acheson, Dean, 65–66
Afghanistan, Soviet invasion of, 284
Agricultural Producers' Cooperatives, 86–89, 91–95, 100–101, 117, 127. *See also* Agriculture; Communes
Agriculture: early 20th-century conditions, 10–16; greater agricultural regions, 11; collectivization in First Five-Year Plan, 85–89; socialist transformation of, 91–95, 96; poor performance and retrenchment after High Tide, 100–103, 114–15; during Great Leap Forward, 131–33; after Great Leap Forward, 142–46, 149–50; growth in 1970s, 219–20, 229–30; condition in late 1970s, 239; new policies under Deng Xiaoping, 243, 258–60; growth in 1980s, 274–75, 278. *See also* Agricultural Producers' Cooperatives; Economy; Industry and commerce; Land distribution; Land reform campaign; Responsibility system
Aksai-Chin border region, 165, 169
Anti-Rightist campaigns, 6, 108, 116–18, 139, 161, 247, 249, 281
APC. *See* Agricultural Producers' Cooperatives
Association of Poor and Middle Peasants, 68, 153, 155

Barrett, David, 52
Beethoven, Ludwig van, 243
Beijing Opera Festival on Contemporary Themes, 164–65
Bhutto, Zulfikar Ali, 233
Boxer uprising, 20–21, 204
Brezhnev, Leonid, 297
Brezhnev Doctrine, 198
Bureaucratism and elitism, 5–6, 76–77, 98–99, 115, 119, 151, 154–55, 201–2, 230, 261–62, 265–67, 279–82, 296

Cambodia: American forces in, 211; 1970 coup, 255. *See also* Kampuchea; Foreign relations
CCP. *See* Chinese Communist Party
Central America, as factor in Sino-American relations, 286
Central Commission for Inspecting Discipline, 265
Central Committee of CCP: size and structure, 56–57; actions, 276; reorganization after Great Proletarian Cultural Revolution, 206, 212; reorganization in 1982, 279. *See also* Plenums of the Central Committee of CCP
Central People's Government Council, 33, 62

Chen Boda: biographical sketch, 37–38, 74; editor of *Red Flag*, 122; on communes, 127–28; member of Mao's inner circle, 165; during Great Proletarian Cultural Revolution, 179; after Great Poletarian Cultural Revolution, 206–7, 212; fall from power, 214–15; formal expulsion from CCP, 222; trial, 267–70

Chen Yi: biographical sketch, 39; attempt to attain U.S. and British aid, 53; foreign minister, 63; moderate position on agricultural collectivization, 89; at Eighth Party Congress, 104; speech on education, 158; attacked during Great Proletarian Cultural Revolution, 190, 192

Chen Yongguei, 230, 264, 266

Chen Yun: biographical sketch, 36–37; role in economic recovery, 55; member of Politburo Standing Committee, 59; against entry into Korean conflict, 66; role in First Five-Year Plan, 84; moderate position on agricultural collectivization, 89, 101, 114–15; eclipsed during Great Leap Forward, 124–25; after Great Leap Forward, 145, 150–52, 243, 246; connections to Wei Jingsheng, 250; influence on economic reforms, 258; head of Central Commission for Inspecting Discipline, 265; honored at 1984 National Day celebrations, 294

Chiang Kai-shek: emergence as Nationalist leader, 23–26, 28; policies during anti-Japanese war, 26; civil war policies, 30–31; retreat to Taiwan, 32, 52; friendship with United States, 113–14. *See also* China, Republic of; Nationalist Party; Taiwan

China, People's Republic of: establishment, 32, 50; consolidation, 51–65; state organization, 61–64

China, Republic of: 23, 80, 113–14; and Korean War, 66; Taiwan straights crisis, 126; factor in Sino-American relations, 284–85. *See also* Taiwan; Nationalist Party

China Writers' Association, 281

Chinese Academy of Social Sciences, 242–43

Chinese Communist Party: values, 6; establishment, 18; congresses, 19, 23, 56, 102–5, 124, 199, 205–6, 222, 244, 265, 279, 284; early development, 23–26; growth during anti-Japanese war, 26–29; organizational structure, 56–61; relationship to state bureaucracy, 61–64; growth in 1950s, 93; effect of Great Leap Forward on, 139; rebuilding after Great Proletarian Cultural Revolution, 211–13, 222–23, 235; crisis of faith in, 280–81; future role, 296. *See also* Central Committee of CCP, Control Committee of CCP, Politburo of CCP, Secretariat of CCP, Standing Committee of the Politburo

Chinese People's Political Consultative Conference, 32, 33, 62–63, 117, 146

Civil War, 30–32, 38, 39, 40, 41

Communes, 127–41, 144–46, 153, 219, 207–8, 227–30, 239–40, 259–60, 274. *See also* Agricultural Producers' Cooperatives; Agriculture; Great Leap Forward

Communist Youth League, 20, 22, 242, 262

Control Committee of CCP, 59

CPPCC. *See* Chinese People's Political Consultative Conference

"Criticize Lin, Criticize Confucius" movement, 224–25

Cultural Revolution. *See* Great Proletarian Cultural Revolution

Cultural Revolution Small Group, 179, 189, 193–96, 212

Czechoslovakia: invaded by Warsaw Pact countries, 198

Daqing: 173–74; campaigns to emulate, 208, 240

Dazhai Brigade, 157; campaign to emulate, 207–8, 219; waning influence, 219–20, 230; attempt to rehabilitate, 233, 240; eclipse, 246, 264

Democracy Wall movement, 247–254

Deng Xiaoping: biographical sketch, 39–40; member of Politburo Standing Committee and Party general secretary, 59, 103–4; during Great Leap Forward, 126; after Great Leap Forward, 144–45, 149, 157; and criticism of Wu Han, 175; support for Mao against Peng Zhen, 176; failure to satisfy Mao's wishes, 181; support for Mao against Peng Zhen and Liu Shaoqi, 181; downfall during Great Proletarian Cultural Revolution, 189, 192–93, 198, 206; first rehabilitation, 222–23, 225–27; second downfall, 231–33; second rehabilitation, 241–42; emergence as national leader, 242–61; criticized by Wei Jingsheng, 252; consolidation of power, 261–72; quoted on Jiang Qing, 269–70; impact on modernization, 4, 273; and political reforms, 279–83; foreign policies in 1980s, 283–86; education policies in 1980s, 286–88; population and environmental policies in 1980s, 288–93; at 1984 National Day celebrations, 293–94

Deng Zihui, 88–89, 101

Dewey, John, 18, 73

Dubček, Alexander, 198

Economy: early 20th-century conditions, 10–22, 49; First Five-Year Plan, 84–89, 114–15; during Great Leap Forward, 110–122, 114–16, 122–35; after Great Leap Forward, 42–50; after Great Proletarian Cultural Revolution, 207–9; Fifth Five-Year Plan, 226–27; in late 1970s, 239–40; new policies under Deng Xiaoping, 243, 246, 258–61; performance and problems in 1980s, 273–79, 296–98. *See also* Agriculture; Industry and Commerce

Education: after liberation, 56; during First Five-Year Plan, 89–90; during Great Leap Forward, 130–31; after Great Leap Forward, 157–60, 174; in Great Proletarian Cultural Revolution, 182–84; after Great Proletarian Cul-

tural Revolution, 207–8; rebuilding in 1970s, 219–20; radical criticism of, 231; new policies under Deng Xiaoping, 243, 286–88

Engels, Friedrich, 44, 132

Environment, 291–93

Ethnic minorities, 51, 291

Fallaci, Oriana, 269

Family system, 16, 56

February Outline Report, 176

Finance and Economic Committee, 36, 62

First Ten Points, 153–54

"Five-Anti" campaign. *See* "Oppose Corruption" campaign

Five-Year Plan: First (1953–57), 4, 84–91, 93, 111; Fourth (1971–75), 219; Fifth (1976–80), 226–27

Foreign Ministry, 190, 192

Foreign relations: "lean to one side" policy of 1950s, 7, 52–55, 107; isolation of 1960s, 7–8, 168–70; opening up in 1970s, 220–22, 249–50, 254; open door in 1980s, 284–86; prospects for future, 297

  Individual countries: Burundi, 170; Burma, 169; Cambodia (Kampuchea), 255–56; Congo, 169–70; Cuba, 173; Egypt, 190; Great Britain, 53, 193, 286; Hong Kong, 192–93, 286; India, 133, 139, 165, 210, 256; Indonesia, 169, 173; Japan, 8, 221, 284–85; Laos, 169, 257; Mongolia, Soviet Republic of, 51–52, 169; Pakistan, 173, 210; Soviet Union, 7–8, 22–25, 53–55, 65, 80–81, 83–85, 114, 118–20, 136–41, 168–70, 187, 190, 198, 209–11, 221–22, 254–57, 283–86; Taiwan, 23, 66–67, 80, 111, 113–14, 126, 220, 284, 286; United States, 7–8, 52–53, 54–55, 70, 113–14; 133, 171, 198–99, 209–11, 248, 250, 254, 280, 283–86; Vietnam, 171–73, 252, 254–57; Yugoslavia, 140, 243. *See also* United Nations

Forum on Art and Culture, 74

"Four basic principles," 253

"Four Modernizations," 226, 240, 284, 297

Fu Yuehua, 251–52, 254, 267

Gang of Four: arrest and detention, 234–37; denunciation, 244, 249; trial of, 267–70. *See also* Jiang Qing; Wang Hongwen; Yao Wenyuan; Zhang Chunqiao

Gao Gang, 41, 137

General Line, 125, 131, 133

General Political Department of People's Liberation Army, 65, 167

Great Britain, 7, 122. *See also* Foreign relations

Great Leap Forward, 4–5, 7, 95, 110–41, 142–43, 249. *See also* High Tide

Great Proletarian Cultural Revolution: use of term, 205; origins, 176; principal participants, 179–81; pattern of, 5–6, 180; first phase, 182–94; latter phase, 194–200; assessments, 200–204; in retreat, 206–35; injustices of reversed, 281

Grenada as factor in Sino-American relations, 286

Guomindang (Nationalist Party), 229, *See also* Nationalist Party

"Hai Rui Dismissed from Office," 146, 161, 174–75, 246

Harrison, James, 60

Health, 91, 295

High Tide, 91–96, 100–102, 115, 118, 121, 122, 125, 141. *See also* Great Leap Forward

Ho Chi Minh, 236

Hong Kong: emigration to, 74, 280; Great Proletarian Cultural Revolution in, 192–93. *See also* Foreign relations

"How to Be a Good Communist," 192

Hu Qili, 281

Hu Shih, 73, 75

Hu Yaobang: biographical sketch, 242–43; appointment to Politburo and as CCP general secretary, 246; growing influence, 262; CCP head, 265, 270,

280; and political reforms, 282; at 1984 National Day celebrations, 293; as possible successor to Deng Xiaoping, 297

Hua Guofeng: biographical sketch, 213; rise to power, 223, 230, 233; as Party, state, and PLA leader, 234–35, 237–42; loss of power, 242–47, 261–65, 270; criticized, 249

Hundred Flowers campaign, 6, 100, 105–9, 112–13, 161, 247, 248, 253

Hungary: uprising of 1956, 105, 113; economic system, 274

Ibsen, Henrik, 42

Imperialism, 6–7, 19–22, 47

Industry and commerce: early 20th-century development, 20–21; socialist growth during First Five-Year Plan, 85, 111, 96–97, 115; transformation, 95; during Great Leap Forward, 122–23, 129, 133, 139; after Great Leap Forward, 142–43, 150, 173, 208, 219; condition in late 1970s, 239–40; new policies under Deng Xiaoping, 243, 258–59; foreign trade, 259, 275–76; reforms and growth in 1980s, 275–77; open door trade policy, 283–86

Japanese aggression, 7, 18, 22–23, 25–30. *See also* Foreign relations Jiang Qing: biographical sketch, 41–43; in thought reform campaign, 72; after Great Leap Forward, 148, 1670–65; and Mao's inner circle, 165; criticism of Wu Han, 174; during Great Proletarian Cultural Revolution, 179, 194, 196, 198; after Great Proletarian Cultural Revolution, 206–7, 213, 217–18; attempts to gain power, 225–27; attacks upon moderates, 230–31; arrest and detention, 234–37; expulsion from CCP, 244; criticized, 247, 265–66; trial, 267–70

Jiangxi Soviet, 25, 40

Jinmen, 52, 124, 127, 133

Johnson, Lyndon B., 171

Kampuchea: conflict with Vietnam, 255–
  56. *See also* Cambodia; Foreign relations
Kang Sheng, 264
Khmer Rouge, 255
Khrushchev, Nikita; and Sino-Soviet relations, 84; de-Stalinization, 97, 100,
  103, 105; 1957 trip to China, 126; attitude toward Great Leap Forward, 137–
  40, 146, 294; 1959 trip to United
  States, 139; 1959 trip to China, 139;
  recall of Soviet advisers, 140, 146;
  criticized by Mao, 163
Kissinger, Henry A., 211, 217
KMT. *See* Nationalist Party; Guomindang
Korean War, 7, 41, 54–55, 65–70, 71,
  75, 79, 104, 111, 171
Kosygin, Aleksei, 209, 297

Land distribution: preliberation, 12–16;
  after land reform, 69. *See also* Agri-
  culture; Land reform campaign; Responsibility system
Land reform campaign, 67–69
Lan Ping. *See* Jiang Qing
Laos: invaded during Vietnam war, 211.
  See also Foreign relations
Lei Feng, 167, 281
Lenin, Vladimir Ilyich, 5, 47–48, 132.
  See also Marxism-Leninism Mao Zedong Thought
"Life of Wu Xun, The," 72, 75
Lin Biao: biographical sketch, 38–39; associated with Chen Yiu, 39; member
  of Politburo Standing Committee, 59;
  minister of defense, 62; during Korean
  conflict, 80; at Eighth Party Congress,
  104; during Great Leap Forward, 125–
  26, 136, 138; after Great Leap Forward, 148; people's war thesis, 171–
  72; and criticism of Wu Han, 176;
  during Great Proletarian Cultural Revolution, 179, 181, 185, 198–99, 206;
  after Great Proletarian Cultural Revolution, 206–7; falling out with Mao
  and death, 213–17, 295; formal expul-

sion from CCP, 222–23; mention during Gang of Four trial, 268
Liu Jiemei, 121
Liu Shaoqi: biographical sketch, 33–34;
  Chen Boda's patron, 37; associated
  with Chen Yi, 39; opposed to seeking
  U.S. aid, 53–54; member of Politburo
  Standing Committee, 59; talk to Tianjin businesspeople, 78; on socialist
  transformation of agriculture, 86, 89;
  at Eighth Party Congress, 104; in
  Hundred Flowers campaign, 105–8,
  113; on heavy industry, 115; during
  Great Leap Forward, 116–17, 124–25,
  135; speech in praise of Soviet Union,
  147; after Great Leap Forward, 149,
  152, 154–57, 159; on cultural reform,
  164; seen with Mao, 170; opposed to
  Lin Biao's radical policies, 172; promotion of industry, 173; diplomatic
  trip, 176; failure to satisfy Mao, 181;
  during Great Proletarian Cultural Revolution, 183, 189–90, 192–93; detention and death 206; Lin Biao compared
  to, 217; criticized, 247; posthumous
  rehabilitation, 262, 265; honored in
  Chairman Mao's Memorial Hall, 282;
  honored at 1984 National Day celebrations, 294
Lon Nol, 255
Long March, 25–26, 28, 34, 36, 38, 39,
  40, 41, 42, 186, 242
"Long Live the Victory of People's War,"
  172
Luo Ruiqing: opposed to Lin Biao, 172–
  73; dismissal, 176, 181; rehabilitation,
  227–28

MacArthur, Douglas, 66–68, 294
McCarthyism, 69
Malenkov, Georgi, 230
Malthus, Thomas, 289
Manchukuo, 23
Mao Yuanxin, 233
Mao Zedong: general assessment, 5; fam-
  ily background, youth, and education,
  10–22; emergence as Communist

Mao Zedong (*continued*)
leader, 23–26; during anti-Japanese war, 26–30; personality cult surrounding, 28, 37, 155, 282; poems, 3, 163, 169; member of Politburo Standing Committee, 59; decision to enter Korean conflict, 66; attitude toward intellectuals, 73–74; 1950 negotiations in Moscow, 80; on socialization of agriculture, 88–89, 91–95; "On the Ten Major Relationships," 96–99, 104; on the transformation of intellectuals, 99–100; at Eighth Party Congress, 102–5; in Hundred Flowers campaign, 105–9; "On the Correct Handling of Contradictions Among the People," 106, 108, 119; during Great Leap Forward, 116–41; 1957 trip to USSR, 118–20; retirement as head of state, 135, 148; moderation and dissatisfaction after Great Leap Forward, 147–49, 151–77, 298; "On Khrushchev's Phony Communism and Its Historical Lessons for the World," 169; and the Great Proletarian Cultural Revolution, 179–204; swim in Yangzi River, 181; quoted by Red Guards, 187; surprised by Red Guard violence, 188; rejection of Shanghai Commune, 191; criticism of civil disorder and Red Guards, 195; renewed attacks against moderates, 196; suppression of Red Guards, 197; assessment of Great Proletarian Cultural Revolution, 201; after Cultural Revolution, 205, 212; falling out with Lin Biao and Chen Boda, 213–26; uncertain support of radicals, 223–29; failing health, 229–30; criticism of Deng Xiaoping and support for Hua Guofeng, 231, 238; death and commemoration, 233–36; criticized, 246–49, 264, 269; Central Committee document on contributions and errors, 271–72; honored at 1984 National Day celebrations, 294. See also *Quotations of Chairman Mao; Selected Works of Mao Zedong;* Marxism-Leninism Mao Zedong Thought

Mao Zedong Thought. *See* Marxism-Leninism Mao Zedong Thought
Marriage Law campaign, 70–71
Marshall, George C., 52–53
Marx, Karl, 44–46, 132. *See also* Marxism-Leninism Mao Zedong Thought
Marxism-Leninism Mao Zedong Thought, 5, 8, 18–19, 33, 43–48, 61, 73, 75, 99, 103–4, 121, 132, 146, 182, 196, 199, 203, 206, 222, 264, 272, 280–83, 296
Mass line theory, 27, 68, 86, 88, 116, 151, 191, 202
Matsu. *See* Mazu
May 7 Cadre schools, 200, 263
May 7 Directive, 182, 184
May 16 Circular, 182
May 16 Corps, 195, 212
Mazu, 52
Middle East, as factor in Sino-American relations, 286
Military Affairs Committee of People's Liberation Army, 65; meetings, 126, 136, 227; reorganization during Great Proletarian Cultural Revolution, 184, 189, 193; headed by Hua Guofeng, 235; Deng Xiaoping's position in, 244, 265, 270–71
Ministry of Defense, 252
Ministry of Education, 130, 157–58
Ministry of Higher Education, 131
Minorities, 51
Mongolia: Lin Biao's death in, 215–16. *See also* Foreign relations

National People's Congress, 63, 91, 121, 124, 134–35, 146, 164, 226–27, 240–41, 253–54, 264
Nationalist Party: reorganization and growth, 22–23; stagnation during anti-Japanese war, 26; defeat in civil war, 30–32; development on Taiwan, 80. *See also* Chiang Kai-shek; China, Republic of; Guomindang; Taiwan
"Nemesis," 7
New Fourth Army, 39
"New Young Man Arrives at the Organization Department," 107

Nie Yuanzi, 182, 186
Nixon, Richard M., 210–11, 220, 254, 283, 295
Nixon doctrine, 210
NPC. *See* National People's Congress
Nuclear weapons, 119, 166, 171, 209, 221

Olympic games of 1984, 286, 294
Opium War, 7, 20
"Oppose Bureaucracy" campaign, 76–77
"Oppose Corruption" campaign, 77–79
"Oppose Counterrevolutionaries" campaign, 71–72

Paris Commune, 127, 185, 189–90
Peach Blossom Brigade, 154
Peng Dehuai; biographical sketch, 40–41; minister of defense, 62; during Korean War, 66, 80; poet, 74; at Eighth Party Congress, 104–5; during Great Leap Forward, 126, 133, 135–39; attempted comeback, 147; identification with Hai Jui, 174; Red Guard trial, 193; death, 249; posthumous rehabilitation, 246, 262
Peng Zhen: biographical sketch, 113; during Hundred Flowers campaign, 105–8, 113; during Great Leap Forward, 116–17; confrontation with Khrushchev, 140; after Great Leap Forward, 149; during Socialist Education Movement, 154–57; patron of Wu Han, 161; during cultural reform, 162, 164–65; named "Chairman Mao's Close Comrade in Arms", 170; and criticism of Wu Han, 174–76; attacked by Mao and dismissed, 180–81; detention after Great Proletarian Cultural Revolution, 206; rehabilitation, 262; drafting of legal codes, 267
People's Liberation Army: renamed from Red Army, 36; organization, 64–65; in Korean conflict, 79–80; during Great Leap Forward, 123; radicalization after Great Leap Forward, 148, 165–68; during Great Proletarian Cultural Rev-

olution, 179–80, 189, 191, 194–97, 199; after Great Proletarian Cultural Revolution, 206–7, 212, 223, 226; action against Vietnam, 257; political involvement, 279
People's Republic of China. *See* China, People's Republic of
People's Revolutionary Military Council, 33
PLA. *See* People's Liberation Army
Plenums of the Central Committee of CCP: Third Plenum of the Eighth Central Committee, 117; Tenth Plenum of the Eighth Central Committee, 151–53; Eleventh Plenum of the Eighth Central Committee, 184–85; Twelfth Plenum of the Eighth Central Committee, 198; Third Plenum of the Eleventh Central Committee, 245–47, 255–57; Sixth Plenum of the Eleventh Central Committee, 270–72; other plenums, 133, 134, 214, 226, 244
Pol Pot, 255–56
Politburo of CCP: size and structure, 57–59; meetings, 137; reorganization after Great Proletarian Cultural Revolution, 206, 212, 223; actions of, 117, 225. *See also* Central Committee of CCP; Chinese Communist Party; Standing Committee of the Politburo
Population, 10, 67, 91, 129, 143, 145–46, 150, 220, 261, 277–78, 289–91
Poverty, 3–4, 12–16, 69, 261, 295
PRC. *See* China, People's Republic of

Qing dynasty, 18, 20, 22, 51
Quemoy. *See* Jinmen
Quotations of Chairman Mao, 166, 170, 186, 222

Reagan, Ronald, 284–86
Rectification campaigns, 28, 76–77, 93, 100, 105–9, 116–18, 127, 139, 147, 153–57, 164–65, 279
Red Army, 24, 29–31, 35–36, 40, 41
Red Guards: first use of term, 184; expansion and excesses, 185–88; criticized by Mao Zedong, 195; offended

Red Guards (*continued*)
by Hu Yaobang, 242; continued aggressiveness, 196; suppressed by Mao Zedong, 197, 199
Ren Wending, 250, 252
"Resist America, Aid Korea" campaign, 70–71
Responsibility system, 259–60, 274–75. *See also* Agriculture; Communes; Economy
Revised Second Ten Points, 155–56
Revolution of 1911, 18, 22
Revolutionary committees, 191, 196, 208, 212
Rural People's Communes. *See* Communes
Russell, Bertrand, 19

Second Ten Points, 154–55
Secretariat of CCP, 59, 189
Selected Works of Mao Zedong, 37, 75
Shanghai Commune, 189, 191, 218
Shanghai Communiqué, 220, 254
Shanghai Group. *See* Jiang Qing; Wang Hongwen; Yao Wenyuan; Zhang Chunqiao; Gang of Four
Shakespeare, William, 243
Sino-Japanese War of 1894–95, 20
Sixteen Points, 184–85, 189
Snow, Edgar, 210
Socialist Education campaigns, 108, 116, 120, 142, 153–57, 158, 167, 173
Soviet Union: Bolshevik revolution, 18; assistance to Nationalists and Communists, 22–24; and Korean War, 65; relations with Vietnam, 254–55. *See also* Foreign relations
Spiritual pollution campaign, 282
Sputnik, 117, 118
Stalin, Joseph compared to Mao, 5, 249; attitude toward Chinese Communists prior to liberation, 53–54, 294; and Chinese entry into Korean conflict, 66–67; 1950 reception of Mao in Moscow, 80, 118; death, 83; methods, 85; denounced by Khrushchev, 97
Standing Committee of the National People's Congress, 63, 117. *See also* National People's Congress
Standing Committee of the Politburo: structure and membership, 59; reorganization during Great Leap Forward, 126; reorganization during Great Proletarian Cultural Revolution, 184, 192, 206, 223. *See also* Politburo of CCP
State Council: establishment of, 62; actions of, 117, 227, 290; during Great Proletarian Cultural Revolution, 179, 189–90, 194, 196; after Great Proletarian Cultural Revolution, 218; headed by Hua Guofeng, 235; Deng Xiaoping's position in, 244; Zhao Ziyang's position in, 264; restructuring of, 267, 279, 289, 296
State Family Planning Commission, 289–90
Strauss, Franz Josef, 227
Stuart, John Leighton, 53
Sun Yat-sen, 22–23
Supreme State Conference, 63, 95, 106, 117, 121, 134

Taiwan: Nationalist retreat to, 31–32, 52; emigration to, 74–75. *See also* China, Republic of; Nationalist Party
Taiwan Relations Act, 284
Taiping Rebellion, 203
Tanaka, Kakuei, 221
Tangshan earthquake, 234
Ten-Year Plan of Hua Guofeng, 240–41, 257–58
Thought reform campaign, 72–76, 99–100, 106
"Three-Anti" campaign. *See* "Oppose Bureaucracy" campaign
Three Red Banners, 131, 140
Tian'anmen Incident, 232–33, 241, 246, 248
Tibet: made part of PRC, 51; 1959 revolt, 133, 139
Tito, Broz, 100, 244
Treaty ports, 19–20
Truman, Harry S., 66
Twelve-Year Plan of Mao Zedong. *See* High Tide

Twenty-Three Points, 156–57
"Two-line struggle," 5–6, 81, 121, 142, 152–53, 170–77, 182, 295–96

United Nations: establishment, 30; Korean War, 66–67; foreign relations with, 80, 211, 221, 286; assistance in census, 289
United States: war in Vietnam, 8, 171. *See also* Foreign relations

Versailles treaties, 18
Vietnam: U.S. military operations in, 171; Great Proletarian Cultural Revolution seizures of weapons destined for, 196; U.S. withdrawal from, 210–11; embalmers from, 236; relations with Soviet Union, 254–55. *See also* Foreign relations

Wang Guangmei, 154, 184, 192, 262
Wang Hongwen, 218, 223, 227; arrest and detention, 234–37; expulsion from CCP, 244; trial, 267–70
Wang Meng, 107
Warlords, 23, 42
"Water Margin," 228
Wei Jingsheng, 250–52, 254, 267, 297
"Whateverists," 239, 244–45, 264, 266
"What If I Really Were?" 266
Witke, Roxanne, 218
Women, 16, 41–43, 56, 70–71, 129–30, 251, 288, 290–91
Wu Han: biographical sketch, 161; author of "Hai Rui Dismissed from Office" and critic of Great Leap Forward, 162; attacked by Mao, 165, 174–76
Wu Xun, 72

Yao Wenyuan: biographical sketch, 161; criticism of Wu Han, 174–75; leader of Shanghai Commune, 191, 212; after Great Proletarian Cultural Revolution, 206–7, 218; bid for power, 227–28; arrest, expulsion from CCP, and trial, 234–37, 244, 246, 267–70
Yugoslavia: economic system, 274. *See also* Foreign relations

Zhang Chunqiao: biographical sketch, 160–61; leader of Shanghai Commune, 191, 212; after Great Proletarian Cultural Revolution, 206–7, 218, 223; bid for power, 227–28, 238; arrest, expulsion from CCP, and trial, 234–37, 244, 267–70
Zhang Zhixin, 262
Zhao Ziyang: biographical sketch, 262–64; and agricultural reforms, 260; premier, 265, 270, 280; and political reforms, 282; trip to United States, 285; at 1984 National Day celebrations, 293; economic policies, 296
Zhou Enlai: biographihcal sketch, 34–35; associated with Chen Yi, 39; in favor of U.S. aid, 52–53; member of Politburo Standing Committee, 58–59; premier and foreign minister, 62; warning to United States concerning Korea, 66; and relaxation of High Tide, 101, 114–15; during Hundred Flowers campaign, 105; speech at Fourth National People's Congress, 111–12; self-criticism, 118; during Great Leap Forward, 124–25; and Afro-Asian conference, 173; support for Mao against Peng Zhen, 176; during Great Proletarian Cultural Revolution, 179–82, 186, 193, 195, 198; meeting with Kosygin, 209; rebuilding of state bureaucracy and development policies, 213, 214, 218–29, 263, 283–84; Shanghai Communiqué, 220, 254; cancer and death, 223, 230–31; Tian'anmen Incident, 232–33; death commemorated, 241–42; allegedly attacked by Mao, 249; honored in Chairman Mao's Memorial Hall, 282; honored at 1984 National Day celebrations, 294. *See also* Tian'anmen Incident
Zhu De: biographical sketch, 35–36; member of Politburo Standing Committee, 58–59; honored in Chairman Mao's Memorial Hall, 282; honored at 1984 National Day celebrations, 294